GOOD HOUSEKEEPING
30 Day Diet

A NOTE OF CAUTION

Before beginning this, or any other, diet, it is advisable to obtain the approval and recommendations of your doctor. While you are on this, or any, diet, it is advisable to visit your doctor for periodic checks. This diet is intended for people of all ages in good health.

GOOD HOUSEKEEPING
30 Day Diet

YOUR
MADE TO
MEASURE
WEIGHT
LOSS
PLAN

Sandra Lane

EBURY PRESS · LONDON

ACKNOWLEDGEMENTS

Thank you to Sophie Vincenzi with whom I hatched the 30-Day Diet and who wrote the original article on which this book is based. Also, thanks to the eight stoical dieters – Daniela Brandler, Carl Caddick, Mary Cadogan, Alice Lane, Penny Nathan, Liz Warner, Sue Webster and Rowena Wilson. Many thanks to nutritionist Caroline Bunker and health consultant Linda McKay; and, finally, thanks to Linda Chaddock who helped me when my word processor played up. Photographs by Jeremy Enness and leotards worn by dieters by Freed of London.

Published by Ebury Press
an imprint of Century Hutchinson Ltd.
20 Vauxhall Bridge Road
London SW1V 2SA

First impression 1990

Copyright © The National Magazine Company Limited
and Sandra Lane 1990

The right of Sandra Lane and Stephen Dew to be identified as the author and illustrator of this book has been asserted by them in accordance with the Copyright, Designs and Patents Act, 1988.

All rights reserved. No part of this publication may be reproduced, stored in a retrieval system, or transmitted in any form or by any means, electronic, mechanical, photocopying, recording or otherwise, without the prior permission of the copyright owner.

The expression GOOD HOUSEKEEPING as used in the title of this book is the trade mark of The National Magazine Company Limited and The Hearst Corporation, registered in the United Kingdom and USA, and other principal countries of the world, and is the absolute property of The National Magazine Company Limited and The Hearst Corporation. The use of this trade mark other than with the express permission of The National Magazine Company Limited or The Hearst Corporation is strictly prohibited.

ISBN 0 85223 831 2

Filmset in Great Britain by Tek Art Limited, Croydon
Printed and bound by the Bath Press, Avon

CONTENTS

Chapter 1	**Introducing the first made-to-measure diet**	6
Chapter 2	**Losing weight – the first step**	12
Chapter 3	**Creating your personal diet**	22
Chapter 4	**The eight who tried the diet**	37
Chapter 5	**Portion counters and combinations**	75
Chapter 6	**The recipes**	88
Chapter 7	**A regular exercise plan**	156
Chapter 8	**Now you've lost weight, here's how to keep it off**	184
Useful addresses		190
Index		191

CHAPTER 1

INTRODUCING THE FIRST MADE-TO-MEASURE DIET

No MATTER HOW GOOD AN idea the last diet you tried seemed, the chances are that when a new diet – such as this one – comes along, you will try it, because the weight you've lost always seems to return. There are several reasons for this, but probably the most obvious – and the one that most diets cater for the least – is that there is such a big gap between the way you eat on a diet, and the way you normally eat. This isn't just because you have to eat less (and less of what you like), but because most diets are basically pretty inflexible and can't be adapted to suit you, or your lifestyle, to any great extent. This makes diets hard to follow and hard to stick to. It is difficult to incorporate the new eating patterns into your life once you have finished.

The trouble with most weight-loss programmes is that they demand drastic changes to the diet and exercise habits that have been acquired over a lifetime and have become deeply ingrained. Because of this, each diet is a battle of willpower, a brief period of **struggle during which our natural eating habits and inclinations are suppressed.** Most of us can only follow an eating pattern that doesn't really suit us for so long before reverting to our former eating habits. It is invariably ourselves that we blame for not being able to change our habits, not the diets – and we feel guilty about it. Yet it is a battle we are bound to lose, as diets cater little for individual needs. Many diets, for example, are still based on large amounts of lean protein in an age when people are increasingly eating a so-called demi-veg diet (which is also much healthier). Diets of grilled chicken breasts and steamed vegetables don't suit those who go out to work and eat sandwiches or in restaurants at lunch time. Some diets call for three cooked meals a day when few of us have time to prepare them. And research reveals that nowadays most of us eat just one conventional 'meal' (meat and two veg) a day and a series of snacks in between. Diet demands are often rigid and unrealistic, such as being told that you can eat as much salad as you like (without dressing) or baked potatoes on their own, or that crisps, chocolate and alcohol are banned. Few diets fit in with family or social life (what diet can cater for the fact that a mother will be driven wild with hunger and frustration around tea time when feeding ravening offspring?) Many people, particularly women, lead wildly irregular lives, working part time with children at home some days, at school on others. They may also cook for their partners in the evening, and if they are housewives they may spend most of their lives cooped up, cheek-by-jowl with food. Because of this, many slimmers end up cooking their family one meal and themselves another, or cancelling their social lives in order to diet. It is just impossible for one diet to take all these individual situations into account.

The *Good Housekeeping* 30-day weight-loss programme, however, is designed to take everyone's individual needs into account. It doesn't impose an arbitrary set of new eating and exercising habits, regardless of how you live your life. We have created a diet and exercise programme that can be tailor-made to suit each and every person who reads this book, whether a busy working mother, housewife, office worker, business man, vegetarian or teenage junk foodie. The aim of the book is to help you design a weight-loss programme that suits you so well that it is easier to follow and to stick to. It has been designed so that no one has to give up any item of food they really can't bear to be without. So those who can't abide salads without olive oil, or do without the occasional Mars Bar, glass of wine, hamburger or packet of crisps, won't have to.

On the other hand, the book aims to gently alter your eating and exercising habits from ones that keep you fat and unfit to ones that make you slim and healthy. **In order to make this as realistic a proposition as possible, the starting point for such new eating habits will be your own lifestyle and likes and dislikes.**

To prove that it is possible to work a successful weight-loss and shape-up programme into your lifestyle in this way, we devised individual diet and exercise plans to suit seven women – and one man – who all wanted to lose weight. Each had very different personalities, body shapes, eating habits and ways of living. The one thing they had in common was that they had tried lots of diets and found them all hard to stick to, and had always regained the lost weight fairly soon afterwards. The aim of the 30-day weight-loss programme is to shed a minimum of 3kg (7lb), and gain a firmer, fitter figure. However, most of our dieters lost closer to 6 kg (1 st), and for the first time they found losing weight (relatively) easy, and felt they had found a diet that actually worked with, not against their natural inclinations. In Chapter 4, you can read how we devised their diet and exercise programmes, and we give full details of these programmes, and the eight dieters describe how they progressed. In Chapter 8, on how to maintain weight loss, we follow up our dieters several months later to see how successfully they have kept their weight off. They give their verdicts as to how well their tailor-made weight-loss plan contributed to it.

Why 30 days? The *Good Housekeeping* 30-day weight-loss programme was originally devised and published in *Good Housekeeping* magazine in July 1989. Not all the participants would necessarily be classed as overweight by their doctors, but they nevertheless wanted to shed about half a stone and get firmer and slimmer before it was time to expose themselves in a swimsuit that summer. Hence, as the weight loss goal was relatively low, 30 days was deemed a realistic and healthy pace at which to lose weight. Others genuinely needed to reduce their weight for health reasons as well as appearance. At the time we didn't realise just how effective the diet would be, and that it would prove to be so successful, so quickly. Of course, the more overweight the dieter, the more dramatic the weight loss. A slimmer person cannot expect to lose so much weight as fast as someone fatter.

Another reason for making this diet last over 30 days is a

psychological one. It is easier to stick to a diet if you can count the days till it ends, and 30 days is long enough to effect substantial figure firming and weight loss, while not being so long that you lose heart. However, there is no reason why you can't continue dieting beyond 30 days should you wish and need to – just read the chapter on staying slim (Chapter 8). As the diet is tailor-made to suit you, it is also easier to stick to it for long periods than are most other diets.

HOW THE DIET WORKS

With the help of the *Good Housekeeping* medical and nutritional team, this book shows you how to devise your own made-to-measure diet and exercise plan. For the first time in any diet book, there is a chart enabling you to discover your own personal calorie requirements – how many calories you need each day to keep ticking over, and just how much you need to cut down in order to lose weight effectively. This is important, as everybody has different calorie requirements, they vary enormously depending on your size, sex and the amount of muscle you carry, and your own personal genetic make-up. Most diets ignore this fact, and simply give one amount of calories per day for everyone.

Once you have established your personal calorie requirements, simple questionnaires guide you towards an awareness of your lifestyle and eating habits. The results of the questionnaires produce the blueprint for your own personal diet, one that suits you alone, and one that you can therefore realistically live with. In Chapter 2, the mechanics of dieting and exercising are explained, and we discuss the psychology of eating, in an attempt to help you become more aware of why you eat the way you do. Understanding your eating patterns, and what happens to your body when you diet and take exercise, goes a long way towards forming better new habits.

An important plus of the 30-day weight-loss programme is that no matter what your eating habits – how unhealthy they currently are – it is impossible to devise yourself a diet that isn't nutritionally sound. In fact, any diet devised will be healthy and well-balanced, following the current guidelines for healthy eating; high fibre, low fat, sugar and salt and plenty of fresh fruit, vegetables and whole grain carbohydrates. The diets don't deal in calories but in carefully worked out portions of easy-to-identify food categories: fats and oils (f&o), protein (p), cereal (c), dairy (d), fruit (f), and free foods (ff). These portions make it much faster and simpler to calculate what you are eating than counting calories. They are like simple building bricks from which you put together your daily diet.

When asked to record exactly what we eat, most people under-record dramatically, or we unconsciously curb the amounts we are eating. It seems it is very easy to fool ourselves about food, and counting up thousands of calories each day is an easy way to miscalculate.

Another important part of the *Good Housekeeping* 30-day weight-loss programme is its exercise plan. Again, most diet and exercise books tend to demand unrealistic amounts and types of exercise for most of us. What busy mother, for instance, can make time to go to the gym regularly (or afford to)? Many of us might blanch at the thought of a three mile jog but would find a simple ten minute exercise routine in front of the television, or a brisk 20 minute walk to the shops, perfectly acceptable and easy to accommodate. Others might find it easy to pop into a nearby swimming pool at lunch time or after school with their kids, while others may thrive on competitive sports. Some of us may take a considerable amount of exercise without really realising it, doing housework or mowing the lawn, for instance. And a really beneficial amount of exercise can often be added to our lives, simply by taking the stairs instead of lifts or escalators, by walking for part of a journey to work, or by walking to the shops instead of driving or taking the bus.

So just as the book helps you to devise an eating plan that fits in with your life, it also helps you to devise a regular exercise plan to accompany it, one that is as realistic as possible for the type of person you are, and the kind of life you lead.

Taking some form of exercise is a very important part of the 30-day weight-loss programme, and not just because it helps to burn up calories faster and makes you firmer and fitter. Exercise puts you firmly on the winning side of dieting, it is an active step

> **SMOKING AND FAT**
>
> Smokers often give weight gain as an excuse for not giving up. It is widely assumed that smoking is both a displacement activity for eating, and that the action of inhaling smoke makes us burn up more calories. Smoking does increase BMR, but only by a tiny amount – about 50–60 calories a day – and this is not enough to make a significant contribution to weight loss or control. One recent study of smokers and non-smokers showed that smokers consumed more high-fat foods, more chips, processed meats and full-cream milk, and also more alcohol, and sugar in tea and coffee. Non-smokers had a healthier diet altogether, eating more fruit, salads and cereal products. In another study, a group of doctors gave up smoking and because they were aware of what they were doing, and of the facts, they only gained 2 kg (4½ lb). They feel this raises doubts about the assumptions of automatic weight gain on giving up smoking.

to losing weight and being in control of your body, life and well-being. On page 18, we examine the important psychological effects it can have, and discuss the physical effects, too. Exercise can help reduce fat and tone up lean muscle tissue which actually burns up more calories than fat (helping to tip the scales further in your favour), and exercising helps to keep off weight for good. The more our eight dieters exercised, the greater the weight-loss they achieved.

Finally, there is a large section of healthy, delicious low calorie recipes devised and triple-tested in the kitchens of the Good Housekeeping Institute, together with extensive menu suggestions. They have been chosen bearing in mind that dieters want good food **fast, so the recipes are mostly quick and easy to prepare. They also reflect today's trend of little meat with lots of vegetables, and bear little resemblance to traditional diet foods. In fact, when eating them, you'll find it hard to believe you are on a diet at all.**

CHAPTER 2

LOSING WEIGHT – THE FIRST STEP

*U*NDERSTANDING THE REASONS why and the way in which your body gains fat is the first step towards controlling it.

Being overweight isn't just a problem of the greedy, the lazy or those with no willpower, it is something that affects most of the populations of the industrialized west. At any one time, 65 per cent of British women and 30 per cent of British men are trying to lose weight. Since the Second World War, we've been progressively getting fatter (though in the past couple of decades our actual weight has begun to drop), and the average amount of body fat an adult carries has gone up by 10 per cent.

The reasons for this can be found in the way our diet and lifestyle has changed. We eat more processed foods containing fat, sugar and salt, and the availability of ready-prepared meals and fast foods means that we have speedier access to it. Our diets now contain 40 per cent fat which is higher in calories weight for weight than any other food, sugar included. Thanks to processed foods, we often aren't even aware we are eating it, but all sorts of things, such as biscuits, processed meats or pastry, come loaded with hidden fat. At the same time, the amount of energy expended these days has decreased. Cars, labour saving gadgets and television, all mean less exercise is taken and consequently fewer calories burnt up. This equation has brought about a rise in weight and a reduction in health, with a particular increase in levels of heart disease which can be aided by high blood pressure.

WHAT CONSTITUTES A HEALTHY DIET?

Losing weight and eating a healthy diet isn't just good for your appearance it is also vital for your health. The current concensus of what constitutes a healthy diet is:
- Less fat, particularly saturated fat. Currently, fat makes up 40 per cent of our diet – it should be below 30 per cent.
- Less sugar which is full of empty calories which can make us fat and contribute to tooth decay.
- Less salt.
- Less alcohol. Women should drink no more than 14 units a week and men no more than 21 units a week.
- More fibre rich foods – up to 30 per cent of our diet.
- More carbohydrates – approximately 50–60 per cent of our total energy intake.
- Plenty of fresh fruit and vegetables.

Being overweight contributes to:
- High blood pressure which is a major factor of stroke and heart attack.
- Diabetes, which also makes us more prone to heart disease.

WHY ARE SOME PEOPLE FAT WHEN OTHERS AREN'T?

Of course, there are individual differences too. Not everyone who eats a high-fat, high-calorie diet and takes little exercise is going to get fat. The reasons why some people put weight on when others don't is the subject of hot debate, and the answer can vary according to which expert you consult! There are a number of theories. Fatness may be in our genes; we may inherit a predisposition to gain weight. Some experts think a defective hypothalmic mechanism which fails to tell us we are no longer hungry may be responsible. Others think that the reason some people put on weight and others don't lies in differences in metabolic rates (the rate at which we burn calories). Other research, however, shows that someone who is thin is just as likely to have a slow metabolism as someone who puts on weight easily.

THE PSYCHOLOGY OF EATING

As research into differences in the way we burn up energy has so far failed to reach a firm conclusion, experts are beginning to focus attention on variations in appetite, and what makes different people eat as they do. Our desire to eat is influenced by many factors, both physical and social. The sensations of hunger and appetite are ill-defined feelings of emptiness on the one hand and pleasant anticipation of food on the other. Appetite is more susceptible than hunger to influences such as emotion, habit or stimulation by the sight or smell of delicious looking food. Just the sight of the time on the clock, signalling mealtime, can be a cue for instant hunger pangs as can the sight of other people leaving for lunch. Eating and drinking between meals is also socially influenced. We invariably associate tea breaks with biscuits and cakes, and may automatically want them whether we are hungry or not.

Taste, rather than calories, may be what determines when we stop eating. If a high-calorie cheese is replaced by a low-calorie one and butter replaced with a low-fat substitute, there will be a large reduction in the calories consumed, but not necessarily in the satisfaction it gives.

Many of us eat for comfort – particularly sweet foods which we frequently associate with approval, as they have been given to us as rewards throughout our childhood. We also have an inbuilt liking for sweetness. In experiments, babies suck stronger on sweet solutions. Some psychologists think that overeating is an attempt to literally fill a gap in our lives. This may simply be the gap between the way the media portrays the way we should look – and the way we really are. Women are so bombarded with images of tall, slim girls we end up with the feeling that they are the norm to which we should all conform.

Before going on a diet, it's always best to sit down and think, 'do I really need to lose weight?' Are you just trying to change your own individual body shape (which is just as right as those portrayed in advertisements) to match some arbitrary image of perfection? Or are you hoping that weight loss is going to answer other problems? It's very common for women (and some men) to misinterpret their body size. Recent research shows that women are particularly prone to seeing themselves as larger than they really are, and thinking they need to diet when they don't.

This all sounds rather deep for a diet book, but an important part of the way that the 30-Day Diet works is to make you aware of why you are eating what, and when you do. It is important to become aware of those times when you overeat for comfort or to relieve boredom, as well as simply mapping the pattern of your eating. Realising why you are eating in certain ways is the first step to changing bad habits for better ones.

It seems increasingly clear that weight loss and gain isn't just dependent on our physiology, but on social, emotional and lifestyle factors, too. Thus, as the reasons for being overweight vary from one person to another, it seems entirely reasonable that the way a person loses weight will be individual too. All this adds to the sense of a more holistic approach to weight control, taking into account a person's personality and lifestyle. And this is exactly what this weight-loss programme is all about. The next chapter, which helps you to devise your own diet, takes you through a questionnaire to help you to evaluate your eating habits and your lifestyle in order to work out a diet and exercise routine that fits in with your life.

No matter what lifestyle or eating patterns we have, dieting would be a whole lot easier if we were more aware of what happens to our bodies when we diet. Understanding the mechanisms involved, can help us to work with, rather than against, our bodies.

HOW MUCH FOOD DO WE REALLY NEED?

The term BMR (basal or resting metabolic rate) is the measurement of the energy our bodies use up to carry out functions such as breathing, digesting and so on, without any exercise at all. It used **to be thought that people leading a normal, not particularly energetic, lifestyle, expended energy at about one-and-a-half times their BMR. This meant that the average woman needed about 2,000 calories a day. However, recent research has shown that most healthy women expend energy at only about 1.38 times their BMR, meaning that the total amount of energy used up each day is only 38 per cent more than if we had stayed in bed all day. Thus, Ms average probably needs no more than 1,750 calories a day,** maximum, and in some cases even less. This is further proof of the diminishing activity in our lives. And as we tend to eat more calories than we need for the amount of activity that we take, it is not surprising they end up stored as fat.

Metabolic rates can vary enormously from person to person – by as much as 50 per cent. Babies have the highest BMR of all, and it declines with age, dropping by about 3 per cent for each decade of our lives. Muscle uses more energy than fat so those of us with a lot of lean muscle will have a higher BMR. Men carry much more muscle than women, who carry a greater amount of fat. Because of this, and their greater body size, men always have a higher BMR than women. But puzzlingly, new research has shown that fat people are just as likely as thin people to have a high metabolic rate. In fact, it has been found that the overweight generally have a higher metabolic rate than the slim because they carry more metabolically active tissue. Not all weight gain consists of fat. Indeed, 25–30 per cent is the more metabolically active muscle, needed to support the extra fat. Because of this, overweight people can need up to 500 calories a day more than the slim to maintain their size. Conversely, when someone loses weight, metabolism drops, partly due to a 'starvation response' – the body tries to conserve energy in case of famine – and also because there is less metabolically active tissue to fuel.

Unfortunately, once weight is lost, people don't automatically drop their food intake to match their lower energy needs, which is a major reason why weight regain after dieting is so common. In the next chapter we show you how to work out your own metabolic rate, and calculate how many calories you need a day to maintain your current weight. But, more importantly, we also show you how many calories you need a day in order to lose about 1 kg (2 lb) a week, which is now thought to be the ideal rate of weight loss.

BURNING FAT FASTER

It must be remembered, however, that our metabolic rate isn't static, and it can be altered by a number of things. One of the first consequences of beginning a diet is a drop in BMR, sometimes by as much as 15–20 per cent in the first 24–48 hours of dieting. The more severe the diet, the more dramatically it tends to drop. This is the body's response to being fed less food. The body doesn't think, 'Oh good, I'm shedding unwanted fat', but 'Oh no, I'm starving', and so lowers its BMR in an attempt to conserve energy. This response is then maintained by a reduction of the lean tissues of the body – the muscle. When you reduce the amount of calories you eat, you don't just lose fat, you lose muscle, water and glycogen (the body's instant energy store) as well. The lean parts of the body, the muscle, use up more energy/calories than fat. Research has shown that the faster you lose weight, the more lean tissue you are likely to lose. People who go on very low-calorie diets are particularly vulnerable to this fat/lean exchange. They invariably find the first diet fast and effective, but find that weight is generally regained soon afterwards and successive bouts of dieting become increasingly unsuccessful as the metabolic rate is increasingly lowered by replacing lean tissue with fat. This is one reason why it is so easy to regain weight following a diet, particularly a crash diet, as you end up needing fewer calories than before you started. But inevitably most of us revert to the amount we ate before dieting.

Slower dieting loses more fat alone, leaving you with more lean tissue that burns up calories faster. A loss of about 0.5–1 kg (1–2 lb) a week is the optimum amount of fat you should lose in a week, and is the rate at which the eating plans in this book are set. Any more and you are no longer losing fat alone, but eating into lean tissue, too.

EXERCISE – THE FAT REDUCER

Exercise is, of course, the best way to guard against loss of too much lean muscle, and the best way to prevent the body exchanging lean for fat through repeated dieting. It also helps reduce the amount of slow calorie burning fat, while toning up fast burning lean, which allows you to consume more calories without gaining weight. It is estimated that increased muscle bulk uses approximately 25 calories per kg (12 calories per lb) per day more than the same weight in fat. And exercise can not only increase the rate at which you burn energy while you exercise, but it is thought to raise your BMR by about 5 per cent for 2–4 hours afterwards.

Most people argue that exercise makes you more hungry so you quickly replace the calories you've burnt off by eating more, but this isn't so. In fact, exercise can actually suppress appetite. Exercise and its benefits are discussed more fully in Chapter 7, in which we help you to work out ways of incorporating more into your life in as enjoyable a way as possible.

One of the most important findings about exercise and weight loss is how it helps long term weight control. Dieters who lose weight by dieting only tend to have regained most of the weight lost within a year, but dieters who also exercise, keep it off.

LOSE FAT, NOT WEIGHT

From what has been said above, it is easy to see that the term 'losing weight' is becoming redundant, because what you really want to do is lose fat, and weight loss doesn't automatically equal fat loss. The weight of a woman (or man) bears less relation to the proportion of fat on our bodies than most of us think. And it is the proportion of fat to lean on a body that determines both how good it looks, and whether your fat is a health risk or not. The best way to get slim (and the way this diet plan works) is by combining diet with exercise – which means exchanging fat for muscle – and muscle is slightly heavier than fat, but there will be a net weight loss too.

Weight loss – or gain – can be due to reasons other than fat loss or gain, such as fluid retention. Most of us aren't aware of the part water plays in weight fluctuations, and we expect to lose weight too fast, and then to gain it more easily than we really do. When first starting to diet, weight loss is dramatic – pounds seem to slide off straight away. This is because when beginning a diet, the first thing the body loses is glycogen from the glycogen stores **(the body's source of instant energy). Glycogen is bound up with three times its own weight in water, so when glycogen is jettisoned at the beginning of a diet, massive quantities of water are expelled with it, together with a small amount of fat.**

At this stage, most people attribute the sudden, dramatic loss of weight to having lost a large amount of fat, and expect to continue to lose it at this rate. However, the next stage of weight loss reflects real fat loss and proceeds at a much slower pace. If you stick to your diet at this stage, this fat loss will continue steadily at about 0.5–1 kg (1–2 lb) a week.

Eventually, of course, your metabolic rate is suppressed a little, partly due to the starvation response and partly because your energy requirements have become smaller as there is less of you to fuel. So, the difference between the calories you are eating and your daily requirements has become smaller. (This is where the benefits of exercise come in, to raise energy requirements.) Most people are discouraged by this slower rate of weight loss and think the diet is failing, when it really isn't at all.

SUDDEN WEIGHT GAIN

Another trick water retention can play on the dieter occurs when she or he lapses and eats normally – or a lot – for a day and then suddenly puts on several pounds. At this point, many dieters simply give up. They have been struggling with what seems to them to be an unnaturally slow weight loss, and after one day's lapse, the whole lot seems to have piled back on. This isn't so, however. What has happened, is that the body's glycogen stores are very low because you have been dieting, and if you stop dieting and eat normally – or even a lot, the extra calories you've eaten are instantly converted into glycogen to replenish the body's depleted glycogen stores. As glycogen is bound up with three times its weight in water, the body instantly retains massive amounts of water. Weight gain from this can be enormous. As much as 1.5–3 kg (3–6 lb) in one day isn't uncommon. But the point is that it isn't fat you have regained, but water. In fact, you are unlikely to regain even 0.5 kg (1 lb) of fat after one day of bingeing. If you think that an excess of 3,500 calories over your normal daily requirements are needed to make 0.5 kg (1 lb) of fat, you'll realise how it is impossible to do this in one – or even two days. This is the point when many dieters feel they will never succeed and give up. But if you bear in mind that real fat loss is continuing apace, and weight gained rapidly (or lost rapidly) isn't real, dieting would be much easier to cope with.

Unrealistic expectations are a common cause of diet failure. But just remember – stick to your diet and you should steadily lose around 0.5–1 kg (1–2 lb) of fat a week, no matter what the scales say. For this reason, experts prefer dieters to limit the use of scales to once a week. Any more isn't necessarily an accurate measure of fat loss and can have a negative and discouraging effect on the dieter whose scales won't budge. A more accurate way to measure your changing shape is the tape measure. Even if weight loss is slow, if you are mixing diet with exercise you will lose inches and be able to fit into a smaller size. Improved appearance and fitness, you'll find, doesn't necessarily depend on a low reading on the scales.

ASSESSING YOUR WEIGHT FOR YOUR HEIGHT

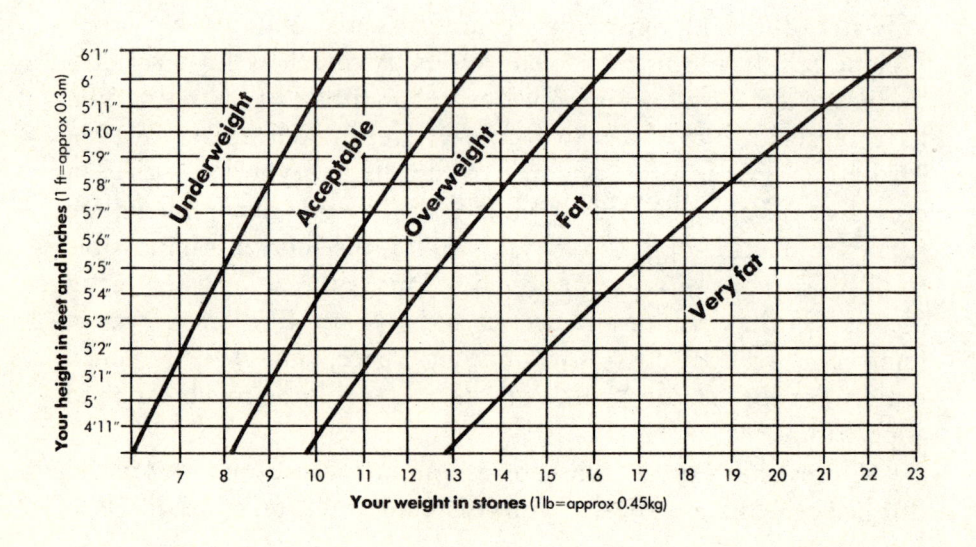

The chart provided here helps you to gauge your ideal weight for your height and build. Please remember, though, that this can only give a rough guide to what your optimum weight should be. It doesn't show you how to work out how much fat you have on your body – which is what you really need to know. Nowadays, when you have a health check at the doctor's surgery or at a gym or health club, the doctor, nurse or fitness assessor uses special calipers to assess the proportion of fat and muscle on your body. This gives the truest indication of whether you need to lose fat or not, and by how much. In many cases the fat/muscle ratio can be altered for the better by exercise alone.

Some research has shown that where you put on fat can dictate how easily you lose it. Those of us who are apple-shaped and carry fat on our tummies, may find they shed fat slightly faster than those who are pear shaped and carry most of their excess weight on hips and thighs.

FORGET CALORIE COUNTING – IT'S WHAT YOU EAT THAT MATTERS

It seems that fat loss may also be influenced by what sort of calories you consume as well as how many. Calories of fat, which are higher in calories weight for weight than any other food, sugar included, are much more readily converted into body fat than the same number of calories of protein or carbohydrate. It is much harder for the body to synthesise fat from protein or carbohydrates. It has also been found that some foods are more naturally filling and able to satisfy hunger than others. Weight for weight, protein is the most satiating food, followed by carbohydrates. High fibre foods are also filling. So the diet that will be easiest to stick to in terms of making you feel least hungry, and most efficient and healthy, is one that is high in starchy, fibre-rich carbohydrates with plenty of protein while being low in fat.

There's some evidence, too, that those who skip breakfast and first eat at lunch time may be slightly reducing their metabolic rate. This may be because the morning starvation induces the body to conserve energy, by slowing down its overall metabolic rate. So, even if you aren't a great breakfast eater, it may be as well to eat a little, or take it to work with you if you can't face eating first thing.

CHAPTER 3

CREATING YOUR PERSONAL DIET

*I*N THIS CHAPTER, WE ARE GOING to show you how to work out your own diet. It won't be the sort that you only use for a few weeks before reverting to your old eating habits, as this is virtually useless. Such dieting may help you lose weight in the short term, but the weight will inevitably be regained once you have finished.

What we are aiming at, is to build you a healthy and slimming eating plan that is based on *what* and *when* you like to eat, substituting fattening foods (which you may not even realise are fattening) with healthier foods, that are nevertheless as satisfying, filling and as enjoyable as possible.

To do this, you must first become aware not only of what you are eating, but of what governs your eating habits. And you must ask yourself what aspects of your diet are so firmly entrenched that you shouldn't attempt to change them, and what changes you feel are more feasible. You may not be able to eat salad without olive oil, for example, but you would be happy to trade butter for low-fat spread and full-cream milk for skimmed or semi-skimmed. In this way, treats are built into the diet, since you are allowed to eat certain foods that are vital to the enjoyment of your diet. At the same time, you are cutting back on those things that are easier for you to do without.

The way we helped our eight dieters in Chapter 4 to become more aware of their eating habits was by asking them to keep a food diary. They recorded everything they ate – however small – for two week days and the weekend, so that they could monitor changes in their eating patterns on different days of the week, and see how weekday or weekend activities influenced their eating patterns. This is the first step that you, too, will need to take in order to build your own diet programme.

While keeping your diet diary, you should also keep an activity log. Include details of all exercise taken as well as normal daily activities like walking, shopping, housework, climbing stairs and gardening. Keep this activity log for a week (see page 158) – you are going to analyse it later, in Chapter 7.

MAKING YOUR FOOD DIARY

To help assess your eating habits, fill in details of everything you eat and drink from the moment you get up, to the moment you go to bed, in the chart overleaf. Make no attempt to modify your diet at this stage. Weigh yourself at the beginning and end of the period. As well as recording food and drink intake, make a note of the following in the relevant columns:

1 The type of food you eat (or drink) and how much, either as a simple estimate of portion size or as an actual weight using kitchen scales. Note if the food is weighed with or without bones as this can make quite a difference.

2 Note the time the food was eaten, and where and why you ate it – perhaps you were hungry and it was the first thing available, or it was simply what you fancied at the time. Were you aware of eating to help you concentrate, because you felt under pressure; or did you eat because you felt it would be comforting?

3 Beneath the chart, jot down details of how your eating patterns fit in with work, both inside and outside the home, and with your social life. Make notes of how what you are doing influences what and when you eat. For example, do you attend evening classes regularly after work and so only eat snacks on those evenings? Or perhaps you work irregular hours and so you cannot plan to eat regular meals.

This record will enable you to examine your normal eating patterns to see what influences what you eat and drink, and why.

YOUR FOOD DIARY

	FOOD	DRINK	WHEN EATEN	WHERE	WHY

Weekday 1

Breakfast

Morning

Lunch

Afternoon

Evening

Weekday 2

Breakfast

Morning

Lunch

Afternoon

Evening

MAKING YOUR FOOD DIARY

	FOOD	DRINK	WHEN EATEN	WHERE	WHY
Saturday					
Breakfast					
Morning					
Lunch					
Afternoon					
Tea time					
Evening					
Sunday					
Breakfast					
Morning					
Lunch					
Afternoon					
Tea time					
Evening					

Eating patterns:

Now, looking carefully at your diet diary, tick the relevant columns in the food preferences chart below, for each time you have eaten the type of food heading the column. Choose just one, typical, day. There are portion counters on pages 76–80 which will help you analyse what type of food you are eating if you need help.
Protein includes eggs, meat, fish, pulses and cheese.
Cereal includes bread, flour, starchy vegetables, pasta and rice.
Dairy foods include milk, yogurt, fromage frais and cream.
Fats & oils include butter, margarine and oils.
Fruit includes apples, bananas, oranges (there are many other fruits which come under the free food category [see page 81]).

FOOD PREFERENCES CHART

Meal/Snack	Time	Protein (p)	Cereal (c)	Dairy (d)	Fats & oils (f&o)	Fruit (f)
Breakfast						
Morning						
Lunch						
Afternoon						
Evening						
Other						

An example is outlined here. For example, if you ate a meal consisting of vegetable soup (c), roll (c) and butter (f&o), chicken (p), chips (c, f&o) and broccoli (f) followed by apple pie (c, f) and custard (c, d), you would fill in the chart as follows:

Meal/Snack	Time	Protein (p)	Cereal (c)	Dairy (d)	Fats & oils (f&o)	Fruit (f)
Lunch	1 pm	✓	✓✓✓✓✓	✓	✓✓	✓✓

Now add up how many ticks you have for each food category and put them in these boxes. You can now clearly see where your inclinations lie in relation to the food categories p, c, d, f&o and f.

p	c	d	f&o	f

ASSESSING YOUR FOOD DIARY

When you have completed your food diary and discovered your food preferences answer the questions on the Dietary Assessment Questionnaire (overleaf). Jot down the answers in the space provided so that you have a record of them. This is important, as a thorough examination of all your responses will help guide you towards a way of eating that fits in with your life.

The information you write down in the Dietary Assessment Questionnaire will reveal your 'eating personality'. Once you have completed the Assessment, look at both it and the diary and answer the questions listed in the second questionnaire on page 30.
  Your answers will point the way to realistic changes for you. They will enable you to identify, for example, the weak points in your day when you should provide yourself with low-calorie snack alternatives. Let your personality work positively for you by letting it help you pin-point your strengths and weaknesses.

QUESTIONNAIRE 1: YOUR DIETARY ASSESSMENT

1 Is there room for improvement in your diet, or is it better than you originally thought?

....

....

2 Are some days better than others? If so why?

....

....

3 Are weekdays and weekends very different? If so, in what ways?

....

....

4 Do you feel more tired as the week progresses? If so, how does it affect what you eat? (For example, you might rely more on ready cooked meals.)

....

....

5 What foods and drink dominate your diet?

....

....

6 What foods do you only eat occasionally?

....

....

7 Do you eat roughly the same foods each day, or does your diet vary a great deal from day to day?

....

....

8 How much starchy, high-fibre foods, such as cereals, fresh vegetables and fruit, do you eat? (Give a rough percentage if you can.)

....

....

9 What proportion of the foods in your diet are processed and made up of large amounts of fat or sugar? (Look at the labelling on the package if you are not sure. Ingredients are given in order of quantities the food contains.)

....

....

10 Do you eat at the same time each day, or does it vary? Do you eat three meals a day; or a series of snacks; or a mixture of small snacks and one large meal?

....

....

QUESTIONNAIRE 2: DISCOVERING WHAT CHANGES CAN BE MADE

1 Is your eating associated with stress?

....

2 If you are a woman is your eating related to your menstrual cycle? If you are not sure, keep a note of how your eating habits change at different times of the month. Do you find you eat more at some times of the month than at others? And less at other times?

....

3 Do you eat extra food at children's tea time, or finish their leftovers?

....

4 Do you eat snacks or drink in the car, bus or train on the way to or from work?

....

5 In what situations do you buy chocolate or sweets? When you are at a supermarket where they sell them at the checkout? When you buy petrol?

....

6 Do you eat, or drink alcohol whilst preparing a meal?

....

7 Do you have snacks in your desk at work?

....

TREATS YOU CAN'T DO WITHOUT

Which of the following fattening foods can you simply not live without? State how often you would like to be able to eat these foods – the least amount you could cope with – and make a note of it. Being allowed to have some of the foods you value sometimes will make your diet easier to stick to.

skimmed milk	low-fat yogurt ....
semi-skimmed milk	low-fat fromage frais ....
low-fat spreads	reduced-fat cheeses ....
low-calorie salad dressings	lower-fat cheeses such as Brie, Edam, cottage cheese ....
low-calorie mayonnaise	low-calorie beer ....
salad without dressing	low-calorie wine ....
artificial sweetener	low-fat crisps ....

PAINLESS CALORIE SAVERS

Having become more aware of what you like to eat, which of these could you change to? Try to change as many as possible as they make big calorie savings for little effort. They will help you whittle down your weight even before you've begun dieting.

butter	crisps	croissants ....
cream	alcohol	full-fat fromage frais ....
bacon	cakes	fatty cheeses e.g. cheddar .....
chocolate or sweets	pastry	olive oil ....

CALCULATING YOUR DAILY CALORIE REQUIREMENT

The next stage in building your own diet is to calculate your normal daily calorie requirement. To do this, you will need a calculator, ruler, pen and paper, and the two charts below. First find your body surface area on Chart 1 by placing a ruler across your height and weight measurements. The point where the ruler crosses the central column is your personal body surface area measurement.

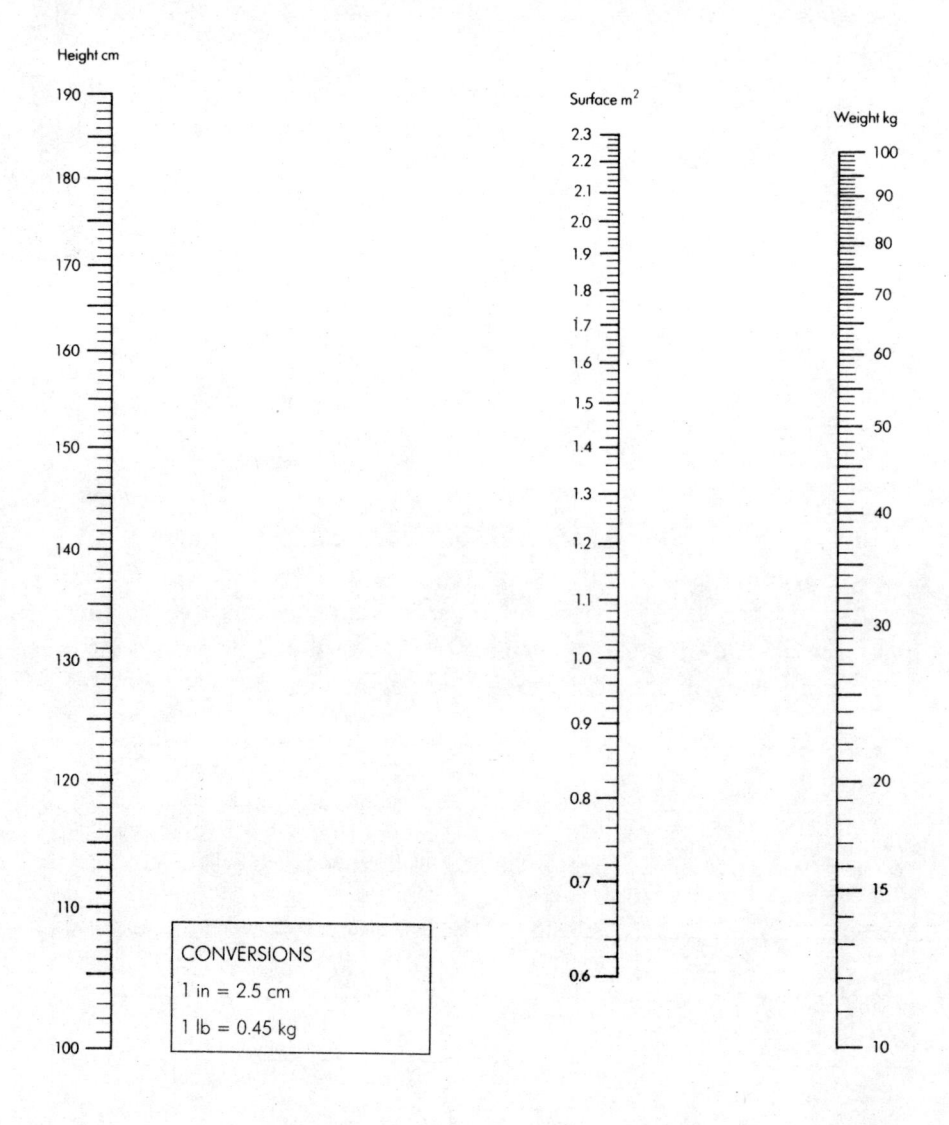

Height cm

Surface m^2

Weight kg

CONVERSIONS
1 in = 2.5 cm
1 lb = 0.45 kg

CALCULATING YOUR DAILY CALORIE REQUIREMENTS

Then place a ruler vertically across Chart 2 to find your basal metabolic rate per hour according to your age. Multiply this figure by your body surface area, then multiply the result by 24 for a daily reading of the calories you consume when simply 'ticking over' without any physical movement. Multiply this by 1.38 to find your daily calorie requirement when averagely active. (To gauge your activity levels more accurately turn to Chapter 7 which will help you assess your activity diary.) Add 15% if you are very active and take regular exercise, and subtract 15% if you have a sedentary job and rarely exercise.

Example: Height 173 cm; weight 65 kg; therefore body surface area 1.8 sq m.

Age 23; sex female; therefore calories per hour = 36.

36 (calories) × 1.8 (sq m) × 24 × 1.38 = 2,146 calories per day.

Subtract 15 per cent for an inactive lifestyle: 1,824 calories per day.

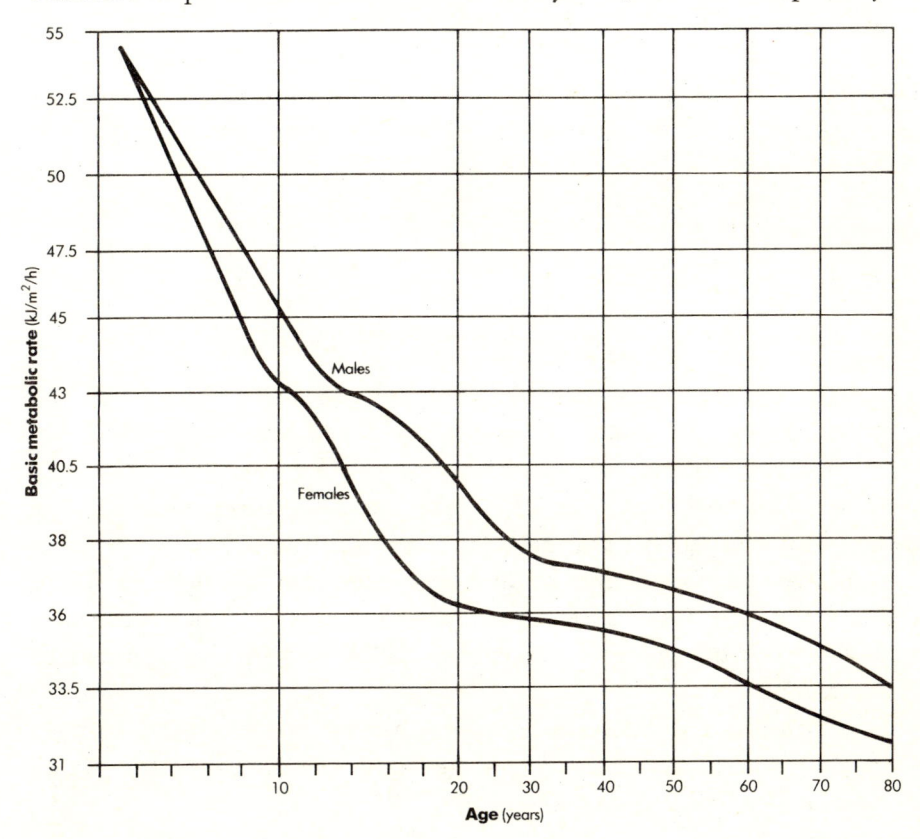

In laboratory test tube experiments it has been found that 0.45 kg (1 lb) of fat yields 3,500 calories. Because of this, some diets require that one must have 3,500 calories a week less than your normal requirements in order to lose a pound of fat a week. Thus, in theory you would need to subtract 1,000 calories a day to lose 1 kg (2 lb) a week. In practice, people can lose weight at this rate with a much smaller cut in their calories and, in any case, it is unwise to drop below 1,000 calories a day. How much you need to reduce your calories varies from person to person, and depends on how active you are. In devising the diets for our eight dieters we reduced their daily calorie requirement by between 500 and 700 calories a day. In some cases, it was less. We suggest that to lose 1 kg (2 lb) a week you should subtract between 500 and 700 calories from the figure you have calculated to be your daily calorie intake. How efficiently you lose weight will also be determined by how much exercise you take. We help you work more activity into your life in Chapter 7. Many people lose weight simply by making changes such as swapping butter for low-fat spread, and taking on regular exercise. So, write your daily calorie requirements in order to lose 1 kg (2 lb) a week in this box:

Now convert your daily calorie allowance into the food portions that are the building blocks of your diet. Take a good look at the boxes on page 27 which indicate where your food preferences lie, and match them up to one of the five diets, A, B, C, D or E, opposite, choosing the one which most closely corresponds to your natural preferences. Then go to the column marked with the letter you have chosen which is headed by the amount of calories you are allowed a day (in the box you filled in above). When you have chosen your diet, enter your daily portion allowance into the boxes overleaf.

You are also allowed 2 units of alcohol a week (see chart on page 82) and a treat a day (see page 80) to replace a portion of fats and oils if you really feel the need.

CHOOSING YOUR PORTION COMBINATIONS

Choose column A if you like plenty of protein foods
Choose column B if you like plenty of cereal foods
Choose column C if you have no particular food group preferences
Choose column D if you like plenty of fibre-rich foods and fruit
Choose column E if you like plenty of dairy foods/fats & oils

1,000 Calories a Day Diet

A	B	C	D	E
5 protein	3 protein	4 protein	3 protein	3 protein
4 cereal	5 cereal	4 cereal	4 cereal	4 cereal
2 dairy	3 dairy	3 dairy	2 dairy	3 dairy
2 fats*	1–2 fats*	2 fats*	1 fat*	3 fats*
3 fruit	1–2 fruit	2 fruit	5 fruit	3 fruit

1,100 Calories a Day Diet

A	B	C	D	E
6 protein	3 protein	5 protein	3 protein	3 protein
4 cereal	6 cereal	5 cereal	5 cereal	4 cereal
3 dairy	2 dairy	2 dairy	2 dairy	4 dairy
2 fats*	2 fats*	2 fats*	2 fats*	3 fats*
3 fruit	2–3 fruit	3 fruit	5 fruit	2 fruit

1,200 Calories a Day Diet

A	B	C	D	E
7 protein	4 protein	5–6 protein	4 protein	3 protein
5 cereal	6 cereal	6 cereal	6 cereal	5 cereal
2 dairy	2 dairy	2 dairy	2 dairy	4 dairy
2 fats*	2 fats*	2 fats*	2 fats*	3 fats*
2–3 fruit	2–3 fruit	2–3 fruit	4–5 fruit	3–4 fruit

1,300 Calories a Day Diet

A	B	C	D	E
7 protein	4 protein	5 protein	6 protein	4 protein
5 cereal	7 cereal	6 cereal	6–7 cereal	4 cereal
2 dairy	2 dairy	2 dairy	2 dairy	4 dairy
2 fats*	2 fats*	2 fats*	2 fats*	2 fats*
3 fruit	2–3 fruit	4 fruit	4 fruit	3–4 fruit

1,400 Calories a Day Diet

A	B	C	D	E
7 protein	4–5 protein	6 protein	6 protein	5 protein
5 cereal	8 cereal	6 cereal	7 cereal	6 cereal
3 dairy	2 dairy	3 dairy	2 dairy	4 dairy
2–3 fats*	3 fats*	3 fats*	2 fats*	3–4 fats*
3 fruit	3–4 fruit	2–3 fruit	4–5 fruit	3–4 fruit

continued over

1,500 Calories a Day Diet

A	B	C	D	E
8 protein	5 protein	7 protein	5 protein	5 protein
5–6 cereal	8 cereal	7 cereal	7 cereal	6 cereal
3 dairy	2–3 dairy	3 dairy	3 dairy	4 dairy
2 fats*	3 fats*	3 fats*	2 fats*	4 fats*
2–3 fruit	3–4 fruit	2–3 fruit	4–5 fruit	3–4 fruit

1,600 Calories a Day Diet

A	B	C	D	E
8 protein	5 protein	7 protein	6 protein	6 protein
6 cereal	8–9 cereal	8 cereal	8 cereal	6 cereal
4 dairy	3 dairy	3 dairy	3 dairy	4 dairy
3 fats*	2–3 fats	3 fats*	2 fats	4 fats
2–3 fruit	3 fruit	2–3 fruit	4–5 fruit	4 fruit

- You may exchange 1 fat portion for 1 treat portion each day if you prefer.
- If you find your daily calorie requirements match those of one of our eight dieters (Chapter 4), and you feel their portion choice would suit you, you can simply slot into their diet plan rather than choosing your daily portions from the chart above.

Protein [ ]

Cereal [ ]

Dairy [ ]

Fats & Oils [ ]

Fruit [ ]

Now, armed with all you know about what you like to eat and when, whether you like a series of snacks or big meals, and armed with your daily portion numbers, you can turn to Chapters 5 and 6 and begin putting together your daily eating plan.

CHAPTER 4

THE EIGHT WHO TRIED THE DIET

ROWENA, MARY, DANIELA, SUE, Penny, Alice, Liz and Carl had one thing in common; they all wanted to lose weight. All had tried diets before and always regained their weight, yo-yoing up and down over the years. Apart from this one similarity, they had little else in common. They were different sizes and shapes, had different eating habits and levels of activity, and all led different lifestyles. This is exactly why they were the perfect subjects to illustrate how the *Good Housekeeping* 30-Day Diet plan can be made to measure to suit every one who tries it. Out goal was to see results – a loss of at least 3.5 kg (8 lb) and a firmer, fitter figure within a month.

We asked our health consultant to appraise the energy requirements and exercise habits of our eight dieters. She established what each dieter's calorie intake should be to lose weight, and the amount and type of exercise they could realistically maintain. 'There's a very fine line between changing habits that can and should be changed, and aiming too high,' she says. 'Activity is the key to fitness and weight loss.'

It is important to remember that the rate of weight loss can vary enormously from person to person. Those who have more to lose, lose it the quickest, and those who exercise the most also tend to lose weight faster, as the exercise helps to counteract the drop in metabolism that dieters experience. Also, men, who don't have to battle with female hormones that fluctuate throughout the month, and influence the way they lay down fat, tend to lose fat faster. An important factor contributing to the successful weight loss of our dieters was their determination to lose weight, and what was going on in their lives at the time. Those who had other concerns in their lives, making them less whole-hearted about losing weight, lost less.

After we had appraised the energy requirements and exercise habits, our nutritionist then analysed the dieters' eating habits. She looked at whether they liked to eat little and often, or if they had a sweet tooth, for example. In this way she showed them how to devise a diet they could really live with. In the last chapter we have already shown you how to work out your own energy requirements, keep a diet diary and devise your own diet. In Chapter 7 we will show you how to work out your own exercise plan.

ROWENA WILSON: THE GOOD LIFE

Height: 1.72 m (5ft 9 in)
Age: 55 years
Start weight: 92 kg (14 st 9 lb)
Finish weight: 86 kg (13 st 9 lb)
Loss: 6 kg (14 lb)
Family: Married, grown-up children and grandchilden

Rowena works full-time as careers advisor at a school. Like many women of her age, she was shocked to discover how much weight had crept on unnoticed. She is a breakfast-skipper, as she rises at 6 am every weekday and leaves for work early. She cannot face eating so early in the morning apart from the juice of three to four oranges. Her first meal each day, then, is lunch in the school dining room. She usually chooses salads from the salad bar but these are loaded with high-calorie dressings. She eats cold meat with the salad, no bread, and two pieces of fruit for dessert. As she leaves for work early she doesn't want to prepare her own packed lunches. She also likes the companionship and bustle of the school dining room. She eats out at least twice a week and often takes afternoon tea at weekends. Her alcohol intake has crept up, too: she drinks three sherries each evening (136 calories per medium glass) and half a bottle of wine twice a week. Alcohol is a major source of unwanted calories that few people are aware of. Just by cutting back on alcohol consumption alone can be enough to lose weight for many people.

BEFORE 92 kg (14 st 9 lb)

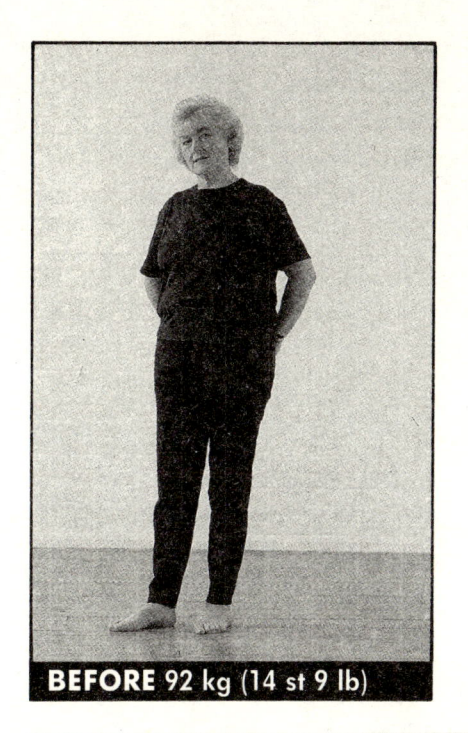

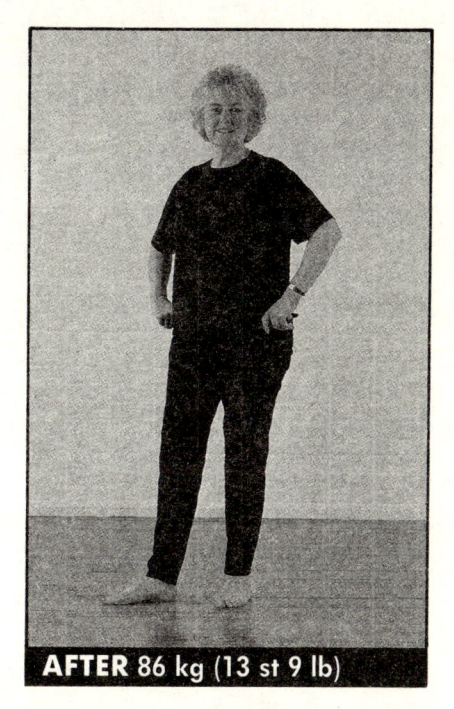

AFTER 86 kg (13 st 9 lb)

ROWENA'S DAILY CALORIE REQUIREMENT

Rowena was consuming at least 1800 calories a day – 100 a day more than the 1700 we estimated she requires. But since she wanted to lose over 6 kg (14 lb), and the more overweight you are, the faster your weight loss tends to be, we calculated her weight should drop about 1 kg (2 lb) a week on 1,200 calories a day.

Analysing Rowena's food diary and lifestyle revealed the following:

Breakfast:
Weekdays – juice of 3–4 oranges.
Weekend – eats brunch: omelette or poached egg on toast or cheese and salad.

Lunch:
Weekdays – salad from the salad bar at work, plus cold meats. No bread, two pieces of fruit.

Weekend Tea time:
- Tea and cakes – no sugar in tea.

Evening meal:
- 3 sherries.
- Half a bottle of wine twice a week.
- Mainly chicken or fish dishes, grilled, plus two potatoes or two spoons of rice or pasta. Vegetables.
- Occasionally eats dessert.

General summary of current eating habits:

- Eats at mealtimes only, with no snacks in between.
- Leaves for work very early in the morning so cannot face breakfast apart from orange juice.
- Eats lunch provided by school, usually from salad bar. Does not want to take packed lunch with her from home.
- Doesn't take sugar in or on anything.
- Drinks 3 sherries every evening and half a bottle of wine twice a week. Would like a small allowance of alcohol, but could cut the sherries out and drink Perrier instead.
- Eats out twice a week.
- Likes 300 ml (½ pint) skimmed milk daily.

All these details enabled us to build up a clear picture of the sort of diet profile Rowena needed, one that took into account her likes and dislikes. Rowena naturally favoured a healthy, well-balanced diet, liking mainly low-fat protein with lots of fresh fruit and vegetables. So we converted her daily calorie allowance of 1,200 calories into daily 'portions' that gave her a satisfying amount of these foods. The portions allowed were:

Protein (p)   6
Cereal (c)   3
Dairy (d)   1
Fats & oils (f&o) 1
Fruit (f)   5

SAMPLE DAILY MENU

Daily allowance:
1d   300 ml (½ pint) skimmed milk for tea and coffee

Breakfast:
3f   juice of 3 oranges

Lunch or Brunch:
3p   75 g (3 oz) lean ham or other cold meat or 2 egg omelette with 25 g (1 oz) Edam cheese
1c   one 25 g (1 oz) slice wholemeal bread
ff   plenty of salad from the free food list
1f&o 15 ml (1 tbsp) low-calorie mayonnaise
1f   1 piece of fruit

Evening Meal:
2p   175 g (6 oz) grilled white fish or chicken
2c   175 g (6 oz) boiled potatoes
1p   100 g (4 oz) peas
ff   plenty of vegetables from the free food list
1f   1 piece of fruit

SAMPLE WEEKEND MENU

Most of us like to relax and indulge ourselves at the weekend. If this is the case with you, it is important for a diet to take it into account. Rowena's diet had just such extra 'treats' built into her weekend eating plan. Eating – particularly at weekends – is an important part of socialising, and by preventing yourself from, say, eating tea, or having the occasional sociable drink, you will be denying yourself part of the pleasure of socialising, and it will therefore make your diet very difficult to stick to. For this reason, we gave some of our dieters an extra portion or two to build into their diets at the weekend. For others, their sample weekend menu merely reflected their different eating patterns, as weekends tend to be less rigid.

Protein (p)   6
Cereal (c)   3
Dairy (d)   1
Fats & oils (f&o) 2
Fruit (f)   5

Daily allowance:
1d   300 ml (½ pint) skimmed milk for tea and coffee

Breakfast:
1f   100 ml (4 fl oz) unsweetened fruit juice
1c   one 25 g (1 oz) slice wholemeal toast
1p   poached egg
1f&o 5 ml (1 tsp) butter or margarine
ff   grilled tomatoes and mushrooms from the free food list

Mid-morning:
1f   1 piece of fruit

Lunch:
1c   25 g (1 oz) pitta bread stuffed
1p   with 25 g (1 oz) low-fat cheese
ff   plenty of vegetables from the free food list
1f   piece of fruit

Dinner:
3p   75 g (3 oz) lean lamb or beef or 150 g (6 oz) chicken
1c   75 g (3 oz) baked potato
1p   100 g (4 oz) peas
ff   plenty of salad from the free food list
1f&o 15 ml (1 tbsp) low-calorie mayonnaise
2f   baked apple filled with 25 g (1 oz) dried fruit
or:
4p   Chicken Kebabs (see recipe on
1f&o page 123)
1c   75 g (3 oz) baked potato

ff   plenty of salad or vegetables from the free food list
2f   baked apple filled with 25 g (1 oz) dried fruit

Extras:
1 small plain cake, *e.g.* small slice victoria sandwich, mini-roll, teacake or 1 chocolate digestive

EXERCISE
Metabolism drops continuously throughout adulthood (by about 1.5 per cent between the ages of 20 and 40), but at a much faster rate (about 7 per cent) between 40 and 60. So at this stage of your life you either need to counteract the drop in metabolism by doing more exercise, or reduce your food intake, or a mixture of both. Although Rowena walks about 1 mile a day in the course of her work, and takes a walk at the weekends, she needs to do more if it is to contribute to her weight loss and to exercise her cardiovascular system (heart and lungs) enough to be beneficial to her health. Rowena felt she would like to return to an aerobics class she used to attend nearby, once a week, and that she could go swimming with a friend once a week. She also felt she could realistically manage a short exercise routine at home. We recommended she try a 20 minutes stretch and strength exercise routine every day at home – you'll find the same exercises on pages 169–183. These will improve muscle tone, stamina and suppleness as well as helping to burn up extra calories.

GENERAL GUIDELINES
For Rowena, a great calorie saving could be made simply by cutting down on alcohol. She also needs to

get the better of school lunches by taking her own low-calorie salad dressing and making sure her other food choices keep within the limits of her diet. Alternatively, she could take a packed lunch to avoid temptation in the dining room. As eating is an important part of her social life, we showed her the low-fat route around a restaurant menu. Go to a place where you have a good relationship with the staff and explain that you must avoid fatty food (imply medical reasons – it gets more cooperation). Choose foods on the menu that appear in your diet and specify that you want your fish without buttery sauce (choose lemon juice instead), your salad without dressing (ask for yogurt) and your potato without butter. Finally, have only fruit salad for pudding.

ROWENA'S PROGRESS

'Cutting out the sherries alone has helped enormously. I can't believe I've lost a stone! I've never been able to stick to a diet before, but this took into account my strengths and weaknesses and so I felt able to cope with it, and didn't have to reorganise my life in order to diet. I had no trouble when I was eating out or with school lunches, and I solved the problem of a social life by inviting people to dinner at our house, where I could control the food. Since I was allowed a glass of wine twice a week, I didn't feel at all deprived.'

Rowena found that the exercises instantly made her feel fresher and more alert, and once she had started, this feeling provided motivation to continue. Taking exercise is an important way to focus attention on your body and is a step towards taking pride in its fitness, well-being and shape. 'I couldn't exercise every day, as I had planned, because my job is so demanding. But I swam on Tuesdays, went to aerobics on Thursdays and did my own exercises all through the weekend,' says Rowena. 'The 30 days of the diet were enough to form good new habits.'

MARY CADOGAN: WORKING MOTHER

Height: 1.61 m (5 ft 3½ in)
Age: 36 years
Start weight: 57.5 kg (9 st 2 lb)
Finish weight: 52 kg (8 st 4 lb)
Loss: 5.5 kg (12 lb)
Family: Married with two children aged 4 and 6 years

Mary is a freelance cookery writer. As well as devising new recipes for magazines and books, she also tests and prepares them for photography in photographic studios. Her work is irregular and often hectic, and as a result, her eating patterns are erratic and she has put on 6 kg (1 st) in weight in a year. Mary may spend two or three days at a time cooped up in a photographic studio where only relatively fattening foods are available to eat. Other days she will spend writing at home or doing housework and looking after her children. She needed a diet and exercise programme which would suit her days at work as well as her days at home with her children.

If she's working at a photographic studio she often skips breakfast and eats cold meats and ready-prepared salads, thinking that they are probably the most slimming foods on offer. This is a common misconception among would-be slimmers. In fact, salads can be laden with fatty dressings, and cold meats can be high in fat.

Mary's two young sons come in hungry for their tea every day after school, and Mary tends to nibble biscuits while preparing it. She and her husband enjoy eating together in the evening. It is the one time of day they can relax and talk. However, as Mary spends much of her working life cooking, her husband often prepares their food and he tends to choose fattening dishes and ingredients. Added to this, Mary takes very little exercise – she says her life isn't routine enough to attend classes. It's easy to see how Mary's lifestyle has led to accumulated pounds.

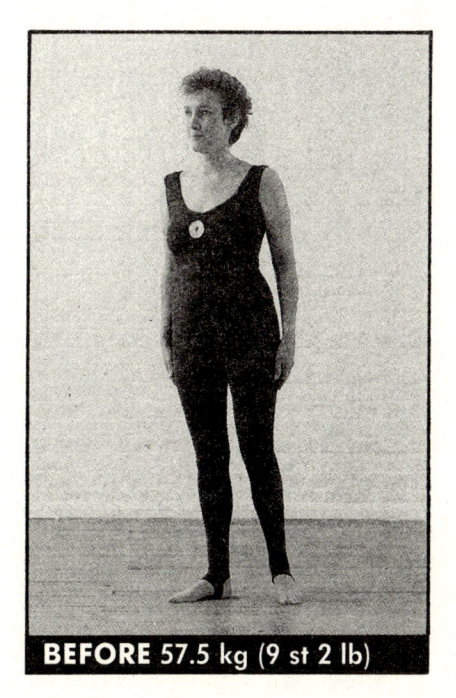

BEFORE 57.5 kg (9 st 2 lb)

AFTER 52 kg (8 st 4 lb)

> **MARY'S DAILY CALORIE REQUIREMENT**
>
> Mary's height, weight and age revealed that her calorie requirements for her current weight are approximately 1,900 calories a day. Going by the average drop of calories of between 500 and 700 a day in order to lose 1 kg (2 lb) a week we calculated that if Mary were to stick to the exercise we'd alotted her, she would need a diet of around 1,200 calories a day. The combined effects of exercise and diet can be remarkable with results exceeding pen and paper calculations. Exercise alone is often enough, especially for those who have already dieted and are on a 'plateau'.

Analysing Mary's diet and lifestyle revealed the following:

Breakfast:
- Mary only eats breakfast when not working but she is prepared to start taking it to the studio with her as she can't face eating it before work.
- She eats 1–2 slices of toast with butter (she isn't prepared to try low-fat spread like St Ivel Gold, but could be persuaded to have a half-fat butter.)
- During morning, if at work, she nibbles at fruit, biscuits or anything that's around – she's hungry because she hasn't had breakfast.

Lunch:
- Work – normally around 2 pm. Mary eats cold meat and ready-prepared salads, often in dressings such as mayonnaise.
- Home – sandwich filled with salami, corned beef and salad. Fruit and biscuits.

Afternoon and early evening:
- Nibbles at bread, crisps, etc, particularly when preparing children's tea at 5 pm.

Evening meal with husband 7–10 pm
- Either Mary or her husband cook – never eat convenience food. Could be pasta, risotto, stir-fry, Spanish omelette. (Husband tends to use a lot of butter and olive oil when he cooks.)
- Rarely dessert, occasionally natural yogurt.
- Likes wine – 1–2 glasses a day.

General summary of current eating habits:
- Very erratic – no set pattern to meals depending whether she's working or not (works 3–4 days a week).
- Tends to nibble.
- Alcohol is an important contributor to excess calories. Doesn't want to cut it out completely when dieting but would be happy with 1–2 glasses a week.
- Can do without desserts – doesn't often eat them.
- Takes 7.5 g (½ tsp) sugar in drinks. Not a lot of calories but feels she could probably do without.
- Takes about 300 ml (½ pint) semi-skimmed milk a day – hates skimmed.

All these details enabled our nutritionist to build up a clear picture of the sort of diet profile Mary needs to be able to incorporate it into her lifestyle and stick at it. Her daily calorie allowance (1,200) was converted into the more simple 'portions' that are the currency of the diets in this book. The portions allowed were:

Protein (p)	6
Cereal (c)	6
Dairy (d)	2
Fats & Oils (f&o)	3
Fruit (f)	3

SAMPLE DAILY MENU

Daily allowance:
1d   200 ml (⅓ pint) semi-skimmed milk for tea and coffee
1f&o   5 ml (1 tsp) butter or margarine

Breakfast:
2c   two 25 g (1 oz) slices wholemeal bread or 2 Weetabix; with milk or butter from allowance

Mid-morning
1f   1 piece of fruit

Lunch:
1c   one 25 g (1 oz) slice wholemeal bread
3p   75 g (3 oz) lean ham or 175 g (6 oz) pilchards in tomato sauce
ff   large salad from the free foods list
1f&o   15 ml (1 tbsp) low-calorie mayonnaise

Tea time:
1c   2 rich tea biscuits
ff   raw vegetables as crudités from the free food list
1f   75 g (3 oz) grapes or cherries

Evening Meal:
3p   125–150 g (4–5 oz) chicken
2c   100 g (4 oz) wholegrain rice
ff   plenty of vegetables from the free food list
1f&o   5 ml (1 tsp) butter or oil
1d   150 ml (¼ pint) low-fat natural yogurt
1f   1 piece of fruit
or:
2p   Fish Kebabs (see recipe on page 86)
2c   100 g (4 oz) cooked brown rice or pasta, or 50 g (2 oz) wholemeal pitta bread
1p   100 g (4 oz) peas
ff   tomato salad from the free food list with
1f&o   15 ml (1 tbsp) low-calorie salad dressing
1d   60 ml (4 level tbsp) fromage frais
1f   1 piece of fruit

SAMPLE WEEKEND MENU

Mary's weekend menu is similar to her weekday menu because her eating problems are caused by the irregularity of her working day. We've tried to introduce a routine into her eating habits which follows through into the weekend.

Daily allowance:
1d   200 ml (⅓ pint) semi-skimmed milk for tea and coffee

Breakfast:
1p   1 boiled or poached egg
1c   one 25 g (1 oz) slice wholemeal toast

Mid-morning:
1f 1 piece of fruit

Lunch:
2c 50 g (2 oz) wholemeal bap filled with
2p 50 g (2 oz) sardines
1f&o 5 ml (1 tsp) butter or margarine
ff plenty of salad from the free food list

or:
1p Spicey Bean Pâté (see recipe on
1c page 93)
1f&o
1p 50 g (2 oz) low-fat soft cheese
1c 25 g (1 oz) pitta bread

Tea-time:
1c 1 digestive biscuit
1f 1 piece of fruit

Dinner:
2p 100 g (4 oz) peeled prawns
1p 100 g (4 oz) peas
2f&o vegetables from the free food list, stir fried in 10 ml (2 tsp) vegetable oil and soy sauce
2c 100 g (4 oz) cooked noodles or rice
1d 150 ml (¼ pint) low-fat fruit yogurt
1f 1 piece of fruit

or:
3p Farmhouse Chicken Breasts
1f&o (see recipe on page 124)
ff vegetables from the free foods list
1f&o 15 ml (1 tbsp) low-calorie salad dressing
2c 175 g (6 oz) boiled new potatoes
1f 1 piece of fruit
1d 60 ml (4 tbsp) fromage frais

EXERCISE

Having devised her diet, we asked Mary what sort of exercise she liked and disliked, and what she felt she could realistically incorporate into her day. Her life is so lacking in routine that she can't attend regular classes, and she doesn't want to spend her spare time away from her children if possible. Mary admitted she would like to go swimming and could manage an exercise routine in the morning when she was at home. She also felt that she could probably put aside about 20 minutes in the evening for exercise on days when she was working. We advised Mary to exercise for 20–30 minutes every morning using the exercise routine on pages 169–183 which aims to improve muscle tone, stamina and suppleness while helping her burn up calories and relieve some of the pent-up stresses that can accompany a busy lifestyle. We also recommended she go swimming twice a week with her children when she wasn't working. This is a good way of combining exercise she enjoys with having fun with her children.

GENERAL GUIDELINES

We showed Mary that if she plans ahead, she can fit a steady diet and exercise programme into her less-than-steady routine. She can ensure that meals are regular by preparing them in advance when necessary. We explained that by skipping breakfast, her body learnt to burn up very few calories until lunch time, so the habit could be counterproductive to overall calorie loss.

For lunch, we advised Mary to have a salad without dressing, and to avoid fatty cold meats like salami (three slices are as fattening as a Mars bar!). To help her succeed, we suggested that Mary involve her husband and children in her new eating plan. Less fat and more fibre would benefit them too, and they could fill up with extra brown bread, rice and potatoes.

MARY'S PROGRESS

Having rapidly lost the first kilogram, Mary realised that discipline and organisation could reap results and she became dedicated to her programme. 'It worked around my lifestyle, so it was easy to follow,' she comments. She enjoyed her exercises and did them every morning and evening. She found they made her feel fresher, more alert and energetic and felt they positively fuelled her enthusiasm to get fit and slim. After four weeks she was able to do 50 sit-ups in one go! Her husband and *au pair* lost weight, too.

'I lapsed once or twice, but it didn't set me back. In fact, letting go occasionally helped me to be more restrained the rest of the time,' she says. 'Tea time was still difficult, but I was allowed a couple of rich tea biscuits (only 36 calories each) as well as unlimited raw vegetables, which kept me going. The *Good Housekeeping* team phoned me twice a week, which was very motivating, but anybody could ask a friend to do this for them.'

DANIELA BRANDLER: YOUNG MOTHER AT HOME

Height: 1.75 m (5ft 10in)
Age: 29 years
Start weight: 70 kg (11st 2lb)
Finish weight: 67 kg (10st 10lb)
Loss: 3 kg (6lb)
Family: Married with a one-year-old child

Daniela had an active, healthy lifestyle until she became pregnant with her son Joshua, after which she found the extra weight she had gained hard to shift. And now that Joshua is one, she is at home all day and eats irregularly, nibbling sweet things through boredom and stress – particularly just before her periods.

Daniela eats many foods that are classic emotional crutches. Many of us associate sweet foods with comfort. This usually stems from childhood when sweet foods are given as treats or rewards. Hopefully, as children tend to be brought up on healthier foods these days, they won't rely on sweet foods in the same way.

BEFORE 70 kg (11 st 2 lb)

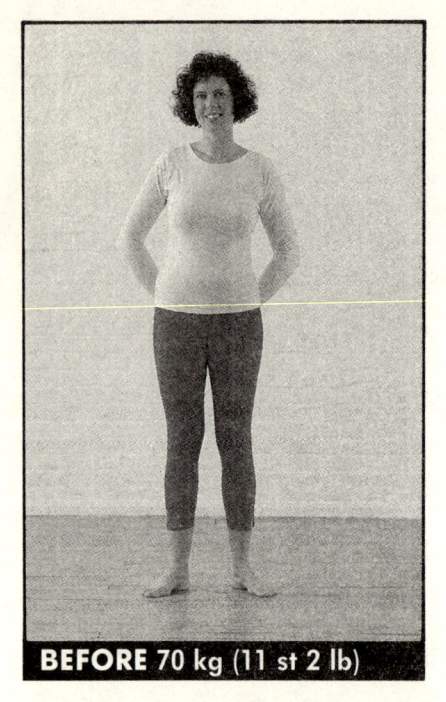

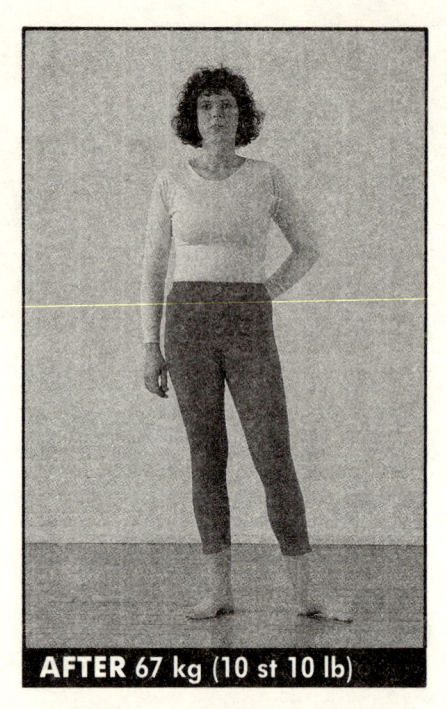

AFTER 67 kg (10 st 10 lb)

Often the menstrual cycle is to blame for a greater impulse to eat. Many women eat an extra 500 or so calories a day just before a period. As long as you eat healthy, filling food, this is nothing to worry about, because your body naturally compensates by stepping up the metabolic rate and demanding less food later on – just after a period. Turn this to your advantage by starting a diet just after a period when it's naturally easier to cut down for many women.

Daniela wants food that's quick and easy to prepare, and because Joshua still needs constant attention, she finds it hard to make time for herself and so takes little exercise.

DANIELA'S DAILY CALORIE REQUIREMENT

Daniela's weight should be more or less stable on 2,000 calories a day. So, on a diet of 1,200 calories we estimated that she should lose around 600 g (1½ lb) a week.

Daniela's food diary revealed the following details about her eating habits:

Breakfast:
- 2–3 slices of bread (white or brown) spread thinly with butter and jam.
- An occasional glass of orange juice.

Mid-Morning:
- Chocolate biscuits (anything up to half a packet).

Lunch:
- Jacket potato with cheese, or
- a sandwich.

During afternoon:
- Biscuits, bread and butter.

Evening:
- Mainly chicken and fish (doesn't eat a lot of red meat).
- Often eats tinned tuna in oil.
- Rice/potatoes.
- Occasional fruit or yogurt when she can be bothered.

Late evening:
- Often makes a sandwich last thing before going to bed.

Takes about 300 ml (½ pint) full-fat milk in drinks throughout the day.

General summary of current eating habits:
- Has recently been over-eating, feels it is due to boredom.
- Daniela is at home during the day with a one-year-old toddler, so she has plenty of time to nibble. May eat half a packet of chocolate biscuits or half a loaf of bread and butter in one go.
- Has a sweet tooth, especially pre-menstrually. She has a very irregular cycle so is never sure when this time really is. Doesn't want a chocolate allowance as part of her diet. Has decided that she will cut out chocolates, sweets and biscuits feeling that if she doesn't have them in the house the craving will subside.
- All food eaten is quick and simple to prepare as she cannot be bothered to spend a lot of time in the kitchen.
- Rarely eats fruit or salads (through 'laziness').
- Rarely eats desserts.
- Has the occasional glass of wine, but would not miss it if she didn't.
- Rarely eats out.

All these details enabled our nutritionist to build up a picture of the sort of eating patterns Daniela's diet should consist of, and the sorts of foods it should contain. Her daily calorie allowance of 1,200 was converted into a diet that consisted of lots of small snack meals throughout the day that were high in cereal allowing her plenty of filling carbohydrate in the form of crunchy crispbreads, savoury biscuits, pasta, rice and potatoes. As she like fatty foods, her allowances of fats and oils and dairy were also relatively high. Her diet is based on the following portions:

Protein (p)	5
Cereal (c)	7
Dairy (d)	2
Fats & Oils (f&o)	3
Fruit (f)	2

SAMPLE DAILY MENU
Daily allowance:
1d   200 ml (⅓ pint) semi-skimmed milk for tea and coffee

Breakfast:
- 2c — two 25 g (1 oz) slices wholemeal bread spread with
- 1f&o — 10 ml (2 tsp) low-fat spread

Mid Morning:
- 1f — 1 piece of fruit

Lunch:
- 2c — 175 g (6 oz) baked potato
- 2p — 100 g (4 oz) cottage cheese
- ff — plenty of salad from the free food list with
- 1f&o — 15 ml (1 tbsp) low-calorie mayonnaise
- 1d — 150 ml (¼ pint) low-fat fruit yogurt

or:
- 2p — Stir-fried Liver (see recipe on
- 1f&o — page 128)
- 2c — 50 g (2 oz) pitta bread/ wholemeal bap
- 1d — 60 ml (4 tbsp) fromage frais

Mid-afternoon
- 1c — one 25 g (1 oz) slice wholemeal bread or 2 plain crackers

Evening Meal:
- 3p — 125–150 g (4–5 oz) white fish or tuna canned in brine
- 2c — 175 g (6 oz) boiled potatoes
- ff — plenty of vegetables from the free food list with
- 1f&o — 15 ml (1 tbsp) low-calorie salad dressing

or:
- 3p — Farmhouse Chicken Breasts
- 1f&o — (see recipe on page 124)
- 2c — 175 g (6 oz) baked potato
- ff — plenty of salad from the free food list
- ff — fruit from the free food list

Late evening:
- 1f — 1 piece of fruit

SAMPLE WEEKEND MENU

Protein (p)	6
Cereal (c)	7
Dairy (d)	2
Fats & Oils (f&o)	3
Fruit (f)	2

There is little difference between Daniela's weekday and weekend routine, except that she may socialise and see friends who drop round to eat with her. Consequently, we allowed her one more protein portion and included more treat foods in her weekend menu.

Daily allowance:
- 1d — 200 ml (⅓ pint) semi-skimmed milk for tea and coffee

Breakfast:
- 2c — two 25 g (1 oz) slices wholemeal toast
- 1f&o — 5 ml (1 tsp) low-fat spread
- 1f&o — 20 ml (4 tsp) marmalade
- 1f — 100 ml (4 fl oz) unsweetened orange juice

Mid-morning:
- 1f — 1 piece of fruit

Lunch:
- 3c — 75 g (3 oz) bap
- 2p — 50 g (2 oz) reduced-fat hard cheese
- ff — plenty of salad from the free food list

or:
- 3c — 75 g (3 oz) pitta bread
- 2p — Peppery Cheese Souffles (see recipe on page 144)
- ff — plenty of vegetables from the free foods list
- ff — fruit from the free food list

Mid-afternoon:

ff	fruit from the free food list
1f&o	1 fun-size chocolate bar

Dinner:

2p	175 g (6 oz) grilled white fish
1p	100 g (4 oz) peas
ff	plenty of vegetables from the free food list
2c	175 (6 oz) baked potato
1d	50 ml (¼ pint) low-fat yogurt with
1p	25 g (1 oz) chopped walnuts mixed in

or:

4p	Tandoori Chicken (see recipe on page 126)
1c	1 small chapati
1c	2 small grilled popadoms
ff	salad from the free food list
1d	150 ml (¼ pint) low-fat natural or fruit yogurt
ff	plenty of fruits from the free food list

EXERCISE

Having devised a diet that fitted in with Daniela's lifestyle, we asked her what exercise she felt she could realistically incorporate into her life. As she has little free time to herself, Daniela didn't want to spend it in an exercise class, so her exercise had to be of the sort that could become part of her daily routine.

So, Daniela felt she could exercise at home for half an hour every evening after Joshua has gone to bed. She was also able to extend her short daily stroll to a more brisk 30 minute walk to get more real benefit from it.

GENERAL GUIDELINES

As Daniela likes to eat little and often, her diet consisted of five or six small, well-balanced meals or snacks a day. Gradually she found she needed less food to satisfy her appetite. In addition, Daniela could also feast on free foods (raw vegetables and certain fruits), if she felt tempted to snack at other times. Daniela can't resist nibbling on biscuits and cakes if they are in the house, so we advised her not to include them on her shopping list. To help her resist them when she goes shopping we told her never to shop on an empty stomach, but always when she has just eaten. Her interest in food is then at its lowest ebb. Good advice for any dieter!

DANIELA'S PROGRESS

The month in which Daniela embarked on her weight loss programme was a very stressful one. First her mother was ill, then Joshua, and she had to spend time in hospital with him. Needless to say, she found the diet hard to follow with so much on her mind. She fell prey to bouts of stress eating, and attacked cakes and biscuits at her mother's house since she had none in her own home!

Our nutritional and medical team feel that there are times when we have other worries on our minds, and it is only possible to stick to a diet if it's a high priority when embarking on it and in order to stick to it. In a situation such as Daniela's, we felt it was far better for her to shelve her weight problems and tackle the more urgent issues in her life. Failing in a diet at such a time would only add to her stresses.

In fact, life settled down for Daniela in the last week-and-a-half of the 30 days and she found she was able to lose 2.5 kg (6 lb) quite easily. 'I found the fact that there was never long to wait until the next meal or snack, was a great help, and the great variety of food that I could eat meant I never got bored.'

SUE WEBSTER: FOODIE

Height: 1.67 m (5ft 7 in)
Age: 46 years
Start weight: 69 kg (11st 1lb)
Finish weight: 64 kg (10st 4lb)
Loss: 5 kg (11lb)
Family: Married with grown-up children

Sue works at home, is an enthusiastic cook and loves to spend a lot of time and effort creating spectacular weekend feasts for family and friends. She enjoys having dinner with her husband each evening, too. She had gradually put on weight over the years, partly due to the hormone replacement therapy she has been given for osteoporosis (or brittle bones). She already has a healthy lifestyle, and has been trying to cut back on her food, and says she is quite careful about how much she eats, but she had found that weight loss had so far been extremely slow. She enjoys exercise and she goes jogging for 20 minutes twice a week.

Our nutritionist suspected that Sue was unaware of how many calories there were in the foods she was cooking. Sue particularly loves French cooking, with liberal use of cream and rich olive or nut oils. When she asked Sue to record everything she ate and drank in her food diary, she also encouraged Sue to record the ingredients used in her recipes. While food might not be piled high on Sue's plate, generous amounts of oil can literally double the amount of calories she consumes without her realising it.

SUE'S DAILY CALORIE REQUIREMENT

With an initial daily intake of 1,500 calories, Sue's weight loss was slow, so she cut down even further to 1,000. She should subsequently be able to maintain her weight at its current level with 2,000 calories a day, provided she keeps up her exercise.

BEFORE 69 kg (11 st 1 lb)

AFTER 64 kg (10 st 4 lb)

Analysing Sue's diet revealed the following:

Breakfast:
- ½ grapefruit.
- 1 dry slice of wholemeal toast, sometimes with jam, or
- 1 Weetabix with 5 ml (1 tsp) sugar and skimmed milk plus prunes drained of juice.

Sunday:
- Cooked breakfast of microwaved bacon, kidney and mushrooms, tinned tomatoes, poached or dry fried egg.

Lunch:
- Findus Lean Cuisine meal
or:
- Baked beans
or:
- Cottage cheese.

- 1 dry slice wholemeal bread.
- Salad with low-calorie dressing, although she does love Hellman's mayonnaise!
- French-style fruit, or natural, yogurt.
- Occasionally eats fruit as well.

Evening meal:
- Meat or fish (sometimes fried) with a rich sauce.
- Baked or sauté potatoes.
- Vegetables – loves them.
- Likes to follow with cheese such as stilton.
- Likes to drink red wine with meal.
- Rarely eats a dessert.

General summary of current eating habits:
- Has already cut down on what she was previously eating in an attempt to lose weight.

- Loves cooking.
- Eats out about once a week.
- Hardly drinks alcohol or milk. Fluid intake comes from black coffee and Perrier water. Wouldn't miss alcohol much if asked to give it up.
- Never eats between meals.
- Doesn't eat biscuits, chocolates, sweets, cakes, etc.
- Likes cheese, particularly stilton, and doesn't realise how many calories this could be contributing to her diet.
- Rarely eats desserts.
- Tends to dry-fry or microwave meat, when it would be preferable for her to grill it because it makes it release more fat. Doesn't realise calories could be saved by doing this.

All these details enabled our nutritionist to clearly see the pitfalls of Sue's diet. Fattening foods that could be easily substituted with lower calorie ones, without spoiling Sue's pleasure in her food. As Sue naturally likes a well-balanced, healthy diet, her recommended calorie intake of 1,000 a day was converted to a balanced mix of portions of each food category, in a diet based on the three meals a day that Sue's own inclinations and lifestyle dictated. Thus, Sue's diet was as follows:

Protein (p)   6
Cereal (c)   4
Dairy (d)   2
Fats & Oils (f&o)   3
Fruit (f)   2

SAMPLE DAILY MENU

Daily allowance:
1d   200 ml (⅓ pint) semi-skimmed milk

Breakfast:
1c   one 25 g (1 oz) slice dry wholemeal toast or 1 Weetabix with milk from allowance
1f   5 prunes in juice

Lunch:
1c   one 25 g (1 oz) slice wholemeal bread
1f&o 10 ml (2 tsp) low-fat spread
3p   75 g (3 oz) Edam cheese, or 150 g (6 oz) cottage cheese
1d   60 ml (4 tbsp) fromage frais
or:
1c   1 Lean Cuisine
3p
ff   salad from the free food list
1f&o 15 ml (1 tbsp) low-calorie mayonnaise
1d   150 ml (¼ pint) low-fat fruit yogurt

Evening Meal:
3p   75 g (3 oz) lean meat, grilled
2c   175 g (6 oz) baked potato
ff   plenty of vegetables from the free food list
2 f&o 10 ml (2 tsp) butter or oil for cooking
1f   1 piece of fruit
or:
3p   Mango Chicken Parcels (see recipe on page 121)
1f
1c   50 g (2 oz) cooked rice
1c   50 g (2 oz) sweetcorn with
2 f&o 10 ml (2 tsp) butter

SAMPLE WEEKEND MENU

As Sue does most of her entertaining at weekends we built extra portions of protein and cereal into her diet at weekends so that she could enjoy them.

Protein (p)   7

Cereal (c)   5
Dairy (d)   2
Fats & Oils (f&o) 3
Fruit (f)   2

Daily allowance:
1d   200 ml (⅓ pint) semi-skimmed milk
2f&o 10 ml (2 tsp) butter or oil for cooking

Breakfast:
ff   ½ grapefruit
1c   one 25 g (1 oz) slice dry wholemeal toast
2p   1 rasher lean grilled bacon and 1 poached egg or 50 g (2 oz) lambs kidney grilled or microwaved

Lunch:
2c   two 25 g (1 oz) slices wholemeal bread as a sandwich
2p   50 g (2 oz) lean ham
ff   plenty of salad from the free food list
1f&o 15 ml (1 tbsp) low-calorie mayonnaise
1f   1 piece of fruit
or:
2p   Peppery Cheese Souffles (see recipe on page 144)
2c   50 g (2 oz) crusty French bread
1f   1 piece of fruit

Evening meal:
1f   Carrot and Orange Soup (see recipe on page 96)
2p   Baked Gingered Chicken (see recipe on page 121)
1p   100 g (4 oz) peas
2c   175 g (6 oz) potatoes
1d   150 ml (¼ pint) French-style, low-fat fruit yogurt

EXERCISE

As Sue already goes jogging and enjoys it, and felt she could easily take on more, we suggested she increase her twice-weekly runs to three times a week and cover a greater distance each time.

GENERAL GUIDELINES:

Sue simply hadn't realised how fattening cooking oils and cheeses such as stilton were. Her diet had a lower weekday portion allowance when she found it easier to cut back, and a higher portion allowance at weekends so that she could still enjoy social eating.

For her osteoporosis, she takes a supplement of vitamins A and D, to ensure she takes a sufficient amount to these two vitamins. Exercise is also believed to help osteoporosis, as the body builds up extra calcium around the joints if they are used sufficiently. So her increased exercise regime should help, too. However, great care must be taken not to put excessive strain on the joints and bones.

SUE'S PROGRESS

The pounds rolled off. 'I weigh less now than I did 10 years ago,' she commented. 'Everybody's noticed that I look slimmer. I'm feeling very conceited!' Sue found the diet was flexible enough for her to use many of her own recipes, adapting them a little to lower the fat content. By the end of the month, she was running 12 miles a week in total, sometimes for an hour at a stretch. Apart from helping her lose weight while on the diet, Sue felt it would help her keep weight off in the future as she was more aware of which foods were fattening.

PENNY NATHAN: VEGETARIAN WORKING MOTHER

Height: 1.66 m (5ft 5½in)
Age : 39 years
Start weight: 60 kg (9st 7lb)
Finish weight: 57 kg (9 st)
Loss: 3 kg (7lb)
Family: Married with a two-year-old daughter.

Penny works three days a week as a sub-editor on a magazine, a sedentary job involving hard concentration, which tends to make her nibble sweet snacks (she has a very sweet tooth). The rest of the week she is at home with her daughter Naomi ceaselessly trying to thwart her attempts to demolish their flat. She says looking after Naomi is much harder work than going out to work! Penny gained weight when pregnant with Naomi, and had lost a lot soon afterwards, but during the past year it had begun to creep on again.

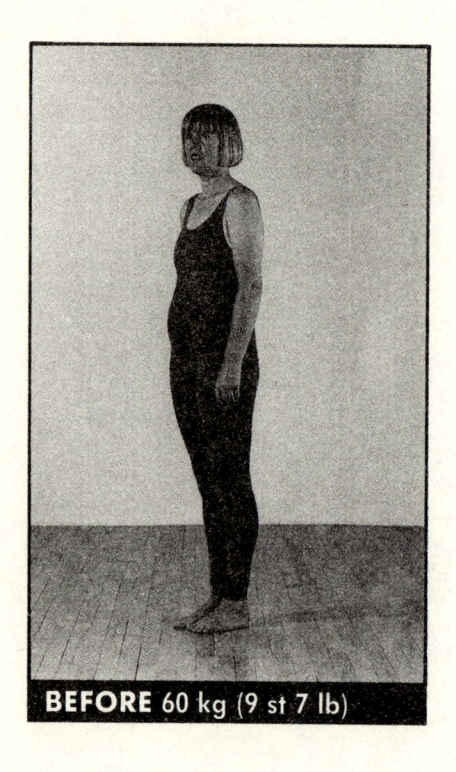

BEFORE 60 kg (9 st 7 lb)

AFTER 57 kg (9 st)

She was eager to get back to her ideal weight before trying to become pregnant again. Penny loves food and is an excellent cook, she is also very aware of what foods are fattening and what aren't. However, a love of food combined with a sedentary and fairly stressful lifestyle with little time to herself, conspired to make her gain weight.

Penny is almost vegetarian, only buying meat when friends come for supper. She finds most diets simply don't cater for vegetarians and, as a result, dieting is extremely monotonous. This is why the 30-Day Diet is so good for Penny, as the food categories aren't divided into meat and vegetables, but cereal, protein and so on. The protein category includes a wealth of vegetarian alternatives to meat. Penny is a member of a gym, and exercising with weights is the form of exercise she most enjoys. However, her lifestyle ensures she currently has little time to spend on herself, and the gym where she is a member is quite far from both home and work. How much free time she has depends on her husband's working patterns which tend to consist of erratic stints of rather long hours.

PENNY'S DAILY CALORIE REQUIREMENT

Penny's current estimated daily calorie intake is 1,620 a day. We estimated that she should maintain her weight on 1,430, and that a daily intake of 1,200 calories a day plus exercise should make her lose weight at about 1 kg (2 lb) a week.

Analysing Penny's food diary and lifestyle revealed the following:

Breakfast:
Weekday
- 1 thick slice wholemeal bread, butter, marmalade or honey.
- Cappuccino using 150 ml (¼ pint) semi-skimmed milk.

Weekend
- Toast as above, and/or porridge or cornflakes using semi-skimmed milk and sugar
- Cappuccino, made as above.

Mid-morning:
Weekday
- Croissant at 10 am on arriving at work.

Weekend
- Occasionally buys doughnut while out shopping.

Lunch:
Weekday
- Sandwich such as avocado/prawn plus mayonnaise.
- 2 small pots of Marks & Spencer rice pudding with apricot purée.

Weekend
• Apple, cheese (cheddar), wholemeal bread and butter.

Afternoon:
Weekday
• Gets very hungry around 5–6 pm and eats Crunchie or Smarties.
Weekend
• Snacks on dried fruit and nuts.

Evening:
Weekday
• Always cooks fresh food, pasta with fresh tomato sauce and plenty of olive oil, eats a large plateful.
• Occasionally cooks pudding – bread and butter pudding, clafoutis, etc.
• Cappuccino, made as above.
Weekend
• Similar to weekday, more likely to have a pudding and maybe a glass of wine.
• Cappuccino, made as above.

General summary of current eating habits:
• Is a keen cook, always likes to prepare fresh food when at home.
• Has a sweet tooth, needs sweet snacks, particularly at work to help her concentrate.
• Eats more during weekdays than at weekends.
• Can do without alcohol.
• Must have at least 2 cappuccinos a day.
• Finds it hard to stick to below about 1,200 calories a day.
• Needs a vegetarian diet with plenty of variety.

As a result of analysing her eating habits, we suggested that Penny stick to the following portions for her diet:

Protein (p)	2
Cereal (c)	5
Dairy (d)	3
Fats & Oils (f&o)	2
Fruit (f)	5

SAMPLE DAILY MENU
Daily allowances:
2d   up to 568 ml (1 pint) skimmed milk
One-a-day multivitamin and mineral tablet

Breakfast:
1c   30 ml (2 tbsp) porridge oats
½d   150 ml (¼ pint) skimmed milk from allowance
1f   12 g (½ oz) raisins or dried apricots
1f   1 piece of fruit, or 100 ml (4 fl oz) unsweetened fruit juice

Mid-morning:
½d   capuccino made with 150 ml (¼ pint) skimmed milk from allowance
1f   1 piece of fruit

Lunch:
2c   sandwich made with two 25 g (1 oz) slices wholemeal bread, or 50 g (2 oz) pitta bread filled with
1p   1 egg or 25 g (1 oz) Edam or Brie, or 50 g (2 oz) cottage cheese, or 15 ml (1 tbsp) peanut butter
ff   salad from the free food list plus
1f&o   15 ml (1 tbsp) low-calorie salad dressing
1d   150 ml (¼ pint) low-fat fruit yogurt
or:
1p   Spiced Bean Sausages (see
½c   recipe on page 138)

1½c	75 g (3 oz) bread roll
ff	salad from the free foods list
1d	60 ml (4 tbsp) fromage frais
1f&o	1 fun-size chocolate bar

Mid-afternoon

½d	cappuccino made with 150 ml (¼ pint) skimmed milk from allowance

Tea time:

ff	can of low-calorie fizzy drink
1f	1 piece of fruit

Supper:

1p	100 g (4 oz) baked beans in tomato sauce
2c	175 g (6 oz) baked potato
ff	large salad or vegetables from the free food list
1f&o	15 ml (1 tbsp) low-calorie salad dressing
1f	1 piece of fruit

Use remaining 150 ml (¼ pint) milk for tea and coffee

SAMPLE WEEKEND MENU

If anything, Penny eats slightly less at weekends so we didn't vary the amount of portions allotted her.

Daily allowance:

2d	up to 568 ml (1 pint) skimmed milk

Breakfast:

2c	two 25 g (1 oz) slices bread or 50 g (2 oz) roll
1f	1 piece of fruit
1f	100 ml (4 fl oz) unsweetened fruit juice

Mid-morning

½d	cappuccino made with 150 ml (¼ pint) skimmed milk from allowance
1f	1 piece of fruit

Lunch:

1c	one 25 g (1 oz) slice bread
2p	50 g (2 oz) Edam, Brie or reduced fat cheese (Shape or Tendale), or 200 g (6 oz) baked beans
ff	plenty of vegetables from the free food list, or large tomato salad dressed with lemon juice and ground black pepper

Mid-afternoon

½d	cappuccino made with 150 ml (¼ pint) skimmed milk from allowance
1f	1 piece of fruit
1f&o	1 fun-size chocolate bar

Supper:

ff	plenty of vegetables from the free food list, stir-fried in
1f&o	10 ml (2 tsp) oil flavoured with herbs, spices or soy sauce
2c	100 g (4 oz) cooked pasta or rice
ff	strawberries, raspberries or other fruit from the free food list with
1d	60 ml (4 tbsp) fromage frais
1f	1 piece of fruit

Use remaining (½ pint) skimmed milk for tea and coffee.

EXERCISE

Penny felt she already took a lot of exercise simply dealing with her daughter Naomi, but it is not the sort to contribute to cardiovascular fitness and burn up extra calories. As she travels between home, work, the childminder and shops frequently, we suggested she walk for some of the shorter journeys rather than take the bus. A brisk 12-minute walk every day from the underground station to her home, making sure she walks fast and takes good long strides will help her keep fit and supple without taking much extra time. As she likes exercising with weights at the gym, we suggested that she works at a balanced body-conditioning programme, two or three times a week, in her lunch hour on the days that she works (the gym is closest to her workplace), plus a stretch and condition class once a week for added suppleness.

GENERAL GUIDELINES

We showed Penny that she could have lots of sweet snacks and still diet and lose weight. We pointed out that painless savings could be made by switching from butter to low-fat spread (such as Flora Light or Low Fat Gold), low-calorie mayonnaise and salad dressing, lower-fat cheeses such as Brie or Edam, or even Shape or Tendale.

When cooking, large calorie savings can be made by cutting down on fats, and substituting the moist juicyness of oily dressings and sauces

THE DIETING VEGETARIAN

It is perfectly possible to obtain all necessary nutrients without meat. Consuming dairy produce such as milk and cheese combined with pulses, whole grain cereals and vegetables will provide more than sufficient amounts of vitamins and minerals. Certain nutrients may be limited in the diet of some vegetarians and vegans such as iron, particularly in the form that is more readily absorbed in the gut which is mostly obtained from animal flesh and organs. Deficiencies can be prevented by ensuring you eat enough of alternative sources of iron; green leafy vegetables, beans, nuts and whole grain cereals. Increasing vitamin C intake by eating plenty of fresh fruit and vegetables will also help improve its absorption. Other nutrients, such as calcium and vitamin B2 may possibly be limited in the diet of strict vegetarians who don't eat meat or animal products, but eating milk and dairy produce reduces the possibility. Despite their restricted choice of food, vegans can obtain all the nutrients they need from plant sources with the exception of vitamin B12. Vegans should take a daily supplement of this vitamin.

Overall, vegetarians and vegans tend to eat more healthily than omnivores, their diets are less high in saturated fats and higher in healthy cereals, fruits and nuts. Cholesterol levels also tend to be lower in vegetarians and vegans.

for those made from tomato juice, puréed vegetables or soy sauce. We pointed out that taking a packed lunch helped to avoid fattening shop-bought ones. If she didn't have time to pack lunch she must make sure to ask for little or no butter and choose a filling such as Edam, Brie, cottage cheese, egg (without mayonnaise) or banana and plenty of salad. As she is such a nibbler we warned her to always have a good stock of free foods to hand – vegetable sticks, fruit, baby tomatoes – at times when she is most likely to be tempted to eat. We also warned her to always throwaway the baby's leftovers – a common pitfall for mothers!

PENNY'S PROGRESS

In common with most dieters, Penny has been on many diets in the past and says with resignation 'dieting is always hard.' Nevertheless, with the 30-Day Diet she found her weight loss programme easier to follow than any other she'd tried. And the weight loss was faster than on her previous diets, in spite of not managing much exercise. 'I found it very easy to follow because there was no calorie counting. You are aware throughout the day just how much you are eating because everything is in such easy-to-calculate units. It is very sensible the way one can build in snacks and rewards (even eating small Mars Bars) to eat at weak points to keep you going.'

Unfortunately, Penny suffered from a lingering virus that left her feeling tired and with joint pains so she managed little of the exercise we'd prescribed. And we felt it was much more important for her to save what little energy she had to spend with her daughter. She found that by the end of the diet, weight loss had slowed right down. This, of course, was due to the fact that she needed less calories because there was less of her to fuel, and because her body had lowered its metabolism slightly in response to dieting. This drop would have been counteracted by the exercise had she been able to do more, helping her weight loss to progress faster. Nevertheless, Penny was really pleased with her 3 kg (7 lb) weight loss, which she said was an exceptionally good rate for her, for relatively little pain!

ALICE LANE: TEENAGE JUNK FOODIE

Height: 1.65 m (5ft 6in)
Age: 16 years
Start weight: 60 kg (9st 7lb)
Finish weight: 57.5 kg (9st 2lb)
Loss: 2.5 kg (5 lb)
Family: Schoolgirl, lives in London flat with mother.

Like most teenagers Alice had little idea which foods were fattening and which weren't. She had begun to eat junk foods with friends at lunch time or after school and also regularly wolfed down chocolate, crisps and fizzy drinks. These foods were beginning to make Alice slightly tubby around the middle, and she would attempt to cut back by trying to skip meals at school, coming home and ravenously consuming half a jar of peanut butter (975 calories!) While she loves junk food, Alice really appreciates healthy foods as well. She enjoys choosing delectable items on trips to the supermarket and cooking them up in interesting combinations. In common with many teenagers, she had got it into her head that dieting meant all enjoyment in food vanished, and that you virtually had to starve on a diet of grated carrots.

Alice is naturally active, enjoying cycling, swimming and horse riding. During term time she is in London where she has access to swimming pools and exercise classes, during the holidays she spends a lot of time in the country, where she is able to cycle and ride. Her eating habits vary depending on where she is, but tend to be very erratic. The chief tasks with Alice were to educate her about food, help her to regulate her eating, and lay down healthy eating and

BEFORE 60 kg (9 st 7 lb)

AFTER 57.5 kg (9 st 2 lb)

exercise habits now, that will benefit her for the rest of her life, rather than effect quick weight loss, that will leave her thinner for a short period until she reverts to her former habits.

> ## ALICE'S DAILY CALORIE REQUIREMENT
> Alice's current daily calorie intake varies enormously from about 1,300 to over 2,000. We calculated that Alice should maintain her body weight on 1,550 calories per day. Teenagers shouldn't reduce their daily calorie intake below 1,300 per day, so this figure was set for Alice.

Analysis of Alice's food diary revealed the following:

Breakfast:
Weekends or holidays
- Toast and butter/Flora, plus home made strawberry jam.

or:
- Porridge or hot oat cereal, both made with milk.

School days
- Skips breakfast, but then feels hungry around break time and eats:

Mid-morning
School days
- Packet of crisps or sweets, Revels, Bounty, Flake, etc.
- May drink can of fizzy drink.
- If has no money may eat lunch at this time.

Weekends or holidays
- May eat biscuits mid-morning.

Lunch:
- Sandwich made with wholemeal bread. Fillings can be cheese and tomato, ham and cheese, peanut butter, plus a piece of fruit.

Afternoon:
School days
- Crisps or iced bun.

- Biscuits, cold meat and cheese and tomatoes from fridge.
- 1 or 2 pieces of fruit, banana or apple, sometimes oranges and satsumas depending on time of year.

Evening:
School days
- Apple, bread and peanut butter when first comes home followed by
- Baked beans on toast

or:
- Scrambled egg on toast.
- Either followed by fruit and fromage frais or yogurt

or:
- Chicken breasts plus salad and baked potato

or:
- Pasta with sauce plus salad or vegetables.
- Smothers any vegetables, particularly potatoes, with butter/Flora.
- Fruit juice.
- Snacks throughout evening on baby tomatoes, hunks of cheese, digestive biscuits.
- Likes to drink lots of full fat milk in holidays when staying at grandparents.

General summary of current eating habits:
- Doesn't like breakfast if has to be eaten early in morning.
- Likes frequent snacks – feels she could adapt to some slimming snack substitutes such as sweet baby tomatoes, rice cake biscuits.
- Likes sweet fizzy drinks – but happy to change to low-calorie versions.
- Takes sugar and milk in tea, is prepared to give up both.
- Never drinks alcohol.
- Is prepared to cut down on milk drunk at grandparents and substitute full fat with semi-skimmed.
- Is prepared to change butter/Flora for low-fat Flora.
- Will eat breakfast on schooldays to help fill her up.
- Feels she must be allowed some sweets sometimes.
- Is prepared to change to low fat crisps.

All these details enabled our nutritionist to build up a picture of what Alice needed in her diet. A diet was devised for her that made full use of the free foods so that she could endlessly snack on slimming foods instead of sweets and crisps. She also had fun-sized Mars Bars built into her diet.

As Alice is only slightly tubby, and still a growing girl, we erred on the side of caution in prescribing her daily calorie allowance and set it at 1,300 per day, preferring to encourage her to switch to a more healthy but satisfying way of eating, and to shape up by taking lots of the sort of exercise she enjoys. As Alice began her diet during the school holidays when she was in the country – where she likes to drink a lot of milk – her diet included a lot of dairy portions, fewer protein, lots of filling cereal and plenty of fruit:

Protein (p)	3
Cereal (c)	5
Dairy (d)	4
Fats & Oils (f&o)	2
Fruit (f)	3

SAMPLE DAILY MENU
Daily allowance:
3d   up to 568 ml (1 pint) semi-skimmed milk

Breakfast:
1c   one 25 g (1 oz) slice toast, preferably wholemeal, with
1f&o   5 ml (1 tsp) low fat Flora
1f   100 ml (4 fl oz) unsweetened orange juice
1d   200 ml (⅓ pint) semi-skimmed milk from daily allowance

Mid-morning:
1c   1 digestive biscuit
1d   200 ml (⅓ pint) semi-skimmed milk from daily allowance

Lunch:
2c   sandwich made with two 25 g (1 oz) slices bread filled with
1p   25 g (1 oz) lean ham or 50 g (2 oz) chicken
ff   plenty of salad from the free food list
1d   low-fat fruit yogurt
ff   Diet Sprite or other low-calorie drink
or:
2c   50 g (2 oz) pitta bread
1p   25 g (1 oz) reduced fat cheddar
ff   plenty of vegetables from the free foods list

1d	60 ml (4 tbsp) fromage frais		1c	75 g (3 oz) potatoes

Afternoon:
1f 1 piece of fruit
1f&o 1 packet low-fat crisps
1d 200 ml (⅓ pint) semi-skimmed milk from daily allowance

Dinner:
2p 200 g (8 oz) baked beans
1c one 25 g (1 oz) slice toast (no Flora)
1f 1 piece of fruit
or:
2p Lamb Chops with Rosemary
1f (see recipe on page 131)
1c 50 g (2 oz) pasta
ff plenty of salad from the free foods list

SAMPLE WEEKEND MENU

Alice's diet consists of small snack meals during the week and weekend. To keep things simple for her we didn't vary her portion amounts.

Daily allowance:
3d up to 568 ml (1 pint) semi-skimmed milk

Breakfast:
1c one 25 g (1 oz) slice of toast with
1f&o 15 ml (1 tsp) Flora
1f 100 ml (4 fl oz) unsweetened orange juice

Mid-morning
1½d 300 ml (½ pint) semi-skimmed milk from allowance
1f 1 piece of fruit

Lunch:
2p Serving of casserole (about 100 g [4 oz]), or 100 g (4 oz) chicken
ff plenty of vegetables or salad from the free food list

Afternoon:
1d 150 ml (¼ pint) low-fat fruit yogurt, or 60 ml (4 tbsp) fromage frais
1f 1 piece of fruit

Supper:
2c 50 g (2 oz) bap filled with
1f&o 5 ml (1 tsp) Flora
1p 50 g (2 oz) chicken meat
ff salad from the free food list
or:
1p Spicy Bean Pâté (see recipe on
1c page 93)
1 f&o 25 g (1 oz) pitta bread

Late night snack:
1½d 300 ml (½ pint) semi-skimmed milk from allowance
1c 1 digestive biscuit

EXERCISE

Next we worked out an exercise plan for Alice that she would enjoy and be able to stick to. She loves cycling in the countryside around her grandparents' home, so we allotted her an hour's bike ride each day. She had also recently joined the local community-centre gym and was happy to work at a balanced exercise programme. This included running, rowing, cycling and exercising with weights, for about an hour, 2–3 times a week.

GENERAL GUIDELINES

We advised Alice to follow the diet closely, and memorise the list of foods to avoid! We told her that if the diet didn't suit her after the first week we'd adapt it to suit her better. We advised her to try to eat regularly and avoid sweet shops altogether, and to arm herself with plenty of free foods that she liked to eat whenever she felt peckish. Also, to stock up on low-calorie fizzy drinks and to use artificial sweetener in her tea instead of sugar. (Nutrasweet type of sweeteners taste more like sugar than saccharine.) We told Alice to keep the packet of crisps as a stand-by in case of desperation only.

ALICE'S PROGRESS

All went well with Alice's new eating plan for the first ten days, she lost 1.5 kg (3 lb) without any trouble and had fun doing all the exercise. Being unused to planning her own meals, she found it hard to think ahead and to work out different combinations of food that she could eat – it's as well for parents to do this for this age group, otherwise they run short of ideas on what to eat and get desperate. 'The portion counting helps because the temptation with diets that give you say, 1,200 calories a day, is to eat three Mars Bars and nothing else. With this diet you can eat the odd chocolate or packet of crisps while still eating a healthy diet.'

Alice liked the diet, but unfortunately went away first on holiday to Ireland, where food choice was limited and the weather was bad so there was little to do but eat, and then she was invited to go camping with friends – again she had too little control over what she could eat. The final stage of her diet was spent in Cornwall where she succumbed to cream teas, gave up and decided to start again at the beginning of the new school term. On starting again, Alice realised she was several pounds heavier than when she had first started! She now weighed in at 61 kg (9st 10lb). This time she stuck to the diet much better. Her life had a predictable and stable routine to it, lacking during the first attempt.

Even though Alice's finish weight was only 2.5 kg (5lb) less than her start weight, she had actually lost 3.5 kg (8lbs) as she had put on more weight in between.

NB: Teenagers should consult their doctor before they go on this or any diet, to make sure they approve.

LIZ WARNER: BUSY JOURNALIST

Height: 1.65 m (5ft 6 in)
Age: 25 years
Start weight: 67.5 kg (10st 10lb)
Finish weight: 61 kg (9st 10lb)
Loss: 6 kg (14lb)
Family: single, shares flat with friend

Liz has a busy, lively life both at work (where she is under some pressure which she finds nibbling helps to relieve), and she goes out a lot in the evenings with friends to pubs, wine bars and restaurants.

BEFORE 67.5 kg (10 st 10 lb)   **AFTER** 61 kg (9 st 10 lb)

Nearly every day she meets friends in the evening and has 2–3 glasses of wine (up to 100 calories each) and consumes bags of crisps, nuts and porky scratchings along with them!

Liz admits she had absolutely no idea which foods were fattening – when she wanted to lose weight, she cut out bread rather than fat. She simply never thought about whether she was eating a healthy or fattening diet. She had slowly got into bad eating habits without realising it, and her diet was full of unhealthy high fat, high salt snacks, almost no fruit and vegetables, little fibre and lots of sugar. An exact reverse of the current healthy eating recommendations. She also took little or no exercise (her job is sedentary) so she was pretty inactive. By using the chart on page 20 we estimated she had about 10 kg (22 lb) to lose, but felt that Liz was so unaware of what she was eating, that a lot of calories could be cut out painlessly just by making her more aware of food values.

Liz's food diary gave her quite a surprise. She hadn't realised how much she ate, or how lacking in wholesome nutritious food it was, being a series of high calorie, high fat, high sugar snacks! An almost inevitable routine for someone with Liz's lifestyle.

> ## LIZ'S DAILY CALORIE REQUIREMENT
> Liz's current daily intake is about 2,140 calories, and she should maintain her body weight on 1,540. As she has quite a lot of weight to lose she will lose it relatively easily, so 1,200 calories a day, combined with regular exercise, should enable her to lose about 1 kg (2 lb) a week.

An analysis of Liz's diet revealed the following:

Breakfast:
Weekday
- Croissant plus coffee
- Second croissant on reaching work at 10am plus cappuccino with 150 ml (¼ pint) milk.

Weekend
- 2 Croissants.

Lunch:
- Sandwich – usually with mayonnaise, chicken or bacon and egg.
- Follows with Kitkat, Minstrels or chocolate.

Afternoon:
- Eats 2–3 biscuits or a piece of cake plus cup of tea with sugar

Evening:
- Frequently goes out, drinks wine or cider – 2–3 glasses.
- Eats porky scratching, nuts, crisps in pubs.
- At weekend can drink up to 7 glasses of wine/cider.
- Eats pasta with lots of sauce, pizza.
- If home for supper, snacks first on tortilla chips, nuts.
- Cooks herself quick-to-prepare foods such as pasta plus mushroom and cream sauce, or a ready-made meal.

General summary of current eating habits:
- Works full time, and often eats out at lunch time or in evening.
- Isn't aware of nutritional value of foods and eats lots of extra calories without realising it.
- Loves foods like croissants, fatty dressings on salads and pasta, cheese and pâté, all of which are high in calories.
- Drinks quite a lot of alcohol, mostly wine when socialising.
- Eats crisps, nuts or fatty dips with drinks before eating later on.
- Mid-afternoon is a problem time when she needs something sweet.
- Feels she can easily cut down on alcohol.
- Feels she could survive on lower-calorie snacks and meals providing they are filling.

As Liz doesn't have the time or inclination to do a lot of cooking, most of her food must be quick to prepare or instant, and there's no reason why fast foods should be bad foods if you know which to eat. In devising Liz's diet, we took her love of croissants and snacks into account, but as our main aim was to re-educate her about food, we allotted her a balanced selection of food portions, as follows:

Protein (p)	5
Cereal (c)	5
Dairy (d)	1
Fats & oils (f&o)	1
Fruit (f)	2

SAMPLE DAILY MENU
Breakfast:
2c   1 croissant with
½f&o   5 ml (1 tsp) low-fat spread
1f   1 piece of fruit

Lunch:
2c   two 25 g (1 oz) slices of wholemeal bread with
½f&o   5 ml (1 tsp) low-fat spread
2p   50 g (2 oz) Brie, Edam or reduced-fat cheese
ff   salad from the free food list
1d   50 ml (¼ pint) low-fat fruit yogurt
1f   1 piece of fruit
or:
2c   175 g (6 oz) baked potato
½f&o   5 ml (1 tsp) low-fat butter
2p   100 g (4 oz) carton cottage cheese with pineapple
1d   60 ml (4 tbsp) fromage frais
1f   100 ml (4 fl oz) unsweetened orange juice

Dinner:
ff   vegetable sticks with
1p   25 g (1 oz) taramasalata or other low-fat dip
2p   100 g (4 oz) lean chicken
1c   50 g (2 oz) sweetcorn
ff   salad and or vegetables from the free food list

or:
2p   Marinated Steak Salad (see
1c   recipe on page 100)
ff   large mixed salad from the free food list with
1p   75 g (3 oz) kidney beans mixed in

SAMPLE WEEKEND MENU
Breakfast:
2c   two 25 g (1 oz) slices of toast with
1f&o   10 ml (2 tsp) low-fat spread
1f   1 piece of fruit

Lunch:
2p   small kebab or 50 g (2 oz) burger
ff   salad from the free food list
2c   50 g (2 oz) pitta bread
1f   1 piece of fruit

Supper:
2p   225 g (8 oz) baked beans, or 50 g (2 oz) Edam or reduced-fat cheese with
1c   one 25 g (1 oz) slice of toast
1d   60 ml (4 tbsp) low-fat fruit fromage frais
or:
2p   2 egg mushroom omelette
1c   25 g (1 oz) pitta bread
ff   plenty of salad from the free foods list
1d   150 ml (¼ pint) low-fat fruit/ natural yogurt
ff   fruit from the free food list

EXERCISE
Liz didn't like the sound of doing much exercise and reluctantly volunteered to cycle to and from work (4–5 miles, 25 minutes each way) twice a week. As her office is right next to a swimming pool which also runs exercise classes Liz agreed to

take a vigorous 20 minute swim once a week and to attack one lunchtime aerobics class a week. She didn't feel at all sure she could stick to it!

GENERAL GUIDELINES

We showed Liz that large calorie savings could be made simply by cutting down on alcohol and fatty snack foods such as cheese, crisps, croissants, pasta sauces, salad dressings, sausages and pâté. We showed her that she could keep up her nibbling habits by switching to different snacks – baby tomatoes, raw vegetables and fruits from the free food list. We pointed out how high in calories alcohol was and advised her to switch to low-alcohol beer and choose dry white wine, mixing it with Perrier when possible which halves the calories and makes it last longer. As Liz eats out a lot we told her to enlist the help and support of her friends – she should explain that she wants to go where she can get food that fits in with her diet, and she should scrutinize the menu closely before she goes in to ensure that there is something to fit in with her diet.

LIZ'S PROGRESS

'Without realizing it, I'd got into really bad habits', remarked Liz. I was fired with enthusiasm by the diet and it has made changes to my diet completely. I have rediscovered fruit and vegetables, Ryvita and wholemeal bread. I really like fruit again and buy apples instead of a Twix. I was drinking much too much alcohol, and just realising this made me cut back. At first I thought, oh I'll save all my alcohol allowance for one day a week, in fact I didn't, having done without it, I actually wanted it less and I mostly drank diet coke instead. It made me realise what an enormous amount I ate between meals. And now I've cut down on fat in my diet so much, I've lost my taste for it – butter or Flora on bread tastes horribly solid and fatty to me now. I stuck to the diet rigidly, I felt that if I broke it at all my willpower would collapse. I found the diet easiest in the first week when I was fired with enthusiasm, and again in the last week because the end was near! It was the easiest diet I've been on though, by far.

I really got into doing the exercise, I ended up cycling to work every day, going to exercise classes and swimming three times a week. It really helped me feel like I was becoming slimmer and fitter. I never dreamt I'd lose so much – I've lost over a stone, I want to lose two more pounds so that I'm 9½ stone.'

CARL CADDICK: Designer with Own Business

Height: 1.75 m (5ft 10in)
Age: 30 years
Start weight: 87 kg (13st 11lb)
Finish weight: 81 kg (12st 11lb)
Loss: 6 kg (14lb)
Family: Single, living on own

BEFORE 87 kg (13 st 11 lb)

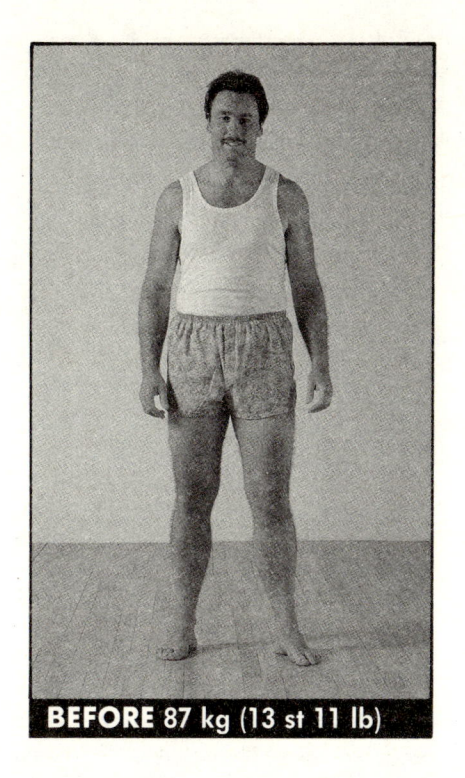

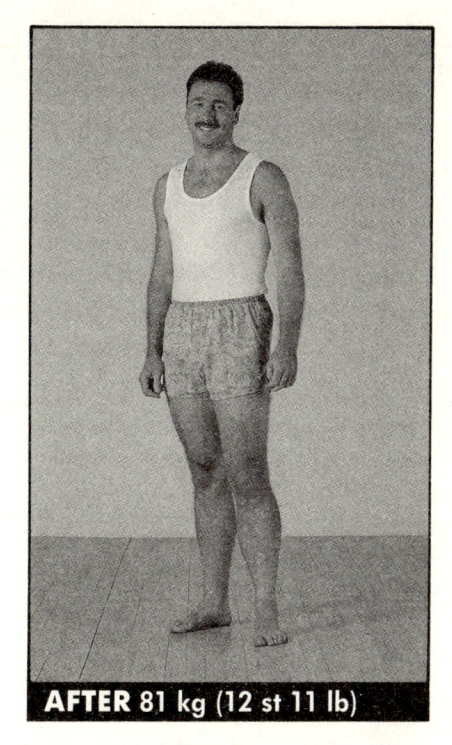

AFTER 81 kg (12 st 11 lb)

Five years ago, before Carl's working life became quite so busy, he used to enjoy running, going to the gym and playing sport. All of this he has since abandoned which, coupled with sedentary work and home life, has contributed to his steady weight gain over the last couple of years. Added to this, Carl didn't think twice about the amounts of food and drink he was consuming, and wouldn't know a calorie if it hit him. When we added up his daily consumption – it totalled a staggering 3,300, 900 more than it should be, probably not uncommon for many men. Carl also needed to be educated about food, to make him aware of how much he was eating and what its energy values were, and to make him aware of less fattening substitutes. Carl spends a lot of time in pubs and restaurants and needs to be shown the slimming route round the menu as well as be converted to drinking low-alcohol beers some of the time. Carl was actually looking for motivation to get him back into the exercising habit, he felt he'd become a slob and wanted to change.

CARL'S DAILY CALORIE REQUIREMENT

Carl needed to lose around 19 kg (42 lb) plus become fit, and he was eating about 3,300 calories a day! At the weekends he was consuming double what he consumed during the week, mostly due to his alcohol intake. He should maintain his body weight on 2,500 calories a day and we decided he would lose weight efficiently on 1,600–1,650 calories a day, combined with regular exercise.

Carl's food diary was the largest one we'd seen so far. This is what it revealed:

Breakfast:
Weekday
- Starts the day with coffee with full fat milk (but no sugar) and two thick slices of toast spread with lashings of peanut butter to which he's addicted.

Weekend
- has a full fry-up – eggs, bacon, tomato, fried bread, sausages if he has any, and at least two of everything!

Mid-morning
- Eats a bun, sometimes iced.
- Drinks coffee throughout day with milk but no sugar.

Lunch:
Weekday
- Large bap bursting with steak, salad and mayonnaise.
- Sometimes eats out, eats meat or pasta in rich sauces, may drink a glass of wine or two.

Weekends
- At least 2 pints beer, plus sandwich, maybe crisps.

Afternoon:
Weekend
- Snacks on crisps or biscuits.

Evening:
Weekday
- Snacks on crisps about 6pm.
- Supper tends to be a ready-made stew, chicken in cream sauces and rice.
- Always buys packet for 2 and eats it all!
- Drinks 1–2 pints of beer.
- Sometimes eats out – pasta or curries.
- Sometimes gets take-aways – burger, chips and milkshake.

Weekend
- Generally eats out – 2–3 course meal (possibly curry).
- Drinks about half a bottle of wine with it.
- May drink 1–2 beers as well as those drunk earlier in evening.

General summary of current eating habits:
- Doesn't realise how many calories he's consuming.
- Loves peanut butter, would find it hard to give up.
- Eats out a lot or buys ready-prepared food – either way he has little control over the contents of his meals.
- Goes to the pub a lot and drinks with friends, more so at the weekend.
- Never buys or eats fresh

vegetables, salads or fruit but likes them when he has them.
- Feels that he needs educating about what he should and should not be eating.

Carl's recommended daily calories were 1,600–1,650 a day. He likes protein and carbohydrate so we gave him plenty of protein and cereal foods, and plenty of fruit to snack on. His portions were as follows:

Protein (p)	5
Cereal (c)	7
Dairy (d)	1
Fats & oils (f&o)	2
Fruit (f)	3

SAMPLE DAILY MENU
Daily allowance:
1d   300 ml (½ pint) skimmed milk

Breakfast:
2c   2 Weetabix with
½d   150 ml (¼ pint) milk (no sugar) from allowance
1f   100 ml (4 fl oz) unsweetened orange juice
1c   1 slice of toast with
1p   15 ml (1 tbsp) peanut butter

Lunch:
2c   sandwich made with medium sized brown bap or two 25 g (1 oz) slices of bread with no butter, filled with 50 g (2 oz) lean ham or 100 g (4 oz) plain tuna
ff   plenty of salad or vegetables from the free food list
1f   1 piece of fruit, diet coke or other low-calorie drink

or:
2c   175 g (6 oz) baked potato

2p   50 g (2 oz) chopped lean ham
ff   salad from the free food list
1f   1 piece of fruit

Dinner:
3p   175 g (6 oz) cooked chicken
ff   plenty of vegetables or salad from the free food list
1c   75 g (3 oz) baked potato with
1f&o   5 ml (1 tsp) butter
1f   75 g (3 oz) grapes

or:
2p   Stir-fried Liver (see recipe on
1f&o   page 128)
1p   25 g (1 oz) Brie
1f   1 piece of fruit

Snack:
1c   1 digestive biscuit

SAMPLE WEEKEND MENU
Daily allowance:
1d   300 ml (½ pint) skimmed milk

Breakfast:
2c   two 25 g (1 oz) slices of toast
½f&o   5 ml (1 tsp) low-fat spread
1p   1 poached egg
1p   25 g (1 oz) lean grilled bacon
1f   100 ml (4 fl oz) unsweetened orange juice

Lunch:
1c   one 25 g (1 oz) slice of wholemeal bread with
½f&o   5 ml (1 tsp) low-fat spread and
2p   50 g (2 oz) lean ham
ff   plenty of salad from the free food list
1f&o   15 ml (1 tbsp) low-fat, salad dressing
1f   1 piece of fruit

Supper:
2p   Baked Gingered Chicken (see recipe on page 121)
2c   100 g (4 oz) plain boiled rice

2c   50 g (2 oz) bread roll
ff   plenty of vegetables from the free foods list
1f   100 g (4 oz) fresh fruit salad

EXERCISE

As Carl was eager to get back into the exercising habit we gave him plenty of it. He works right next to a local authority-run swimming pool which also has a gym and runs exercise classes which makes it easy for him. We recommended a balanced exercise routine in the multi-gym (weights, rowing, cycling, etc) followed by a 20-minute aerobic swim (at a pace to make you pant a bit but not be breathless) three times a week. Carl had been an enthusiastic runner and was keen to start again. He was going to start to run each weekend.

GENERAL GUIDELINES

As Carl's diet had been so full of the foods on the 'Foods to Avoid' list (see page 82), we told him to memorise it carefully! We pointed out that large calorie savings can be made easily and painlessly by simply cutting down on fatty foods such as chips, burgers, curries, fatty meats, rich sauces and dressings such as mayonnaise. As Carl eats out a lot we advised him to choose a restaurant where he knows the staff and can explain that he wants to avoid fatty foods, or to go somewhere where he could dictate toppings, sauces, etc. We warned him to watch out for pasta sauces, curries and garlic bread and poppadoms, pâtés, pastries, salads in mayonnaise or oily dressings, crisps, peanuts and other nibbles. Also cheese, which he had wrongly assumed to be slimming. Instead, we told him to choose lean meats, poultry and fish with plenty of fresh vegetables (without butter) and salad. And to choose fresh fruit or fruit salad for dessert and avoid cream.

We also pointed out how high alcohol is in calories, so he could make big savings by cutting down and switching to lower-calorie drinks such as low-alcohol beer, slimline tonic and other mixers.

Ready-prepared meals are another pitfall of the single person's diet, as they are often loaded with calories you'd never suspect were there. Choose those with calories counted on the box such as those by Marks & Spencer or Findus Lean Cuisine, avoiding those over 300 calories.

CARL'S PROGRESS

Carl was surprised at how easy it was to stick to the diet. 'You quickly adapt to thinking in portions, it was quite good fun, and provides you with a really easy means to work out what you are eating, and how much you can have. I ate vegetables for the first time, and granary bread, and really liked it. It made me realise what I was eating for the first time. The diet has completely changed my awareness about my food and health.'

Carl started his diet when London's tube strike was on – this gave him the incentive to run into work (about 4 miles), and once he started, he enjoyed it so much he decided to run in every other day. He also went to the gym and for a swim, as recommended, and really enjoyed it, finding exercise made him feel instantly fitter and more alert.

Carl was delighted to have lost a whole stone so painlessly, 'I like the way my stomach doesn't hang over my trousers any more.'

CHAPTER 5

PORTION COUNTERS AND COMBINATIONS

THE FOLLOWING PAGES CONvert everyday foods into the portions that are the building blocks of your diet. There is no fiddly calorie counting, instead, precise amounts of each food is converted into one of five portions – protein (p) (meat, fish, pulses, cheese, nuts tofu etc); cereal (c) (bread, biscuits, starchy vegetables, rice, pasta); dairy (d) (milk, yogurt, etc); fats & oils (f&o) (butter, oils, cream etc); fruit (f) (fruit, fruit juices); free foods (ff) (many vegetables and some fruits); and finally a list of extras – treats such as chocolate, which can be swapped with 1 f&o portion a day in times of need!

Alongside each of the food categories, is a box for you to fill in your own personal number of daily portion, which you will have decided upon by the end of Chapter 3. So, if you can have 6 protein portions a day, write 6 in the box alongside the protein portions, and so on. In this way, you will always have a handy reminder close at hand when working out your daily menus.

When selecting your food portions, try to get as broad a selection from each category as possible. This is particularly **important when choosing from the protein, cereal and free food categories. For instance, if you have 5 cereal portions a day, don't choose all bread or all potatoes, try to have pasta, rice, sweetcorn and so on, too. The greater the variety in your diet, the bigger the variety of vitamins and minerals you are likely to consume, and the better nourished you will be.** If you like to plan ahead, plan out your daily/weekly menu and write it down so that you can take it shopping with you.

THE PROTEIN PORTION COUNTER

YOUR DAILY ALLOWANCE ☐

Each of the following quantities is the equivalent of one portion of protein.

Meat:
25 g (1 oz) lean beef, duck, ham, lamb, pork, bacon, veal, partridge, pheasant
50 g (2 oz) turkey or chicken (meat only, skin removed)
25 g (1 oz) liver, kidney, heart
1 rasher grilled lean bacon
25 g (1 oz) low-fat sausage or low-fat burger, grilled
25 g (1 oz) corned beef
15 g (½ oz) liver sausage or luncheon meat

Fish:
75 g (3 oz) white fish *e.g.* haddock, plaice
25 g (1 oz) oily fish (weight without skin and bones) *e.g.* herring, salmon, mackerel, trout, sardines, kippers
1 grilled fish finger or fish cake
50 g (2 oz) hard fish roe
50 g (2 oz) tuna canned in brine
50 g (2 oz) pilchards in tomato sauce
25 g (1 oz) sardines canned in tomato sauce or oil (drained)
50 g (2 oz) shelled prawns, shrimps, cockles or mussels, crabmeat or lobster flesh

Dairy products:
1 egg size 3
25 g (1 oz) reduced-fat hard cheese, *e.g.* Shape or Tendale, or medium-fat cheese *e.g.* Brie, Camembert, Fetta, Edam, Ricotta, medium fat Mozarella
15 g (½ oz) full-fat cheese *e.g.* Cheddar, Cheshire, Double Gloucester, Danish Blue, Stilton, Parmesan, Emmenthal, Gruyère, Mozarella or cream cheese, processed cheese or cheese spread
50 g (2 oz) low-fat soft cheese such as cottage cheese or curd cheese

Vegetables:
100 g (4 oz) tofu (plain or smoked)
75 g (3 oz) canned or cooked beans or pulses *e.g.* kidney beans, butter beans, chick peas, lentils
25 g (1 oz) dried beans or pulses
100 g (4 oz) cooked peas
100 g (4 oz) baked beans in tomato sauce
25 g (1 oz) vegetable burger, grilled

Nuts:
15 g (½ oz) shelled nuts *e.g.* almonds, walnuts, peanuts
15 ml (1 level tbsp) peanut butter or tahini
15 g (½ oz) sunflower, sesame seeds, pine kernels or other seeds
50 g (2 oz) chestnuts (weighed with shells)

THE CEREAL PORTION COUNTER

YOUR DAILY ALLOWANCE ☐

Each of the following quantities is the equivalent of one portion of cereal.

Remember to choose a varied selection of cereal portions. Each type of food below contains a different mix of vitamins and minerals, all vital to keep you healthy, particularly important while you are dieting.

Bread:
25 g (1 oz) slice bread (preferably wholemeal or high fibre white or brown)
25 g (1 oz) bread roll (preferably wholemeal)
25 g (1 oz) pitta bread (equal to approximately half one standard pitta bread or 1 mini)
15 g (½ oz) enriched bread *e.g.* chollah, brioche, croissant or teabread
1 small chapati (made without fat) approximately 25 g (1 oz)
2 small grilled popadoms

Biscuits:
2 crackers
2 rich tea biscuits
1 digestive biscuit or plain biscuit
1 crumpet

½ plain muffin or scone (preferably wholemeal)
25 g (1 oz) plain grilled waffle
15 g (½ oz) dried breadcrumbs
2 grissini bread sticks

Cereals:
25 g (1 oz) wholegrain breakfast cereal e.g. Branflakes, Sultana Bran, All-Bran, or unsweetened cereal e.g. puffed rice, cornflakes
20 g (3/4 oz) muesli
25 g (1 oz) porridge oats
1 Weetabix or Shredded Wheat

Vegetables:
75 g (3 oz) potato (boiled or baked) or sweet potato
50 g (2 oz) sweetcorn or ½ corn on the cob
100 g (4 oz) parsnip
100 g (4 oz) beetroot

Miscellaneous:
50 g (2 oz) cooked pasta or rice (preferably wholegrain)
25 g (1 oz) dried pasta or rice
15 g (½ oz) plain, unsweetened popcorn
15 g (½ oz) flour (including wheat, rice, soya, cornflour, buckwheat, arrowroot, etc)
20 g (4 level tsp) custard powder
100 g (4 oz) canned spaghetti in tomato sauce
1 can low-calorie soup (any variety)

THE DAIRY PORTION COUNTER

YOUR DAILY ALLOWANCE ☐

Each of the following quantities is the equivalent of one portion of dairy food.

The lower the fat content of the milk you use, the more you're allowed. Some people find skimmed milk much too thin, however, in which case, semi-skimmed is a good compromise as it has only half the fat of full-fat milk. Always choose low-fat yogurts and fromage frais, there's very little difference in taste, particularly in the fruit fromage frais. But there is a big difference in the amount of calories they contain.

150 ml (¼ pint) full-fat skimmed milk (cow or goat)
200 ml (⅓ pint) semi-skimmed milk or soya milk
300 ml (½ pint) skimmed milk or buttermilk
150 ml (¼ pint) low-fat natural yogurt
150 ml (¼ pint) very low-fat or 'diet' fruit yogurt
60 ml (4 level tbsp) low-fat fruit fromage frais
50 g (2 oz) natural Greek-style strained yogurt (cow or sheep)

THE FATS & OILS PORTION COUNTER

YOUR DAILY ALLOWANCE

Each of the following quantities is the equivalent of one portion of fats & oils.

Fat is more fattening, weight for weight, than any other food – sugar included. In Britain, our diet is made up of too much fat, particularly saturated fats. Polyunsaturated oils (vegetable oils such as sunflower), however, are better for our health than saturated animal fats (butter, cream).

5 ml (1 level tsp) butter or margarine
10 ml (2 level tsp) low-fat spread, very low-fat spread or half-fat butter
5 ml (1 tsp) vegetable oil
10 ml (2 tsp) double or whipping cream
15 ml (1 tbsp) single, soured or reduced-fat cream
10 ml (2 tsp) salad dressing
15 ml (1 tbsp) low-calorie salad dressing
15 ml (1 tbsp) low-calorie mayonnaise

THE FRUIT PORTION COUNTER

YOUR DAILY ALLOWANCE ☐

Each of the following quantities is the equivalent of one portion of fruit.

100 ml (4 fl oz) unsweetened fruit juice
1 medium sized apple, orange, pear, peach, nectarine
125 g (4 oz) apricots or pineapple
small pomegranate
1 small banana
2 clementines, satsumas or tangerines
1 kiwi fruit or persimon
4 lychees
5 prunes in juice
½ mango or papaya
75 g (3 oz) grapes or cherries
3 medium plums
125 g (4 oz) apricot, peach, pear, pineapple, mandarine or fruit salad canned in natural juice
25 g (1 oz) dried fruit
25 g (1 oz) avocado pear
40 g (1½ oz) olives (with stones, stoned or stuffed)

EXTRAS

You won't have a number to put by these foods for this category is simply an optional extra in case you feel the need for a 'treat' food. If you really feel the need, you can exchange one of your daily fat & oil portions for one item from this list per day.

15 g (½ oz) milk or plain chocolate
1 fun-size (bite-size) chocolate bar
½ packet (approximately 15 g [½ oz]) crisps
15 ml (1 level tbsp) jam, marmalade or lemon curd
20 ml (4 tsp) low-sugar jam or marmalade
10 ml (2 level tsp) honey, sugar or golden syrup
150 ml (¼ pint) jelly (made up)
25 g (1 oz) ice-cream

FREE FOODS

You can eat as many of these as you like – well almost, up to 550 g (1½ lb) in fact, although you may find it hard to eat this much. You can also drink any amount of the beverages and add as much of the flavourings and sauces to your food as you wish.

These delicious fresh fruits and vegetables are full of vitamins and minerals – choose as varied a selection as you can in order to get as much goodness as possible.

These foods won't be free, however, if you smother the vegetables in butter, or the fruit in sugar. If you need dressing, use a low-calorie one (taking it from your fats & oils portions, of course), and use artificial sweetener in place of sugar.

A totally free food meal is a simple vegetable stir fry using soy sauce in place of oil. To make it more filling, serve it on a 50 g (2 oz) bed of rice (1c).

Fruit:
Blackberries, blackcurrants, cranberries, gooseberries, grapefruit, melon, lemons, loganberries, raspberries, redcurrants, rhubarb, strawberries, tomatoes.

Vegetables:
Artichokes, asparagus, aubergine, bamboo shoots, beansprouts, broccoli, brussels sprouts, cabbage, carrots, cauliflower, celeriac, celery, chicory, Chinese leaves, courgettes, cucumber, endive, fennel, leeks, lettuce, mange-tout, marrow, mushrooms, mustard & cress, okra, onions, peppers, pumpkin, radish, runner beans, spinach, spring greens, swede, turnips, watercress.

Beverages:
Coffee, tea, water, sugar-free (low-calorie) fruit squash, sugar-free (diet) fizzy drinks, tomato juice

Flavourings and sauces:
Salt, pepper, herbs, spices, garlic, vinegar, mustard, curry powder, soy sauce, chilli sauce, Worcestershire sauce, mint sauce, horse radish sauce, tomato ketchup, brown sauce. Artificial sweetener, clear soup, yeast and meat extract, stock cubes, oil-free vinaigrette, pickled vegetables.

ALCOHOL

Everyone is allowed 2 units of alcohol a week. Each of the following is 1 unit:

1 standard measure of spirits
½ pint ordinary strength beer, lager or dry cider
1 glass wine
1 pint low-alcohol/alcohol-free beer or lager
½ pint lager or beer
2 glasses alcohol-free wine
2 glasses wine with Perrier water

FOODS TO AVOID

Sugar, glucose, chocolate, sweets, nuts, crisps, jam, marmalade, honey, syrup, treacle, sweetened fizzy drinks, sweetened fruit squash, tinned fruit in syrup, jelly, ice cream, cream (except from fats and oils or extras allowance), butter and oil in cooking (except from fats and oils allowance), fried foods (bake, boil, grill, microwave, poach or stew instead), salami and other fatty meats, avocado pears, alcoholic drinks other than the 2 units permitted per week.

DIET NOTES

- Eat large portions of vegetables and salads from the Free Food list.
- Trim all fat off meat before cooking.
- Never fry anything (except with fat from allowance).
- Grilling meat drains away more fats than microwaving.
- Measure or weigh all portions carefully.
- Eat meals as regularly as possible.

EATING OUT

Eating out can be the dieter's downfall because it is so hard to tell what ingredients have gone into items on a menu, and ready-made sandwiches in sandwich bars tend to come loaded with mayonnaise and butter.

In restaurants:
- If possible go to a place where you have a good relationship with the staff and explain that you must avoid fatty food (imply it's for medical reasons – it gets better co-operation)
- Specify that you want your fish without buttery sauce (choose lemon juice instead), ask for meat to be grilled.
- Sauces to eat are those made from puréed vegetables without butter or cream.
- Eat salad without dressing, ask for yogurt instead.
- Have fruit salad for pudding.
- Have wine mixed with soda – a spritzer.

In the sandwich/snack bar:
- Always go to snack bars that make your sandwiches up for you fresh so you can dictate exactly what goes in them.
- Ask for wholemeal bread – it's more filling and better for you.
- Specify you don't want butter.
- Avoid fatty dressings such as mayonnaise.
- Choose fillings such as chicken without skin, sardines, tuna fish, lower-fat cheeses such as Edam or Brie, egg.
- Combine with liberal helpings of tomatoes and salad
- Ask for salad without dressing – keep your own low-calorie dressing at work.
- Buy a baked potato and choose fillings of mixed vegetables, sweetcorn, tomatoes, kidney beans, add yogurt if liked. Make your own dressing by mixing yogurt with tomato juice and a dash of Tobasco and/or lemon juice.
- Advice about choosing pizzas.

BREAKFAST, LUNCH AND SUPPER IDEAS

To give you inspiration and help you put together an interesting and varied daily menu we've come up with lots of breakfast, lunch/snack and supper ideas, as well as some well-balanced three-course menus to be found in the next chapter. All are clearly marked with their portion contents. You won't have to rack your brains for ideas any more, we've done all the thinking for you. Take this book when you go shopping so you'll know which foods to stock up on.

BREAKFAST IDEAS

- 1 rasher lean grilled bacon, grilled tomatoes and mushrooms, 25 g (1 oz) slice wholemeal toast, 100 ml (4 fl oz) unsweetened orange juice (**Total: 1p,1c,1f**)
- 100 g (4 oz) low-fat cottage cheese, 25 g (1 oz) slice wholemeal bread, 1 peach, apple or pear (**Total: 2p,1c,1f**)
- 175 g (6 oz) strawberries, 150 ml (¼ pint) low-fat fruit yogurt, 25 g (1 oz) slice wholemeal toast, 15 ml (1 tbsp) peanut butter (**Total: 1p,1c,1d**)
- 50–75 g (2–3 oz) dried fruits soaked overnight in 150 ml (¼ pint) apple juice served with 100 ml (4 fl oz) Greek-style natural yogurt (**Total: 2d,3–4f**)
- 50 g (2 oz) reduced-fat hard cheese grated over 25 g (1 oz) slice wholemeal bread, grilled and topped with tomato slices, 100 ml (4 fl oz) unsweetened orange juice (**Total: 2p,1c,1f**)
- 1 egg boiled or poached, 25 g (1 oz) slice wholemeal bread, 5 ml (1 tsp) butter or margarine, grilled tomatoes and mushrooms (**Total: 1p,1c,1f&o**)
- ½ grapefruit, 25 g (1 oz) wholegrain breakfast cereal sprinkled with 25 g (1 oz) raisins, 150 ml (¼ pint) skimmed milk (**Total: 1c,½d,1f**)
- 150 g (6 oz) grilled white fish or smoked haddock, 25 g (1 oz) slice wholemeal bread, 5 ml (1 tsp) butter or margarine, grilled tomatoes, 150 ml (¼ pint) fruit juice (**Total: 2p,1c,1f&o**)
- Combine 25 g (1 oz) muesli, 1 apple, pear or peach, chopped and 150 ml (¼ pint) low-fat fruit yogurt (**Total: 1c,1d,1f**)
- 25 g (1 oz) porridge oats soaked in 150 ml (¼ pint) apple juice and served with 1 chopped apple and 25 g (1 oz) raisins (**Total: 1c,2f**)

- Breakfast Shake – 200 ml (⅓ pint) skimmed milk, 150 ml (¼ pint) low-fat natural yogurt, 1 small banana, 10 ml (2 tsp) honey, blended together until smooth **(Total: 2d,1f,1f&o)**
- ½ grapefruit, 50 g (2 oz) lamb kidneys sautéed in 5–10 ml (1–2 tsp) vegetable oil, 25 g (1 oz) slice wholemeal toast, grilled mushrooms and tomatoes **(Total: 2p,1c,1–2f&o)**

LUNCH IDEAS

- 50 g (2 oz) hummus, raw vegetable sticks, 25 g (1 oz) pitta bread, 150 ml (¼ pint) low-fat fruit yogurt **(Total: 2p,1c,1d,1f&o)**
- 25 g (1 oz) dried pasta, cooked, cooled and tossed in 20 ml (4 tsp) low-calorie salad dressing; 50 g (2 oz) peeled prawns, shredded lettuce, diced cucumber, bean sprouts and chopped tomato; season and sprinkle with herbs, 1 small banana **(Total: 1p,1c,1f,1f&o)**
- 75 g (3 oz) canned, drained butter beans tossed with 75 g (3 oz) tuna in brine, drained and flaked; add half a red pepper diced and 10 ml (2 tsp) low-calorie salad dressing; 25 g (1 oz) slice wholemeal bread, apple, pear or peach **(Total: 2½p,1c,1f,½f&o)**
- Bean sprout, cabbage and carrot salad tossed in 20 ml (4 tsp) low-calorie salad dressing in a 50 g (2 oz) wholemeal pitta bread; 50 g (2 oz) wedge of Brie, Camembert or reduced fat hard cheese; 150 ml (¼ pint) carton fruit juice **(Total: 2p,2c,1f,1f&o)**
- Poached mushrooms (as many as you like) in vegetable stock, strain and serve on 50 g (2 oz) wholemeal toast; 1 orange and 1 small banana peeled, chopped and mixed together topped with 150 ml (¼ pint) low-fat natural yogurt. **(Total: 2c,1d,2f)**
- Can of low-calorie vegetable soup; 50 g (2 oz) wholemeal bap filled with 50 g (2 oz) cottage cheese and grated carrot; 60 ml (4 tbsp) fruit-flavoured fromage frais **(Total: 1p,3c,1d)**
- Chicken sandwich made with 2 slices (50 g [2 oz]) wholemeal bread, 10 ml (2 tsp) low-fat spread, 50 g (2 oz) cooked chicken, shredded lettuce and beansprouts or other salad from free food list; ½ packet low-fat crisps; small banana or other fruit **(Total: 1p,3c,1f,1f&o)**
- Ploughman's lunch – 50 g (2 oz) crusty bread roll, 10 ml (2 tsp) low-fat spread, 50 g (2 oz) Brie, Camembert or reduced-fat hard cheese, lettuce, tomatoes and onions, 1 apple **(Total: 2p,2c,1f,1f&o)**

- 225 g (8 oz) baked beans, 50 g (2 oz) wholemeal bread, toasted; 100 ml (4 fl oz) unsweetened orange juice; 150 ml (¼ pint) low-fat fruit yogurt (**Total: 2p,2c,1d,1f**)
- 175 g (6 oz) baked potato; 100 g (4 oz) cottage cheese with chives; large mixed salad from free food list; 1 bite-size chocolate bar (**Total: 2p,2c,1f&o swop**)
- 50 g (2 oz) wholemeal bap filled with 100 g (4 oz) peeled prawns; 15 ml (1 tbsp) low-calorie mayonnaise, shredded lettuce and cucumber; 50 g (2 oz) ready-to-eat dried apricots, 60 ml (4 tbsp) fruit-flavoured fromage frais (**Total: 2p,2c,1d,2f,1f&o**)

SUPPER IDEAS

- 100 g (4 oz) chicken breast; 150 g (6 oz) new potatoes, carrots and courgettes cut into thin sticks and steamed; small salad from free food list with 20 ml (4 tsp) low-calorie salad dressing (**Total: 2p,2c,1f&o**)
- Stir-fried vegetables – selection of vegetables from free food list (e.g. green beans, Chinese cabbage, beansprouts, mushrooms plus 50 g (2 oz) sweetcorn and 75 g (3 oz) tofu, stir fried in 5–10 ml (1–2 tsp) vegetable oil serve with 100 g (4 oz) cooked rice or noodles, soy sauce (**Total: 1p,3c,1–2f&o**)
- 250 g (9 oz) baked potato; 5 ml (1 tsp) butter or margarine, 25 g (1 oz) reduced-fat hard cheese, grated, or 50 g (2 oz) cottage cheese; vegetables or salad from free food list (**Total: 2½p,½f&o**)
- 75 g (3 oz) poached salmon; 150 g (6 oz) new potatoes; mange tout, green beans, broccoli or other green vegetables from free food list (**Total: 3p,2c**)
- 75–100 g (3–4 oz) lamb or calves liver, onions; 10 ml (2 tsp) vegetable oil; broccoli or other green vegetables from free food list; 100 g (4 oz) cooked pasta or rice (**Total: 3–4p,2c,2f&o**)
- Fish Kebabs – 100 g (6 oz) white fish steak cubed, mushrooms, strips of green pepper, tomatoes, and thickly sliced courgettes threaded onto skewers. Brush with 5 ml (1 tsp) each lemon juice and oil, mixed, then grill or barbecue until fish is cooked. Serve with 100 g (4 oz) cooked brown rice or pasta or 50 g (2 oz) wholemal pitta bread. (**Total: 2p,2c,1f&o**)
- Cheese and vegetable omelette – made with 2 eggs, vegetables from

SUPPER IDEAS

free food list, 5 ml (1 tsp) vegetable oil, 25 g (1 oz) reduced-fat hard cheese or medium-fat cheese such as Brie, Camembert or Edam. Served with 25 g (1 oz) slice wholemeal bread and large mixed salad from free food list, 20 ml (4 tsp) low-calorie salad dressing (**Total: 3p,1c,2f&o**)

- Burger and milkshake – 50 g (2 oz) beefburger or vegetarian burger grilled, 50 g (2 oz) wholemeal bap, large mixed salad from free food list, 20 ml (4 tsp) low-calorie salad dressing. Milkshake made with 200 ml (⅓ pint) semi-skimmed milk and 1 small banana liquidised together (**Total: 2p,2c,1d,1f,1f&o**)
- 75–100 g (3–4 oz) lamb steak grilled or baked with fresh rosemary; 75 g (6 oz) new potatoes; green beans, broccoli or other green vegetables from free food list; watercress and orange salad made with 1 medium orange, watercress and 20 ml (4 tsp) low-calorie salad dressing (**Total: 3–4p,2c,1f,1f&o**)
- Vegetable curry made with 75 g (3 oz) potato, 75 g (3 oz) cooked beans or lentils and other vegetables from free food list, 150 g (6 oz) cooked rice, 150 ml (¼ pint) low-fat natural yogurt, 1 small banana sliced and slices of cucumber to accompany (**Total: 1p,3c,1d,1f**)
- 50 g (2 oz) lean ham, 75 g (3 oz) new potatoes, 1 medium corn on the cob, 5 ml (1 tsp) butter or margarine, green vegetables or salad from free food list (**Total: 2p,3c**)
- Cauliflower cheese – cauliflower with cheese sauce made with 300 ml (½ pint) skimmed milk, 15 ml (3 tsp) butter or margarine, 12 g (½ oz) flour and 25 g (1 oz) reduced-fat hard cheese. Serve with salad or green vegetables from free food list. (**Total: 1p,1c,1d,3f&o**)

CHAPTER 6

THE RECIPES

THE FOLLOWING RECIPES HAVE been developed to be low in calories while being highly nutritious, satisfying and delicious. When eating these dishes, you will find it hard to believe that you are on a diet, for they are so unlike traditional diet foods.

Each recipe, many of which hail from the healthier diets of other countries, has been developed and tested in the kitchens of the Good Housekeeping Institute, so you can be sure that they work, and that they are healthy and well balanced. Many have also been chosen because they are speedy to prepare, as dieters want good food fast. Each recipe states the amount of food portions it contains, and to make choosing your recipe even simpler, we've opened each recipe section with an at-a-glance portion guide, so that you can see instantly which recipes you can eat, if you've only got a few portions left.

MENU SUGGESTIONS

Opposite we've put together suggestions for balanced three-course meals using the recipes featured on pages 90–155. Depending on how much cooking you want to do, or how many portions you have left to eat, you could subtract a starter or a pudding, or even add in extras such as yogurt, fromage frais, rice, potatoes or salad dressing.

MENU SUGGESTIONS

Carrot and Orange soup (1f)
Baked Gingered Chicken (2p)
Mixed salad (ff)
2 oz Brown Basmati Rice (1c)
Strawberry Cream (½p,1f)
(Total: 2½p,1c,2f)

Lettuce and Mange-Tout Soup (½d,1f&o)
Minted Lamb Meatballs (4p)
Tomato Salad (ff)
Orange Mousse (½d,½f&o,1f)
(Total: 4p,1d,2½f&o,1f)

Gazpacho (½c,1f&o)
Marinated Steak Salad (2p,1c)
Golden Peach Souffle (½p,1f)
(Total: 2½p,1½c,1f&o,1f)

Taramasalata with Toast (1p,1½c)
Mango Chicken Parcels (2–3p,1f)
Ginger Fruit Salad (1½f,½d [optional]
(Total: 3–4p,1½c,½d [optional], 2½f)

Chunky Vegetable Soup (1c)
Spinach and Cheese Quiche with Crisp Potato Crust (2p,1½c, 2f&o)
Mixed salad (ff)
Dried Fruit Compote (1½f)
(Total: 2p, 2½c, 2f&o,1½f)

Watercress Soup (½c,½d,½f&o)
Carrot Onion and Egg Loaf (1p,½c)
Almond and Mango Ice Cream (1p,½f)
(Total: 2p,1c,½d,½f&o,½f)

Crispy Baked Mushrooms (1p,1c)
Chicken Stir-Fry Salad (2p,1f&o)
Raspberry Tofu Ice Cream (½p,1f&o)
(Total: 3½p,1c,2f&o)

Asparagus with Orange Sauce (½d,1f)
Hot Chicken Liver Salad (2p,½c,1f&o)
Barbecued Bananas (½d,2f&o,1½f)
(Total: 2p,½c,1d, 3f&o,2½f)

Spinach Soup (½d)
Haddock-stuffed Courgettes (2p)
2 oz Brown/White Rice (1c)
Spiced Dried Fruit Compote (3f, 1½f&o)
(Total: 2p,1c,½d, 1½f&o, 3f)

Spicy Bean Pâté (1p,1c,1f&o)
Pasta Giorgio (2½c,1f&o)
Salad of Mixed leaves (ff)
Optional low-cal dressing (½f&o)
Apricot and Orange Coupe (½d,2f)
(Total: 1p, 3½c,½d, 2½f&o, 2f)

Stripy Avocado and Cheese Mousses (2f)
Baked Beef and Vegetable Crumble (2p,1½c,1½f&o)
Almond and Mango Ice Cream (1p,½f)
(Total: 3p,1½c,1½f&o, 2½f)

Fresh Pea Soup (1p,½d,1½f&o)
Seafood Spaghetti (2p, 2½c)
Ginger Fruit Salad (½d,1½f)
(Total: 3p,2½c,1d,1½f&o,1½f)

Carrot and Orange Soup (1f)
Pizza Chilli (1p, 4c)
Mixed Salad (ff)
Apricot and kiwi-Fruit Cups (½p,½c,½d,2f&o,1f)
(Total: 1½p, 4½c,½d, 2f&o, 2f)

Warm Vegetable Salad (2f&o,1f)
Chinese Chicken with Rice (2p,1c,1½f&o)
Golden Peach Souffle (½p,1f)
(Total: 2½p,1c, 3½f&o,2f)

SOUPS AND STARTERS

Soups and starters are rarely part of a book on dieting, there are just too few calories to spare. The following recipes, however, have been chosen because they are both delicious and low in calories. If you are not feeling very hungry you might like to eat one of these dishes on its own, perhaps with crusty bread (remember to subtract it from your cereal portions).

Recipe	p	c	d	f&o	f
Crispy Baked Mushrooms	1	1			
Chunky Vegetable Soup		1			
Spinach and Yogurt Soup			1		
Fresh Pea Soup	1			½	1½
Quick Chicken Liver Pâté	4	1½		2	
Spicy Bean Pâté	1	1		1	
Stripy Avocado and Cheese Mousses					2
Taramasalata	1	1½			
Gazpacho		½		1	
Watercress Soup		½	½	½	
Carrot and Orange Soup					1
Spinach Soup			½		
Lettuce and Mange-Tout Soup			½	1	
Asparagus with Orange Sauce			½		1

CRISPY BAKED MUSHROOMS WITH GARLIC DIP

These baked mushrooms can be made in advance and stored in the refrigerator. Spearing the mushrooms on wooden cocktail sticks makes dipping easier.

―――― SERVES 4 ――――
Portions per serving: **1p, 1c**

100 g (4 oz) fine day-old wholemeal breadcrumbs
30 ml (2 tbsp) grated Parmesan cheese
15 ml (1 tbsp) chopped fresh mixed herbs or 7.5 ml (½ tbsp) dried
225 g (8 oz) button mushrooms, trimmed
3 egg whites

GARLIC DIP

100 g (4 oz) low-fat soft cheese
60 ml (4 tbsp) low-fat natural yogurt
1–2 garlic cloves, skinned and crushed
15 ml (1 tbsp) snipped fresh chives

1 Mix the breadcrumbs, Parmesan cheese and herbs together on a large flat plate.
2 Dip each mushroom in the lightly beaten egg whites, then coat in the breadcrumb mixture, pressing on firmly and making sure that the mushroom is completely covered. Repeat until all the mushrooms are coated.
3 Place the mushrooms on a baking sheet and chill for at least 30 minutes. Bake at 190°C (375°F) mark 5 for 15–20 minutes, until golden brown.
4 Meanwhile, put the cheese, yogurt, garlic and chives in a bowl and mix together. Spoon into a serving dish. Serve the mushrooms hot with the garlic flavoured dip.

CHUNKY VEGETABLE SOUP

This is a very hearty soup. Served with some warm crusty wholemeal bread, it can make a complete meal.

―――― SERVES 4 ――――
Portions per serving: **1c**

1 onion, skinned and thinly sliced
3 celery sticks, trimmed and chopped
3 carrots, scrubbed and chopped
1 parsnip, peeled and chopped
100 g (4 oz) swede, peeled and diced
1 potato, scrubbed and diced
1 garlic clove, skinned and crushed
900 ml (1½ pints) chicken stock
40 g (1½ oz) sweetcorn kernels
salt and pepper

1 Put the vegetables, except the sweetcorn, and garlic into a large saucepan with the stock. Bring to the boil, lower the heat and simmer very gently for 25–30 minutes or until the vegetables are just tender.
2 Using a slotted spoon, remove approximately half the vegetables. Place the remaining vegetables and stock in a blender or food processor and purée until smooth.
3 Return the purée to a clean pan and add the reserved vegetables, sweetcorn, and salt and pepper to taste. Heat through, then serve.

SPINACH AND YOGURT SOUP

Spinach combines well with yogurt and spring onions to give a refreshing, chilled summer soup.

───────── SERVES 4 ─────────
Portions per serving: **1d**

225 g (8 oz) young spinach leaves, washed and drained
4 spring onions, chopped
450 ml (¾ pint) low-fat natural yogurt
5 ml (1 tsp) paprika
15 ml (1 tbsp) lemon juice
150 ml (¼ pint) semi-skimmed milk
salt and pepper
4 ice cubes, to serve
paprika, spring onion and spinach, to garnish

1 Put the spinach leaves in a saucepan with only the water that clings to the leaves. Cover and cook for 5 minutes, until wilted. Drain well, pressing out any excess water.
2 Chop the spinach roughly, then place in a blender or food processor with the spring onions and 300 ml (½ pint) yogurt. Purée until smooth. Add the remaining yogurt, the paprika, lemon juice and milk, and add salt and pepper, to taste. Blend until mixed. Chill for 1 hour.
3 Divide the soup between 4 serving bowls and drop an ice cube into each. Sprinkle with a little paprika and garnish with spring onion and spinach before serving.

FRESH PEA SOUP

If fresh peas are not readily available, use frozen; both require the same cooking time.

───────── SERVES 4 ─────────
Portions per serving: **1p, ½d, 1½ f&o**

30 ml (2 tbsp) corn oil
1 small onion, skinned and chopped
1 garlic clove, skinned and crushed
1.1 litres (2 pints) chicken stock
900 g (2 lb) fresh peas, shelled, or 450 g (1 lb) frozen
salt and pepper
low-fat natural yogurt, to garnish

1 Heat the oil in a saucepan. Add the onion and garlic and cook for 5 minutes, until softened. Add the stock and peas and bring to the boil, then simmer for 20–25 minutes, until the peas are very tender.
2 Cool slightly. Purée in a blender or food processor, until smooth. Return to the pan and add salt and pepper, to taste. Reheat and serve hot, garnished with a swirl of yogurt.

QUICK CHICKEN LIVER PATE

This pâté is high in iron, as chicken livers are a rich source. Serve with wholemeal bread.

SERVES 4
Portions per serving: **4p, 1½c, 2f&o**

450 g (1 lb) chicken livers, trimmed
40 g (1½ oz) polyunsaturated margarine
1 small onion, skinned and chopped
2 cloves
8 allspice berries
10 black peppercorns
5 ml (1 tsp) dried thyme
10 ml (2 tsp) dry sherry
salt and pepper
1 egg, hard-boiled, and 15 ml (1 tbsp) toasted sunflower seeds, to garnish
1 stick (approx 150 g [6 oz]) wholemeal French bread, warmed, to serve

1 Rinse the livers and place in a saucepan. Cover with cold water, bring to the boil and simmer gently for 5–7 minutes, until no longer pink.
2 Meanwhile, melt the margarine in a small saucepan. Add the onion and cook for about 5 minutes, until soft. Add the cloves, allspice, peppercorns and thyme and stir over low heat for 2 minutes.
3 Drain the livers and put them into a blender or food processor. Remove the spices from the onion and discard. Add the onion to the livers and blend briefly. Add the sherry and salt and pepper, to taste, and coarsely blend.
4 Scoop the mixture into a dish and smooth the surface. Leave to cool for 1–2 hours, then chill for 1 hour.
5 Finely chop the egg white into a bowl. Sieve in the yolk. Use to garnish the pâté with the sunflower seeds. Serve with warmed bread.

SPICY BEAN PATE

SERVES 4
Portions per serving: **1p, 1c, 1f&o**

400 g (14 oz) can cannellini beans, drained and rinsed
1 garlic clove, skinned and crushed
15 ml (1 tbsp) lemon juice
30 ml (2 tbsp) low-fat natural yogurt
15 ml (1 tbsp) olive oil
15 ml (1 tbsp) chopped fresh parsley
salt and cayenne
black olives, tomato wedges and small lettuce leaves, to garnish
four 25 g (1 oz) slices wholemeal bread, toasted and cut into triangles, or Melba toast, to serve

1 Drain the beans well, patting away any excess moisture with absorbent kitchen paper. Place in a blender or food processor and purée until well blended and smooth.
2 Transfer to a bowl and add the garlic, lemon juice, yogurt, oil and parsley. Mix well and add salt and cayenne to taste. Cover the mixture and chill for at least 1 hour.
3 Serve in a large bowl or on individual plates, garnished with olives, tomato wedges and lettuce leaves. Serve with the toast.

STRIPY AVOCADO AND CHEESE MOUSSES

An easy-to-prepare and impressive starter which can be made the evening before and stored, covered, in the refrigerator.

———————— SERVES 4 ————————
Portions per serving: **2f**

1 large ripe avocado
1 garlic clove, skinned and crushed
1.25 ml (¼ tsp) cayenne
15 ml (1 tbsp) lemon juice
1–2 drops Tabasco sauce (optional)
salt and pepper
30 ml (2 tbsp) natural Quark
2.5 ml (½ tsp) paprika
1 celery stick, trimmed and finely chopped
7.5 ml (1½ tsp) powdered gelatine
strips of red pepper, to garnish

1 Scoop the flesh out of the avocado and place in a blender or food processor. Add the garlic, cayenne, lemon juice and Tabasco sauce, if using, and purée until smooth. Add salt and pepper, to taste.
2 Put the Quark into a bowl, sprinkle in the paprika and mix in the celery and seasoning.
3 Sprinkle the gelatine on to 30 ml (2 tbsp) cold water in a heatproof bowl and leave to soak for 1 minute. Place over a pan of gently boiling hot water and stir until the gelatine is dissolved. Stir 5 ml (1 tsp) into the cheese mixture. Pour the remainder into the avocado mixture and blend briefly until mixed.
4 Pour half of the avocado mixture into 4 wine glasses. Top with the cheese mixture, dividing it evenly. Finish with the avocado mixture.

5 Cover and chill for at least 2 hours or overnight. Just before serving, garnish with strips of red pepper.

TARAMASALATA

This classic Greek dip keeps well for 3–4 days if stored in the refrigerator in an airtight container.

———————— SERVES 4 ————————
Portions per serving: **1p, 1½c**

175 g (6 oz) smoked cod's roe, skinned
50 g (2 oz) fresh wholemeal breadcrumbs
1 garlic clove, skinned and crushed
150 ml (¼ pint) low-fat natural yogurt
juice of ½ lemon or 1 lime
pepper
15 ml (1 tbsp) snipped fresh chives
fresh chives and lemon and lime twists, to garnish
four 25 g (1 oz) slices toasted wholemeal bread fingers, to serve

Blend all the ingredients, except for the garnish and toast, in a blender or food processor until smooth and creamy, then adjust the pepper, to taste. Garnish and serve with wholemeal toast fingers.

GAZPACHO

A traditional chilled Spanish soup.

———— SERVES 4 ————
Portions per serving: ½c, 1f&o

225 g (8 oz) tomatoes, seeded and finely diced
⅓ cucumber, peeled, seeded and finely diced
1 onion, skinned and chopped
1 small green pepper, cored, seeded and diced
1 small red pepper, cored, seeded and diced
1 garlic clove, skinned and finely chopped
450 ml (¾ pint) tomato juice, chilled
150 ml (¼ pint) chicken or vegetable stock, skimmed and chilled
15 ml (1 tbsp) olive oil
45 ml (3 tbsp) red wine vinegar
a few drops of Tabasco sauce
salt and pepper
a few sprigs of fresh chervil, to garnish

TO SERVE

two 25 g (1 oz) slices of wholemeal bread, toasted and cubed
ice cubes

1 Reserve about a quarter of the tomatoes, cucumber, onion and peppers for the garnish. Place the remaining vegetables in a blender or food processor with the garlic and tomato juice and blend until smooth.
2 Add the stock, oil, vinegar and Tabasco sauce and blend well. Add salt and pepper to taste. Pour into a bowl, cover and chill for about 30 minutes.
3 Stir the soup and garnish with the chervil. Serve with the reserved vegetables, wholemeal bread croûtons and ice cubes in separate bowls, to be added to the soup as desired.

WATERCRESS SOUP

———— SERVES 4 ————
Portions per serving: ½c, ½d, ½f&o

15 g (½ oz) polyunsaturated margarine
1 small onion, skinned and chopped
1 bunch of watercress, trimmed and coarsely chopped
20 g (¾ oz) plain wholemeal flour
300 ml (½ pint) chicken or vegetable stock, skimmed
300 ml (½ pint) semi-skimmed milk
1.25 ml (¼ tsp) freshly grated nutmeg
salt and pepper
watercress sprigs and paprika, to garnish

1 Melt the margarine in a saucepan. Add the onion and watercress and cook over a low heat for 3–5 minutes or until the onion is soft but not brown, stirring occasionally.
2 Add the flour and cook for 1 minute, then gradually stir in the stock, milk and nutmeg. Bring to the boil, stirring. Add salt and pepper to taste, lower the heat and simmer, covered, for about 15 minutes or until thickened and smooth.
3 Remove from the heat and leave to cool slightly, then purée in a blender or food processor. Return the soup to the saucepan and reheat. Serve in individual bowls garnished with watercress sprigs and a sprinkling of paprika.

CARROT AND ORANGE SOUP

To make the orange butter, work grated orange rind into butter.

———— SERVES 6 ————
Portions per serving: **1f**

450 g (1 lb) carrots, scraped and finely chopped
1 large onion, skinned and finely chopped
1.7 litres (3 pints) chicken stock
juice and grated rind of 2 small oranges
pinch of ground coriander
salt and freshly ground black pepper

1 Put the carrots and onion into a large saucepan and add the stock. Do not add salt and pepper yet, but bring to the boil and simmer until the carrots are quite soft.
2 Liquidise, return to the saucepan and add the juice of the oranges, and the coriander. Heat through and taste for seasoning.

SPINACH SOUP

———— SERVES 4 ————
Portions per serving: **½d**

450 g (1 lb) fresh spinach
900 ml (1½ pints) vegetable or chicken stock, skimmed
15 ml (1 tbsp) lemon juice
salt and pepper
450 ml (¾ pint) buttermilk
a few drops of Tabasco sauce

1 Strip the spinach leaves from their stems and wash in several changes of water. Place the spinach, stock and lemon juice in a large saucepan and add salt and pepper, to taste. Bring to the boil, then simmer for 10 minutes.
2 Work the spinach through a sieve, or strain off most of the liquid and reserve, then purée the spinach in a blender or food processor.
3 Reheat the spinach purée gently with the cooking liquid, 300 ml (½ pint) of the buttermilk and the Tabasco sauce. Swirl in the remaining buttermilk just before serving.

LETTUCE AND MANGE-TOUT SOUP

———— SERVES 4 ————
Portions per serving: ½d, 1f

15 ml (1 tbsp) polyunsaturated oil
2 shallots, skinned and chopped
30 ml (2 tbsp) chopped celery leaves
900 ml (1½ pints) chicken or vegetable stock, skimmed
225 g (8 oz) mange-tout
½ cos lettuce
5 ml (1 tsp) reduced-sodium soy sauce, preferably naturally fermented shoyu
pepper
15 ml (1 tbsp) chopped fresh mint or lemon balm
45 ml (3 tbsp) chopped fresh parsley or chervil

1 Heat the oil in a large saucepan. Add the shallots and fry gently for about 5 minutes, or until softened. Add the celery leaves and stock and bring to the boil. Simmer, partly covered, for 5 minutes.
2 Meanwhile, string the mange-tout and cut in half if large. Finely shred the lettuce. Add these to the pan with the soy sauce and pepper to taste, then bring back to the boil.
3 Simmer for 5 minutes or until the lettuce is wilted, then stir in the herbs. Serve hot.

ASPARAGUS WITH ORANGE SAUCE

Make the most of the fresh asparagus season and serve this luxurious but healthy starter.

———— SERVES 4 ————
Portions per serving: ½d, 1f

450 g (1 lb) fresh asparagus, trimmed and scraped
150 ml (¼ pint) dry white wine
juice of 1 orange
150 ml (¼ pint) Greek-style natural yogurt
1 egg, size 2
salt

TO GARNISH
finely pared rind of 1 orange, finely shredded orange slices

1 Tie the asparagus in a bundle and cover the tips with a cap of foil. Stand, tips uppermost, in a deep saucepan of boiling water, lower the heat and simmer for 15 minutes or until tender. Drain and arrange in a serving dish.
2 Meanwhile, place the wine and orange juice in a small saucepan and boil for 7–8 minutes or until reduced by two-thirds.
3 Beat together the yogurt and egg in a small heatproof bowl over a pan of simmering water. Cook for about 10 minutes, whisking continuously until thickened, then gradually stir in the reduced liquid. Add the salt to taste and spoon the sauce over the asparagus tips. Garnish with finely shredded orange rind and orange slices.

SALADS

Salads are no longer just a pallid side dish of wilting leaves, they can be a light and refreshing way to combine a variety of both cooked and raw ingredients. They are increasingly served as a whole meal in themselves, as are many of the salads below. To make these salad recipes more slimming, substitute the salad dressings given for a bought low-calorie dressing or one made from low-fat yogurt, tomato juice, tabasco and salt and pepper. Or use the orange and herb dressing (see Fruited Cheese Salad, page 102) or lemon dressing (see Avocado and Chick-Pea Salad, page 102).

AT-A-GLANCE PORTION GUIDE (per serving)

Recipe	p	c	d	f&o	f
Warm Vegetable Salad				2	1
Hot Chicken Liver Salad	2	½		1	
Marinated Steak Salad	2	1			
Hedgerow Salad	1			1½	
Chicken Stir-fry Salad	2			1	
Tuna and Bean Salad with Orange Dressing	2			1	1
Fruited Cheese Salad	1½				1
Avocado and Chick-Pea Salad	2	½			1½
Luncheon Salad	2½				
Burghul Wheat Salad		1½		1½	1
Smoked Chicken and Mint Salad	3½		½		
Spinach Salad				3	

WARM VEGETABLE SALAD

This summer salad can be cooked on a barbecue or under a grill. The vegetables are cooked whole, then thinly sliced and served with an oil and vinegar dressing.

―――――― SERVES 4 ――――――
Portions per serving: **2f&o, 1f**

4 onions, skinned
2 red peppers
2 yellow peppers
6 courgettes
1 aubergine
45 ml (3 tbsp) olive oil
30 ml (2 tbsp) red wine vinegar
2 garlic cloves, skinned and crushed
15 ml (1 tbsp) chopped fresh thyme
salt and pepper

1 Parboil the onions whole for 5 minutes, then drain thoroughly. Rub the onions, peppers, courgettes and aubergine with 15 ml (1 tbsp) of the olive oil.
2 Place the vegetables on the rack over a preheated barbecue, or under a medium grill, keeping the peppers 10 cm (4 inches) away from the source of heat. Cook for 15–20 minutes, turning the vegetables once or twice, until they are tender.
3 Meanwhile, prepare the dressing. Mix the remaining olive oil with the red wine vinegar, garlic, thyme and add salt and pepper to taste.
4 Remove the cooked vegetables from the barbecue or grill with tongs. Leave to cool slightly. Slice the vegetables quite thinly, including any charred pieces of vegetable skin for flavour. Discard the core and seeds from the peppers.
5 Place the warm vegetables in a shallow serving dish. Spoon the prepared dressing over the top and serve immediately.

HOT CHICKEN LIVER SALAD

Hot, piquant chicken livers, spooned over the crisp curly endive, are quite mouthwatering.

―――――― SERVES 4 ――――――
Portions per serving: **2p, ½c, 1f&o**

½ curly endive, broken into sprigs
1 thick slice wholemeal bread
5 ml (1 tsp) sunflower oil
1 shallot or small onion, skinned and finely chopped
225 g (8 oz) chicken livers, trimmed and cut into small pieces
large pinch of dried sage
30 ml (2 tbsp) wine vinegar
15 ml (1 tbsp) walnut oil

1 Line 4 individual salad bowls with the curly endive. Toast the bread and cut into small cubes. Set aside.
2 Heat the oil in a non-stick frying pan and gently cook the shallot for about 5 minutes until soft. Add the chicken livers and sage and fry for about 5–8 minutes until just cooked through. Pour on the wine vinegar and heat.
3 Spoon the livers into the centre of the endive, garnish with the toasted croûtons and sprinkle with the walnut oil. Serve immediately.

MARINATED STEAK SALAD

This warm salad should be eaten as soon as it is ready, otherwise the heat from the steak and rice will speed the loss of vitamin C in the raw vegetables. Marinades should contain an acid such as lemon juice; this helps to tenderise the meat. Marinate for at least 3 hours for flavour absorption.

──────── SERVES 4 ────────
Portions per serving: **2p, 1c**

225 g (8 oz) lean rump steak, trimmed of excess fat, cut in 5 cm (2 inch) long narrow strips
1 garlic clove, skinned and crushed
15 ml (1 tbsp) soy sauce, preferably naturally fermented shoyu
15 ml (1 tbsp) lemon juice
5 ml (1 tsp) finely grated fresh root ginger
2 spring onions, trimmed, chopped
30 ml (2 tbsp) dry red wine
pepper
75 g (3 oz) brown rice
2.5 ml (½ tsp) corn oil
100 g (4 oz) button mushrooms, halved
1 red pepper, cored and seeded
1 bunch of watercress, trimmed, or 100 g (4 oz) fresh spinach leaves

1 Place the steak strips in a glass, ceramic or stainless steel bowl with the garlic, soy sauce, lemon juice, ginger, spring onions, wine and add pepper to taste. Stir. Cover and marinate in the refrigerator for 3 hours or overnight, stirring occasionally.
2 Put the rice in 450 ml (¾ pint) boiling water. Cover and simmer for 30 minutes or until tender and the liquid has been absorbed. Place in a serving bowl and keep warm.
3 Lightly brush a heavy-based frying pan or wok with the oil and heat. Pour in the meat and marinade, then the mushrooms. Cook, stirring constantly, over a medium heat for 1 minute. Cover and simmer for a further 5 minutes. Remove from the heat and set aside to cool slightly.
4 Meanwhile, cut the red pepper into long narrow strips and add to the rice with the watercress or fresh spinach. Stir in the meat and mushroom mixture. Check the seasoning, adding a little more soy sauce, if liked. Serve immediately.

HEDGEROW SALAD

Health food shops and some large supermarkets sell dandelion leaves, primulas and nasturtiums.

──────── SERVES 4 ────────
Portions per serving: **1p, 1½f&o**

1 small bunch of dandelion leaves
a few leaves of chicory
1 small curly endive
50 g (2 oz) sorrel
8 primula or nasturtium flowers

DRESSING

50 g (2 oz) walnuts, halved
30 ml (2 tbsp) walnut oil
60 ml (4 tbsp) lemon juice
1 garlic clove, skinned and crushed
salt and pepper

1 Break the leaves into bite-size pieces and place in a large bowl. Sprinkle over the flowers.
2 Mix together the dressing ingredients, adding salt and pepper to taste, and pour over the salad. Toss and serve immediately.

CHICKEN STIR-FRY SALAD

SERVES 4
Portions per serving: **2p, 1f&o**

450 g (1 lb) boneless chicken breasts, skinned and cut into very thin strips
10 ml (2 tsp) sesame oil
2 garlic cloves, skinned and crushed
2 cm (¾ inch) piece fresh root ginger, peeled and grated
45 ml (3 tbsp) soy sauce, preferably naturally fermented shoyu
1 bunch of watercress, trimmed
½ head Chinese leaves, torn into bite-size pieces
½ head curly endive, torn into bite-size pieces
15 ml (1 tbsp) corn oil
pepper
radish roses and a dill sprig, to garnish

1 Put the chicken strips in a bowl. Add the sesame oil, garlic, grated ginger and soy sauce. Stir well and leave to marinate for 15 minutes.
2 Meanwhile, arrange the watercress, Chinese leaves and endive on a serving platter or individual plates.
3 Heat the oil in a large frying pan or wok. Add the chicken mixture and cook over a high heat for 3–4 minutes, stirring constantly, until the chicken is cooked through.
4 Spoon the mixture over the leaves, add pepper to taste and serve immediately, garnished with radish roses and a fresh dill sprig.

TUNA AND BEAN SALAD WITH ORANGE DRESSING

SERVES 4
Portions per serving: **2p, 1f&o, 1f**

2 oranges
100–150 g (4–5 oz) fresh spinach, cos lettuce or endive leaves, rinsed and dried
½ small onion, skinned and thinly sliced
200 g (7 oz) can tuna in brine, well drained and flaked
100 g (4 oz) button mushrooms, sliced
400 g (14 oz) can cannellini beans, drained and rinsed
8 black olives and 5 ml (1 tsp) chopped fresh parsley, to garnish

ORANGE DRESSING
juice of 1 orange
150 ml (¼ pint) low-fat natural yogurt
1 garlic clove, skinned and crushed
15 ml (1 tbsp) soya oil
salt and pepper

1 Thinly pare the rind from the oranges and cut into thin strips. Remove all white pith from the oranges and segment them. Set aside. Blanch the rind in boiling water for 4–5 minutes, drain and reserve.
2 Arrange the leaves, onion and orange on a platter. Mix the tuna, mushrooms and beans together.
3 To make the dressing, mix together the juice, yogurt, garlic, oil and add salt and pepper to taste. Pour half over the tuna bean mixture and toss lightly.
4 Pile the tuna on the serving platter and garnish with the olives, parsley and orange rind. Pour over the remaining dressing before serving.

FRUITED CHEESE SALAD

A refreshing salad full of goodness – its low-fat dressing has no oil or egg yolk, just juice and the seasonings.

——————— SERVES 4 ———————
Portions per serving: 1½p, 1f

225 g (8 oz) green cabbage, finely shredded
4 courgettes, shredded or coarsely grated
350 g (12 oz) cottage cheese
100 g (4 oz) black grapes, halved and seeded
2 eating apples, quartered, cored and sliced
2 oranges, peeled and segmented
1 bunch watercress, trimmed and divided into small sprigs

ORANGE AND HERB DRESSING
90 ml (6 tbsp) unsweetened orange juice
1.25 ml (¼ tsp) grated nutmeg
30 ml (2 tbsp) finely chopped fresh parsley
15 ml (1 tbsp) snipped fresh chives
1 garlic clove, skinned and crushed
salt and pepper

1 Mix the shredded cabbage and courgettes together in a bowl. To make the dressing, mix together all the ingredients in another bowl, adding salt and pepper to taste.
2 Add all but 15 ml (1 tbsp) of the dressing to the shredded vegetables and toss together. Spoon the shredded vegetables on to a shallow dish or platter.
3 Make 4 hollows in the vegetables and spoon in the cottage cheese. Arrange the grapes, apples, oranges and watercress sprigs over and around the vegetables. Spoon over the remaining dressing and serve.

AVOCADO AND CHICK-PEA SALAD

Quark is used in this recipe with semi-skimmed milk, to make a low-fat dressing. Use Quark in recipes calling for full-fat soft cheese.

——————— SERVES 4 ———————
Portions per serving: 2p, ½c, 1½f

1 avocado
15 ml (1 tbsp) lemon juice
450 g (1 lb) fresh young spinach, with stalks removed, finely sliced
100 g (4 oz) red cabbage, finely shredded
400 g (14 oz) can chick-peas, drained and rinsed
1 slice wholemeal bread, toasted and diced
2 eggs, hard-boiled and sliced
paprika

LEMON DRESSING
juice of ½ lemon
50 g (2 oz) natural Quark
100 ml (4 fl oz) semi-skimmed milk
30 ml (2 tbsp) snipped fresh chives or parsley
salt and pepper

1 To make the dressing, place the lemon juice, Quark and milk in a bowl and whisk until smooth. Add the herbs, reserving some for garnish and add salt and pepper to taste. Set aside.
2 Peel the avocado, discard the stone and dice. Coat with the lemon juice to prevent discoloration.
3 Mix together the spinach and red

cabbage and arrange over a large serving platter. Arrange the avocado around the edge of the platter.
4 Pile the chick-peas in the centre of the spinach and scatter the toast around them. Arrange the egg slices on top and sprinkle over a little paprika.
5 To serve, spoon a little of the dressing over the chick-peas, and garnish with the reserved snipped chives. Serve the remaining dressing separately.

LUNCHEON SALAD

SERVES 4
Portions per serving: 2½p

225 g (8 oz) cold cooked chicken meat, skinned and cut into small cubes
75 g (3 oz) pickled dill cucumber, cut into small cubes
1 orange, rind finely grated and reserved, pith removed and segemented
10 ml (2 tsp) chopped fresh parsley
225 g (8 oz) cottage cheese, sieved
pepper
100 g (4 oz) Webb's Wonder or Iceberg lettuce, shredded
25 g (1 oz) blanched almonds, toasted

1 Put the chicken and cucumber into a bowl, then add the orange rind and parsley. Stir in the cottage cheese and add the pepper to taste.
2 Arrange the lettuce on a serving platter and place the chicken mixture on top. Place the orange segments around the chicken mixture. Scatter the almonds over the chicken mixture and serve.

BURGHUL WHEAT SALAD

SERVES 4
Portions per serving: 1½c, 1½f&o, 1f

100 g (4 oz) burghul wheat
50 g (2 oz) currants, rinsed
6 spring onions, trimmed and chopped
3 tomatoes, diced
juice of 1 orange
30 ml (2 tbsp) chopped fresh parsley
15 ml (1 tbsp) chopped fresh mint
pepper
30 ml (2 tbsp) olive oil
orange segments and mint sprigs, to garnish

1 Put the burghul wheat in a bowl, cover with cold water and leave to soak for 30 minutes. Drain through a clean piece of muslin or cloth and squeeze well to remove all the water.
2 Return the wheat to the rinsed-out bowl. Add the currants, spring onions and tomatoes and mix together well.
3 Blend together the orange juice, parsley, mint and add pepper to taste. Gradually add the olive oil, beating until well blended. Pour over the wheat mixture and leave for 5 minutes.
4 Transfer the salad to a serving dish and garnish with the orange segments and mint sprigs.

SMOKED CHICKEN AND MINT SALAD

Smoked chicken can be found in delicatessens and some supermarkets. The moist, tasty flesh is rich and benefits from the freshness of mint, cucumber and strawberries.

———— SERVES 6 ————
Portions per serving: **3½p, ½d**

1.1 kg (2½ lb) smoked chicken
1 small cucumber
100 g (4 oz) strawberries, hulled
150 ml (¼ pint) Greek-style natural yogurt
45 ml (3 tbsp) chopped fresh mint
salt and pepper
mint sprigs, to garnish

1 Thinly slice the chicken breast, leaving on the skin. Cut the leg flesh into strips, discarding the skin. Thinly slice half the cucumber and all the strawberries. Tightly cover all these ingredients and refrigerate.
2 Coarsely grate the remaining cucumber and mix into the yogurt with the chopped mint and salt and pepper to taste. Cover tightly and refrigerate.
3 About 30 minutes before serving, arrange some of the chicken, cucumber and strawberry slices on each of six individual serving plates. Pile the chicken leg flesh in the centre of each and top with a small spoonful of the yogurt dressing.
4 Garnish the salads with mint sprigs and serve the remaining dressing separately.

SPINACH SALAD

———— SERVES 4 ————
Portions per serving: **3f&o**

450 g (1 lb) young spinach leaves, stems removed and well washed
75 g (3 oz) button mushrooms, sliced
60 ml (4 tbsp) olive oil
6 spring onions, trimmed and chopped
1 small red pepper, cored, seeded and chopped
5 ml (1 tsp) French mustard
5 ml (1 tsp) light muscovado sugar
pepper
30 ml (2 tbsp) white wine vinegar

1 Tear the spinach leaves into small pieces and put into a salad bowl with the mushrooms. Mix together. Chill while preparing the dressing.
2 Put the oil into a small saucepan and heat gently. Add the spring onions and red pepper and cook for 2 minutes. Remove from the heat.
3 Stir in the mustard, sugar and add pepper to taste, then add the vinegar. Return to the heat and cook gently, until nearly boiling. Pour the dressing immediately over the prepared salad, toss and serve.

PASTA DISHES

Pasta is an important part of any diet as it is both satisfying and filling. Most dieters wrongly assume that pasta is out of bounds to them, but what makes pasta fattening is what you put on it. Below we have adapted delicious classic pasta sauce recipes so they won't end up coating your hips.

AT-A-GLANCE PORTION GUIDE (per serving)					
Recipe	p	c	d	f&o	f
Vegetable Lasagne			1½	1	1
Neapolitan Tortelloni			3	½	
Pasta with Pesto		2	2½	1½	
Pasta with Tomato Sauce			4		
Singapore Noodles		1	3½	½	
Seafood Spaghetti		2	2½		
Fettuccini with Clam Sauce		1	4½	½	
Broad Noodles with Smoked Salmon		½	3½	1	
Pasta Giorgio			2½	1	
Pasta con le Zucchine			3½	2	
Simple Tomato Sauce	No portions				
Fresh Tomato Sauce			½	1½	
Uncooked Tomato Sauce				3½	

VEGETABLE LASAGNE

Prepare this quick and easy dish in advance and then cook either later that day or the next day.

——————— SERVES 4 ———————
Portions per serving: **1½c, 1d, 1f&o**

15 ml (1 tbsp) sunflower oil
1 small onion, skinned and chopped
1 carrot, scrubbed and chopped
1 small green pepper, cored, seeded and chopped
1 garlic clove, skinned and chopped
350 g (12 oz) mushrooms, chopped
400 g (14 oz) can tomatoes
30 ml (2 tbsp) tomato purée
5 ml (1 tsp) chopped fresh basil or 2.5 ml (½ tsp) dried
5 ml (1 tsp) chopped fresh oregano or 2.5 ml (½ tsp) dried
pepper
225 g (8 oz) courgettes, trimmed and thinly sliced diagonally
175 g (6 oz) fresh spinach (or wholemeal) lasagne
1 egg
300 ml (½ pint) natural low-fat yogurt
15 ml (1 tbsp) freshly grated Parmesan cheese

1 Heat the oil in a saucepan. Add the onion, carrot, green pepper and garlic. Gently fry for 5 minutes. Add the mushrooms and cook for a further 5 minutes. Add the tomatoes and their juice, tomato purée, herbs and pepper to taste. Bring to the boil, then gently simmer for about 20 minutes, until the sauce has thickened, stirring occasionally.
2 Cook the courgettes for about 3 minutes in a little boiling water. Drain well to remove excess moisture.
3 Cook the lasagne sheets in boiling water for 3–4 minutes or until just tender. Drain and set aside on a clean cloth in a single layer.
4 Pour half the tomato sauce into the base of an ovenproof dish. Top with half the courgettes, then arrange half the lasagne on top. Repeat the layers.
5 Beat together the egg, yogurt and cheese and spoon over the lasagne. Cook at 190°C (375°F) mark 5 for 30–40 minutes, until golden. Serve hot.

NEAPOLITAN TORTELLONI

For best results, use the fresh pasta available at most large supermarkets with your own homemade sauce. Tortelloni are half-moon shaped pasta with fluted edges; in this recipe they are filled with spinach.

——————— SERVES 4 ———————
Portions per serving: **3c, ½f&o**

10 ml (2 tsp) sunflower oil
2 garlic cloves, skinned and finely chopped
225 ml (8 fl oz) passata or other sieved tomatoes
2.5 ml (½ tsp) dried or fresh oregano
pepper
500 g (18 oz) fresh spinach tortelloni
15 g (½ oz) Parmesan cheese, freshly grated

1 Heat the oil in a large non-stick saucepan and gently cook the garlic until beginning to change colour. Add the tomatoes and oregano. Add pepper, to taste. Bring to the boil, turn off the heat and cover. Keep warm while cooking the pasta.
2 Cook the tortelloni according to

packet directions. Drain well.
3 Divide the tortelloni between 4 soup plates, pour over the sauce and sprinkle with the Parmesan cheese.

PASTA WITH PESTO

―――――― SERVES 4 ――――――
Portions per serving: **2p, 2½c, 1½f&o**

225 g (8 oz) wholemeal pasta, any shape
30 ml (2 tbsp) olive oil
1–2 garlic cloves, skinned
about 7 g (¼ oz) fresh basil leaves and stems
50 g (2 oz) pine nuts
25 g (1 oz) Parmesan cheese, grated
semi-skimmed milk, to blend
100 g (4 oz) low-fat curd cheese
pepper
fresh basil, to garnish
Parmesan cheese, preferably freshly grated, to serve

1 Cook the pasta in a large saucepan of boiling water for 10–12 minutes, until just tender.
2 Meanwhile, make the pesto. Put the oil, garlic, basil, pine nuts and Parmesan cheese in a blender or food processor. Add a little milk to moisten the mixture and blend to a thick purée. Transfer to a bowl. Stir in curd cheese and add pepper to taste.
3 Drain the pasta, return to the pan and stir in the pesto. Cook, stirring for 1–2 minutes over a very low heat. Thin the sauce with a little more milk, if needed. Garnish with basil and serve with Parmesan cheese.

PASTA WITH TOMATO SAUCE

In this unusual pasta starter, the pasta twirls are served hot with a cold frothy tomato sauce.

―――――― SERVES 4 ――――――
Portions per serving: **4c**

5 ml (1 tsp) corn oil
100 g (4 oz) dried or fresh wholemeal pasta twirls
225 g (8 oz) dried or fresh spinach pasta twirls
30 ml (2 tbsp) chopped fresh parsley, to garnish

FRESH TOMATO SAUCE
450 g (1 lb) tomatoes, chopped
20 ml (4 tsp) chopped fresh tarragon or
10 ml (2 tsp) dried
5 ml (1 tsp) dried thyme
1 garlic clove, skinned and crushed
salt and pepper

1 Bring a large pan of water to the boil and add the corn oil. Add the pasta, stir and cook for 3 minutes for fresh pasta, 10 minutes for dried.
2 Meanwhile, make the sauce. Purée the tomatoes in a blender or food processor. Add the tarragon, thyme, garlic and salt and pepper, to taste. Blend again, until the sauce is pink and frothy.
3 Drain the pasta and divide between 4 plates. Spoon the sauce on top and sprinkle with chopped parsley.

SINGAPORE NOODLES

Root ginger provides a piquancy to this high fibre dish from the East. If you are unable to find root ginger, substitute 5 ml (1 tsp) lemon juice instead.

―――――― SERVES 4 ――――――
Portions per serving: **1p, 3½c, ½f&o**

275 g (10 oz) wholemeal spaghetti
10 ml (2 tsp) sunflower oil
1 large onion, skinned and chopped
2.5 cm (1 inch) piece of root ginger, peeled and finely chopped
2 large garlic cloves, skinned and crushed
15 ml (1 tbsp) curry powder
45 ml (3 tbsp) chicken stock
30 ml (2 tbsp) dry sherry
15 ml (1 tbsp) tomato purée
15 ml (1 tbsp) soy sauce
125 g (4 oz) mushrooms
125 g (4 oz) beansprouts
125 g (4 oz) prawns
125 g (4 oz) cooked chicken, cut into 2.5 cm (1inch) pieces
3 spring onions, trimmed and finely chopped

1 Cook the spaghetti in boiling water for 10 minutes. Drain and rinse with cold water.
2 Heat the oil in a wok, add the onion and ginger and stir-fry for 2 minutes. Add the garlic and curry powder and stir-fry for a further minute.
3 Add the chicken stock, dry sherry, tomato purée, soy sauce, mushrooms and beansprouts and cook for 4 minutes, stirring frequently.
4 Add the spaghetti, chicken and prawns and cook for 5 minutes. Garnish with spring onions.

SEAFOOD SPAGHETTI

―――――― SERVES 4 ――――――
Portions per serving: **2p, 2½c**

350 g (12 oz) wholemeal spaghetti
3 spring onions, chopped
300 ml (½ pint) dry white wine
2 egg yolks
100 g (4 oz) natural Quark
175 g (6 oz) cooked white fish, skinned boned and flaked
100 g (4 oz) fresh or canned shelled mussels
100 g (4 oz) fresh or canned shelled cockles
salt and pepper

1 Cook the spaghetti in a large saucepan of fast-boiling, lightly salted water for about 10 minutes.
2 Meanwhile, put the spring onions and white wine into a saucepan and simmer very gently for 3–4 minutes, without allowing the wine to evaporate too much. Remove from the heat and whisk in the egg yolks, one at a time, and the natural Quark.
3 Drain the pasta, then spoon into a serving dish and keep warm. Return the wine sauce to the heat and add the white fish, mussels and cockles. Heat through gently and season. Spoon the sauce over the pasta.

FETTUCCINI WITH CLAM SAUCE

———— SERVES 4 ————
Portions per serving: **1p, 4½c, ½f&o**

15 ml (1 tbsp) olive oil
1 medium onion, skinned and finely chopped
2–3 garlic cloves, skinned and crushed
700 g (1½ lb) tomatoes, skinned and roughly chopped, or 397 g (14 oz) and 225 g (8 oz) cans tomatoes
two 200 g (7 oz) cans or jars baby clams in brine, drained
30 ml (2 tbsp) chopped fresh parsley
salt and pepper
400 g (14 oz) fettuccini or other long thin pasta, preferably wholewheat

1 Make the sauce. Heat the oil in a saucepan, add the onion and garlic and fry gently for 5 minutes until soft but not coloured.
2 Stir in the tomatoes and their juice, bring to the boil and cook for 15–20 minutes until slightly reduced.
3 Stir the drained clams into the sauce with 15 ml (1 tbsp) parsley and salt and pepper to taste. Remove from heat.
4 Cook the fettuccini in a large pan of boiling salted water for 8–10 minutes or until just tender.
5 Reheat the sauce just before the pasta is cooked. Drain the fettuccini well, tip into a warmed serving dish and pour over the clam sauce. Sprinkle with the remaining chopped parsley to garnish.

BROAD NOODLES WITH SMOKED SALMON

A simple pasta dish to prepare with the luxurious touch of smoked salmon.

———— SERVES 6 ————
Portions per serving: **½p, 3½c, 1f&o**

450 g (1 lb) fettuccini or tagliatelle, preferably wholewheat
30 ml (2 tbsp) olive oil or 25 g (1 oz) butter
100 g (4 oz) smoked salmon or smoked sea trout, chopped into 1 cm (½ inch) pieces
60 ml (4 tbsp) low-fat Quark or single cream
squeeze of fresh lemon juice
freshly ground black pepper

1 Cook the pasta in a large pan of boiling salted water for 8–10 minutes or until just tender. While the pasta is draining, put the rinsed and dried saucepan back on the stove with the oil or butter and heat gently, but do not let it smoke or brown.
2 Add the drained pasta and turn it gently to coat. Put in the salmon pieces and fold them through the pasta. Stir in the Quark or single cream. Squeeze in the lemon juice, season to taste with a good grind of black pepper and serve at once on warmed plates.

PASTA GIORGIO

This is a very fresh-tasting pasta dish which is easy to make.

———————— SERVES 6 ————————
Portions per serving: **2½c, 1f&o**

350 g (12 oz) pasta spirals or tagliatelle
30 ml (2 tbsp) olive oil
salt
1 large red pepper, cored, deseeded and chopped
2 garlic cloves, skinned and chopped
2 large ripe tomatoes, skinned and coarsely chopped
25 g (1 oz) pinenut kernels
12 black olives, stoned and chopped
15 ml (1 tbsp) chopped fresh basil leaves or 5 ml (1 tsp) dried
freshly ground black pepper
75 g (3 oz) Parmesan cheese, finely grated, to serve

1 Cook the pasta in a large pan of boiling salted water for 8–10 minutes or until just tender. While the pasta is draining, put the rinsed and dried saucepan back on the stove with the olive oil and soften the pepper and garlic. Add the tomatoes and soften thoroughly, mixing well.
2 Gently fold in the drained pasta, then add the pinenut kernels, olives, basil and give a good grind of black pepper to taste. Serve at once on warmed plates, accompanied by Parmesan cheese.

PASTA CON LE ZUCCHINE

This is a Southern Italian dish, simple and delicious. In Italy, it is usually considered too delicately flavoured a dish to eat with Parmesan, but this is a matter of individual choice.

———————— SERVES 6 ————————
Portions per serving: **3½c, 2f&o**

450 g (1 lb) pasta of your choice
60 ml (4 tbsp) olive oil
450 g (1 lb) courgettes, unpeeled, thinly sliced
salt and freshly ground black pepper
30 ml (2 tbsp) low-fat Quark

1 Cook the pasta in a large pan of boiling salted water for 8–10 minutes or until just tender. While cooking, heat the oil and lightly fry the courgettes until soft, but do not allow them to brown. Set aside and keep hot.
2 Drain the pasta and return it to the rinsed and drained saucepan over a very low heat. Gently fold in the courgettes and oil. Add salt and freshly ground black pepper to taste. Finally, gently mix in the Quark and serve at once.

PASTA DISHES

Here are three simple, low-calorie variations on tomato sauce to combine with your choice of pasta.

SIMPLE TOMATO SAUCE

SERVES 4
Portions per serving: **none**

397 g (14 oz) can tomatoes, with their juice
1 small onion, skinned and roughly chopped
1 garlic clove, skinned and chopped
1 celery stick, sliced
1 bay leaf
parsley sprig
2.5 ml (½ tsp) raw cane sugar
salt and pepper

1 Put all the ingredients in a saucepan, bring to the boil then simmer, uncovered, for 30 minutes until thickened. Stir occasionally to prevent sticking to the bottom of the pan.
2 Remove the bay leaf and purée the mixture in a blender or food processor until smooth, or push through a sieve using a wooden spoon. Reheat and serve.

UNCOOKED TOMATO SAUCE

SERVES 4
Portions per serving: **3½f&o**

350 g (12 oz) tomatoes, skinned and seeded
1 garlic clove, skinned and finely chopped
75 ml (5 tbsp) olive oil
1 basil or parsley sprig, chopped
salt and pepper

1 Chop the tomatoes roughly and place in a bowl. Add the remaining ingredients and stir well to mix. Cover and leave to marinate for at least 6 hours. Stir well before serving cold.

FRESH TOMATO SAUCE

SERVES 4
Portions per serving: **½c, 1½f&o**

30 ml (2 tbsp) polyunsaturated oil
1 small onion, skinned and chopped
1 small carrot, peeled and chopped
25 ml (5 tsp) plain wholemeal flour
450 g (1 lb) tomatoes, quartered
300 ml (½ pint) chicken stock
1 bay leaf
1 clove
5 ml (1 tsp) raw cane sugar
15 ml (1 tbsp) chopped fresh parsley or basil
salt and pepper

1 Heat the oil in a saucepan, add the onion and carrot and fry lightly for 5 minutes until soft.
2 Stir in the flour and cook gently for 1 minute, stirring. Remove the pan from the heat and gradually stir in the tomatoes, stock, bay leaf, clove, sugar, parsley and salt and pepper to taste. Bring to the boil slowly and continue to cook, stirring, until the sauce thickens. Cover and simmer for 30–45 minutes, until the vegetables are cooked.
3 Sieve or purée in a blender or food processor. Reheat and serve.

THE RECIPES

FISH DISHES

Most of us don't eat enough fish, but it is an important part of a healthy diet. You can eat your fish alone, simply steamed with lemon juice and black pepper and lots of vegetables from your free food list, or you can try one of the mouth-watering recipes below. Fish is an excellent fast food, taking only minutes to cook – important for dieters who come home hungry and want to eat quickly.

AT-A-GLANCE PORTION GUIDE (per serving)

Recipe	p	c	d	f&o	f
Monkfish and Mussel Brochettes	3½			1	
Smoked Trout Mousse in Lemon Shells	2	1½			
Baked Smoked Salmon Mousses	2		½		
Haddock-stuffed Courgettes	2				
Lemon Sole in Lettuce	3				
Spicy Scallops	1½			1½	
Mediterranean Fish Stew	3			1½	
Seafood Spaghetti	2½	4			
Kedgeree	1	2		1½	
Tuna and Haricot Bake	2½	½			
West Country Cod	1				½
Haddock Quiche	1½	2		4	

MONKFISH AND MUSSEL BROCHETTES

———— SERVES 6 ————
Portions per serving: **3½p, 1f&o**

900 g (2 lb) monkfish, skinned and boned
36 cooked mussels
12 lean bacon rashers, rinded and halved
25 g (1 oz) polyunsaturated margarine, melted
60 ml (4 tbsp) chopped fresh parsley
finely grated rind and juice of 1 lime or lemon
3 garlic cloves, skinned and crushed
pepper
shredded lettuce, bay leaves, and lime or lemon wedges, to serve

1 Cut the fish into cubes. Using a sharp knife, shell the mussels. Reserve the mussels and discard the shells.
2 Roll the bacon rashers up neatly. Thread the cubed fish, mussels and bacon alternately on to six oiled kebab skewers.
3 Mix together the margarine, parsley, lime rind and juice, garlic and pepper to taste.
4 Place the brochettes on an oiled grill or barbecue rack. Brush with the margarine mixture, then barbecue or grill for 15 minutes. Turn the brochettes frequently during cooking and brush with the margarine mixture with each turn.
5 Arrange the hot brochettes on a serving platter lined with shredded lettuce. Garnish with bay leaves and lime wedges.

SMOKED TROUT MOUSSE IN LEMON SHELLS

Smoked mackerel may be used but it does not have such a delicate flavour.

———— SERVES 4 ————
Portions per serving: **2p, 1½c**

175 g (6 oz) smoked trout, skinned
175 g (6 oz) natural Quark
10–15 ml (2–3 tsp) horseradish
pepper
4 large lemons
10 ml (2 tsp) powdered gelatine
2 egg whites
30 ml (2 tbsp) finely chopped fresh parsley, to garnish
50 g (2 oz) hot wholemeal toast, to serve

1 Flake the trout and discard all the bones. Put the flesh in a bowl with the Quark, horseradish and pepper to taste. Mix well, then set aside.
2 Cut the lemons in half lengthways. Scoop out all the flesh, pips and pith into a sieve and press to extract the juice. Reserve the lemon shells.
3 Sprinkle the gelatine over 60 ml (4 tbsp) lemon juice in a small bowl. Soak for 1 minute, then place over a saucepan of simmering water and stir until the gelatine has dissolved.
4 Stir the gelatine liquid into the trout mixture. Whisk the egg whites until stiff, then fold into the mousse until evenly incorporated. Chill for about 45 minutes or until the mousse just holds its shape, then spoon into the reserved lemon shells. Chill for a further 2 hours, until firm. Sprinkle with chopped fresh parsley and serve with the hot toast, cut into triangles.

BAKED SMOKED SALMON MOUSSES

SERVES 4
Portions per serving: **2p**, ½d

75 g (3 oz) smoked salmon, thinly sliced
1 egg, size 2
225 g (8 oz) cooked cod or haddock fillet, skinned and flaked
10 ml (2 tsp) cornflour
75 ml (5 tbsp) whipping cream
75 ml (5 tbsp) Greek strained yogurt
30 ml (2 tbsp) chopped fresh parsley
15 ml (1 tbsp) brandy
salt and pepper
parsley sprigs and lemon twists, to garnish

1 Lightly grease 4 ramekin dishes. Line each with a circle of greaseproof paper and a small piece of smoked salmon.
2 Roughly chop the remaining smoked salmon and place in a bowl. Add the egg, fish, cornflour, whipping cream, yogurt, parsley, brandy and salt and pepper to taste. Mix together well.
3 Divide the mixture between the ramekins and cover each tightly with foil. Bake at 180°C (350°F) mark 4 for about 40 minutes, until firm when lightly touched.
4 Remove foil and run a sharp knife around the edge of each ramekin. Turn out and peel off the greaseproof paper. Serve hot or cold, garnished with parsley sprigs and lemon twists.

HADDOCK-STUFFED COURGETTES

SERVES 4
Portions per serving: **2p**

4 large courgettes, about 100 g (4 oz) each
450 g (1 lb) haddock fillets, skinned
5 ml (1 tsp) ground cumin
5 ml (1 tsp) ground coriander
1.25 ml (¼ tsp) turmeric
45 ml (3 tbsp) low-fat natural yogurt
1 egg, size 2, separated
fresh coriander sprigs, to garnish

1 Trim the ends from the courgettes, then cut them in half and scoop out and discard the seeds. Place the courgette shells in a saucepan of boiling water and cook for about 5 minutes, until just tender. Drain well and set aside.
2 Place the haddock in a saucepan of just enough simmering water to cover. Poach for 8–10 minutes, until cooked through and the fish flakes easily. Drain well, then flake, discarding any bones.
3 Put the fish, cumin, coriander, turmeric, yogurt and egg yolk in a bowl and mix well.
4 Whisk the egg white and using a metal spoon, carefully fold into the fish mixture. Spoon into the prepared courgette shells and place in an ovenproof dish in a single layer.
5 Cook at 200°C (400°F) mark 6 for 25–30 minutes, until the stuffing is pale golden brown and the courgettes are tender. Garnish with coriander sprigs and serve hot.

LEMON SOLE IN LETTUCE

———— SERVES 4 ————
Portions per serving: **3p**

16 large lettuce leaves, thick stalks removed
8 lemon sole fillets, about 100 g (4 oz) each, skinned
15 ml (1 tbsp) lemon juice
salt and pepper
100 g (4 oz) peeled cooked prawns
15 ml (1 tbsp) chopped fresh dill
150 ml (¼ pint) fish stock or dry white wine
lemon slices, to garnish

1 Drop the lettuce leaves into a large saucepan of boiling water and simmer for 2 minutes. Drain and rinse in cold water until the leaves are chilled. Dry on absorbent kitchen paper, then spread out on a flat surface.
2 Sprinkle the fillets with a little of the lemon juice and salt and pepper to taste. Arrange a few prawns in the centre of each fillet and sprinkle over half the dill. Fold the fish into thirds to enclose the prawns.
3 Place each folded fillet on a lettuce leaf and roll up again, folding the edges to form a neat parcel.
4 Place the fish parcels in a non-stick frying pan and sprinkle over the remaining lemon juice, stock or wine and pepper to taste. Cover and cook gently for 15 minutes, until tender.
5 Remove the fish to a warmed serving dish. Boil the cooking juices until reduced to about 90 ml (6 tbsp). Stir in the remaining dill and pour over the fish. Serve with lemon slices.

SPICY SCALLOPS

Serve these delicious scallops on a bed of steamed, shredded Chinese leaves.

———— SERVES 4 ————
Portions per serving: **1½p, 1½f&o**

350 g (12 oz) queen scallops, fresh or frozen, thawed
10 ml (2 tsp) Chinese sweet chilli sauce
100 g (4 oz) carrots, scrubbed
3 celery sticks
15 ml (1 tbsp) dry sherry
15 ml (1 tbsp) soy sauce
5 ml (1 tsp) tomato purée
30 ml (2 tbsp) corn oil
5 ml (1tsp) grated fresh root ginger
15 ml (1 tbsp) chopped spring onion

1 Mix the scallops with the chilli sauce and set aside. Cut the carrots and celery into thin matchsticks. Mix the sherry, soy sauce and tomato purée with 30 ml (2 tbsp) water.
2 Heat half the oil in a large frying pan or wok. Add the carrot and celery and stir-fry over a high heat for 1 minute. Remove vegetables from pan with a slotted spoon and set aside.
3 Heat the remaining oil in the pan, then add the ginger and spring onion and stir-fry briefly over high heat. Add the scallops and turn them in the oil to seal them on all sides.
4 Lower the heat to medium, add the soy sauce mixture to the pan and stir well. Return the vegetables to the pan and stir well. Stir-fry for 3–4 minutes, until the scallops feel firm. Serve the dish hot.

MEDITERRANEAN FISH STEW

Serve sprinkled with parsley.

──────── SERVES 4 ────────
Portions per serving: **3p, 1½f&o**

12 fresh mussels
1 onion, skinned and thinly sliced
30 ml (2 tbsp) olive oil
1 garlic clove, skinned and crushed
450 g (1 lb) tomatoes, skinned, seeded and chopped
300 ml (½ pint) dry white wine
450 ml (¾ pint) fish stock
15 ml (1 tbsp) chopped fresh dill or 5 ml (1 tsp) dill weed
10 ml (2 tsp) chopped fresh rosemary or 5 ml (1 tsp) dried
15 ml (1 tbsp) tomato purée
salt and pepper
450 g (1 lb) monkfish fillet, skinned and cut into large chunks
4 jumbo prawns, peeled
225 g (8 oz) squid, cleaned and cut into rings

1 To clean the mussels, put in a large bowl and scrape well under cold running water. Discard any that are open. Rinse until there is no trace of sand in the bowl.
2 In a large saucepan or flameproof casserole, gently cook the onion in the olive oil for 3–4 minutes. Add the garlic and tomatoes and cook for a further 3–4 minutes.
3 Add the white wine, stock, herbs, tomato purée and salt and pepper to taste and bring to the boil. Lower the heat and simmer for a further 5 minutes.
4 Add the monkfish and simmer for 5 minutes. Add the prawns and squid and simmer for a further 5 minutes. Add the prepared mussels, cover the pan and cook for 3–4 minutes, until the shells open. Discard any of the mussels that do not open. Ladle the stew into individual bowls and serve at once.

SEAFOOD SPAGHETTI

──────── SERVES 4 ────────
Portions per serving: **2½p, 4c**

350 g (12 oz) wholewheat spaghetti
1 small onion, skinned and chopped
300 ml (½ pint) dry white wine
2 egg yolks
100 g (4 oz) natural Quark
175 g (6 oz) cooked white fish, boned and flaked
100 g (4 oz) cooked fresh or canned shelled mussels
100 g (4 oz) cooked fresh or canned shelled cockles
salt and pepper

1 Cook the spaghetti in a large saucepan of fast-boiling, lightly salted water for about 10 minutes or until tender.
2 Meanwhile, put the onion and white wine in a saucepan and simmer very gently for 3–4 minutes, without allowing the wine to evaporate too much. Remove from the heat and whisk in the egg yolks, one at a time, followed by the natural Quark. Add the white fish, mussels and cockles. Heat through gently and add salt and pepper to taste.
3 Drain the pasta and put in a serving dish. Spoon the sauce over the pasta and serve immediately.

KEDGEREE

Before refrigeration and fast transport, fish was heavily smoked to preserve it. Today, fish is usually only lightly smoked to create flavour rather than to improve its keeping qualities.

―――――――― SERVES 4 ――――――――
Portions per serving: **1p, 2c, 1½f&o**

25 (1 oz) polyunsaturated margarine
1 small onion, skinned and finely chopped
7.5 ml (1½ tsp) medium curry powder
175 g (6 oz) brown rice
600 ml (1 pint) fish stock or water
100 g (4 oz) smoked fish
100 g (4 oz) firm-fleshed white fish
1 egg, hard-boiled and chopped
30 ml (2 tbsp) chopped fresh parsley
pepper
finely grated rind of ½ lemon

1 Melt 15 g (½ oz) of the margarine in a large non-stick saucepan and cook the onion for 3 minutes. Add the curry powder and cook for 1 minute.
2 Add the rice with the stock. Cover and simmer gently for about 30 minutes or until the rice is just tender and the liquid absorbed.
3 Meanwhile, place the fish in a large frying pan with just enough water to cover. Simmer for 10–15 minutes or until tender. Drain, flake and discard all the bones.
4 When the rice is cooked, add the fish, egg, remaining margarine and 15 ml (1 tbsp) of the parsley. Add pepper to taste. Stir gently until heated through.
5 Spoon into a warmed serving dish and sprinkle with the remaining chopped parsley and the grated lemon rind. Serve immediately.

TUNA AND HARICOT BAKE

The cooking times for dried beans depends on how long they have been in stock for. The older the beans, the longer the cooking time.

―――――――― SERVES 4 ――――――――
Portions per serving: **2½p, ½c**

175 g (6 oz) dried haricot beans, soaked overnight
200 g (7 oz) can tuna in brine, drained and flaked
60 ml (4 tbsp) chopped fresh parsley
30 ml (2 tbsp) chopped fresh chives
pepper
15 g (½ oz) dried wholemeal breadcrumbs
15 g (½ oz) Parmesan cheese, freshly grated
2 tomatoes, sliced, to garnish

1 Drain the beans and rinse. Put into a saucepan and cover with plenty of fresh water. Bring to the boil and boil for 10 minutes, then simmer for about 50 minutes or until tender.
2 Drain the beans, reserving the cooking liquid. Purée half the beans with just enough of the cooking liquid to make a smooth, thick mixture. Spread over the base of a lightly greased 600 ml (1 pint) shallow, ovenproof dish.
3 Mix the remaining beans with the tuna, parsley and chives. Add pepper to taste.
4 Mix the breadcrumbs with the Parmesan and sprinkle over the top. Garnish with the sliced tomatoes. Bake at 200°C (400°F) mark 6 for 20–30 minutes until crisp on the top.

WEST COUNTRY COD

———— SERVES 4 ————
Portions per serving: **1p, ½f**

4 cod fillets, each about 175 g (6 oz), skinned
1 onion, skinned and thinly sliced
pepper
thinly pared rind of 1 orange, cut into 7.5 cm (3 inch) strips
juice of 1 orange
150 ml (¼ pint) medium-dry cider
100 ml (4 fl oz) fish stock
10 ml (2 tsp) chopped fresh coriander
coriander sprigs, to garnish

1 Wipe the fish with absorbent kitchen paper and put in a shallow 1.1 litre (2 pint) ovenproof dish. Cover the fish with the onion, add pepper to taste and orange rind.
2 Mix the orange juice with the cider and fish stock to make 300 ml (½ pint) liquid. Pour over the fish, cover and cook at 190°C (375°F) mark 5 for 20–25 minutes or until the fish is cooked through and flakes easily when tested with a fork. Place the fish, onion and orange strips on a serving dish and keep warm.
3 Strain the cooking liquid into a small saucepan and boil rapidly for 5 minutes or until the liquid is reduced by half. Pour over the fish and sprinkle with the coriander. Garnish and serve hot.

HADDOCK QUICHE

———— MAKES 6 SLICES ————
Portions per serving: **1½p, 2c, 4f&o**

75 g (3 oz) plain flour
75 g (3 oz) plain wholemeal flour
pinch of salt
100 g (4 oz) polyunsaturated margarine
225 g (8 oz) fresh haddock fillets
100 g (4 oz) smoked haddock fillets
1 onion, skinned and chopped
150 ml (¼ pint) semi-skimmed milk
1 egg
15 ml (1 tbsp) chopped fresh parsley
25 g (1 oz) mature Cheddar, grated

1 Put flours and salt into a bowl, then rub in 75 g (3 oz) of the margarine until mixture resembles fine breadcrumbs. Add 25 ml (1 fl oz) chilled water and mix to make a soft dough. Add a little extra water if necessary.
2 Knead the dough on a lightly floured surface. Roll out and line a 20.5 cm (8 inch), loose based flan tin. Chill for 30 minutes.
3 Meanwhile, place the fish in a saucepan with just enough water to cover. Bring to the boil and simmer gently for 10 minutes. Drain, discard the skin and any bones and flake the fish into small pieces.
4 Melt the remaining 25 g (1 oz) margarine in a saucepan, add the onion and cook gently for 3–5 minutes, until soft. Add the fish and heat through.
5 Spoon the filling into the flan case. Whisk together the milk, egg and parsley and pour over the fish. Sprinkle the cheese on top. Cook at 190°C (375°F) mark 5 for about 40 minutes, until the filling is set.

CHICKEN DISHES

Chicken is a low-fat meat that is firmly on the dieter's side. It is both healthier and lower in calories than red meat as it is lower in saturated fat that is said to contribute to heart disease. Chicken on its own can be bland, especially when it is baked or grilled, so we've chosen a variety of recipes combining chicken with other delicious ingredients; marinated and skewered on kebabs, spiced with coriander, or in fragrant herbed sauces. Removing the skin is advisable as it is quite fatty.

AT-A-GLANCE PORTION GUIDE (per serving)					
Recipe	p	c	d	f&o	f
Spiced Chicken	3		½		
Chicken in Yogurt	3		½		
Baked Gingered Chicken	2				
Mango Chicken Parcels	2–3				1
Chicken and Chicory Sandwiches	2	3		1	
Curried Chicken Toasts	2½	1		½	
Chicken Kebabs	4			1	
Bean and Chicken Tabouleh	1½	1½		3	
Farmhouse Chicken Breasts	3			1	
Chicken and Spinach Loaf with Carrot Orange Sauce	2				
Chicken with Mustard Sauce	2				
Tandoori Chicken	4				
Chinese Chicken with Rice	2	1		1½	

SPICED CHICKEN

Light, aromatic cumin and cinnamon are used to spice the chicken. Accompany the dish with brown rice and green beans.

SERVES 4
Portions per serving: **3p, ½d**

4 chicken breasts on the bone, skinned
5 ml (1 tsp) ground cinnamon
300 ml (½ pint) low-fat natural yogurt
10 ml (2 tsp) sunflower oil
2 large onions, skinned and finely chopped
1 garlic clove, skinned and crushed
1 fresh green chilli, seeded and chopped
15 ml (1 tbsp) paprika
5 ml (1 tsp) cumin seeds
1 small red pepper, cored, seeded and finely chopped
45 ml (3 tbsp) tomato juice
pinch of finely grated lemon rind
pepper to taste
15 ml (1 tbsp) cornflower

1 Rub the chicken breasts with the cinnamon. Put into a dish, pour over the yogurt, reserving 30 ml (2 tbsp), and marinate for at least 30 minutes.

2 Heat 5 ml (1 tsp) of the oil in a non-stick frying pan and gently cook the onions for 5–8 minutes until lightly browned. Remove and transfer to a casserole. Add the garlic and chilli to the pan and gently cook for 2 minutes. Stir in the paprika and cumin seeds and cook for a further 2 minutes. Transfer to the casserole.

3 Remove the chicken from the marinade, reserving the marinade. Heat the remaining oil in the pan and brown the chicken on all sides.

4 Place the chicken, marinade, red pepper, tomato juice, lemon rind and pepper in the casserole. Cover and cook at 180°C (350°F) mark 4 for about 1 hour.

5 Mix the cornflour and reserved yogurt together. Blend in some of the hot liquid from the casserole, then mix with the rest of the casserole juices. Cook until the juices have thickened.

CHICKEN IN YOGURT

Marinating the chicken breasts beforehand flavours and helps keep them moist without adding any fat during the cooking. The spicy coating is equally delicious with turkey breasts.

SERVES 4
Portions per serving: **3p, ½d**

300 ml (½ pint) low-fat natural yogurt
15 ml (1 tbsp) freshly ground coriander
15 ml (1 tbsp) freshly ground cumin
1 cm (½ inch) piece of fresh root ginger, peeled and finely chopped, or 10 ml (2 tsp) ground
5 ml (1 tsp) chilli powder
1 garlic clove, skinned and crushed
4 chicken breasts on the bone, each weighing about 275 g (10 oz), skinned
fresh coriander sprigs, to garnish

1 Mix together the yogurt, coriander, cumin, ginger, chilli and garlic in a bowl.

2 Prick the chicken pieces all over with a fork and spread with half of the yogurt mixture. Cover and marinate for at least 3–4 hours in the refrigerator, turning occasionally.

3 Transfer the chicken to a roasting pan. Bake at 200°C (400°F) mark 6 for 45 minutes. Remove from the pan and keep warm.
4 Put the roasting pan over a gentle heat, stir in the reserved yogurt mixture and heat through, but do not boil, scraping up any sediment and juices from the base of the pan.
5 Pour the sauce over the chicken and serve hot, garnished with coriander sprigs.

BAKED GINGERED CHICKEN

SERVES 4
Portions per serving: **2p**

4 small chicken portions, skinned
10 ml (2 tsp) soy sauce
30 ml (2 tbsp) dry sherry
60 ml (4 tbsp) unsweetened apple juice
2 lemon slices, finely chopped
1 garlic clove, skinned and crushed
10 ml (2 tsp) grated fresh root ginger

1 Arrange the chicken in a baking dish just large enough to take the pieces in one layer, fleshy side down.
2 Mix the rest of the ingredients together and pour over the chicken. Cover and leave to marinate for several hours.
3 Bake at 200°C (400°F) mark 6 for 30–40 minutes or until the juices run clear when a skewer is inserted into the thickest part of the leg. Turn the chicken half way through cooking and baste frequently.

MANGO CHICKEN PARCELS

Cooking the chicken in foil parcels seals in the flavour. Use ripe mangoes, recognized by their sweet aroma.

SERVES 4
Portions per serving: **2–3p, 1f**

4 boneless chicken breasts, each about 100–175 g (4–6 oz), skinned
2 fresh mangoes
2.5 cm (1 inch) fresh root ginger, peeled and finely chopped
pepper
lime slices and wedges and fresh coriander sprigs, to garnish

1 Slash the chicken breasts vertically, but do not cut all the way through. Place on individual pieces of foil large enough to make a secure parcel around the chicken.
2 Peel and remove all the flesh from the mangoes and discard the stones. Place the flesh in a bowl with the ginger and mash with a fork.
3 Spread evenly over the chicken and add pepper to taste. Seal the foil around the chicken and place on a baking sheet. Cook at 190°C (375°F) mark 5 for 25–30 minutes, until the chicken is cooked through. Open the parcels and garnish with the lime and coriander sprigs. Serve immediately, leaving the chicken in the foil.

CHICKEN AND CHICORY SANDWICHES

Low-fat cottage-cheese and yogurt and lean chicken lower the fat content of these tasty layered sandwiches. Wholemeal bread increases the fibre.

―――――― MAKES 4 ――――――
Portions per serving: **2p, 3c, 1f&o**

12 slices wholemeal bread
40 g (1½ oz) low-fat spread
60 ml (4 tbsp) low-fat natural yogurt
30 ml (2 tbsp) chopped fresh parsley
pepper
225 g (8 oz) cooked chicken, shredded
1 head chicory, finely shredded
175 g (6 oz) low-fat cottage cheese
1 small red pepper, cored, seeded and diced
15 ml (1 tbsp) snipped fresh chives
lettuce leaves

1 Spread each slice of bread on one side only with low-fat spread. Mix together the yogurt and parsley in a bowl. Add pepper to taste, then mix in the chicken and chicory. Mix the cottage cheese with the red pepper and chives.
2 Spread 4 of the slices of bread with the chicken and chicory mixture. Line 4 slices with a lettuce leaf, then spread with the cottage cheese mixture.
3 Stack in pairs, sitting a cottage cheese topped slice on top of a chicken one. Place the remaining slices of bread on top, low-fat spread side down. Cut in quarters and serve.

CURRIED CHICKEN TOASTS

―――――― MAKES 4 ――――――
Portions per serving: **2½p, 1c, ½f&o**

60 ml (4 tbsp) low-fat natural yogurt
10 ml (2 tsp) curry paste
350 g (12 oz) cold cooked chicken meat, shredded
pepper
4 slices granary bread
15 g (½ oz) low-fat spread
4 large lettuce leaves
25 g (1 oz) flaked almonds, toasted
pinch of paprika
few cucumber slices

1 Mix together the yogurt, curry paste and chicken in a bowl. Add pepper to taste.
2 Toast the bread, then spread with the low-fat spread. Top each slice with a lettuce leaf.
3 Spoon some of the chicken mixture over each slice of toast. Sprinkle with flaked almonds and paprika. Arrange a few cucumber slices on top.

CHICKEN KEBABS

Herbs and grated orange rind flavour these nutritional kebabs. Serve with boiled brown rice and a salad.

MAKES 4

Portions per serving: **4p, 1f&o**
MARINATING At least 4 hours

100 ml (4 fl oz) dry white wine
60 ml (4 tbsp) lemon juice
30 ml (2 tbsp) olive oil
1 garlic clove, skinned and crushed
15 ml (1 tbsp) chopped fresh tarragon or 10 ml (2 tsp) dried
grated rind of 1 orange
pepper
450 g (1 lb) boned chicken breasts, skinned and cubed
225 g (8 oz) chicken livers, thawed if frozen, halved
2 oranges, peeled and segmented, and watercress sprigs, to garnish

1 Mix together the wine, lemon juice, olive oil, garlic, tarragon, orange rind and pepper to taste.
2 Pour the marinade over the chicken and livers, reserving about 75 ml (5 tbsp) for basting, and set aside for at least 4 hours, turning the pieces several times.
3 Thread the chicken pieces and the livers evenly on to 4 long skewers and place under the grill.
4 Grill the kebabs for about 15 minutes, basting occasionally with the reserved marinade, and turning once during cooking. Serve hot, garnished with the orange segments and the sprigs of watercress.

BEAN AND CHICKEN TABOULEH

Tabouleh is a traditional Middle Eastern dish. It is made with bulgar wheat which is available at health food shops.

SERVES 4

Portions per serving: **1½p, 1½c, 3f&o**

150 g (5 oz) bulgar wheat
400 g (14 oz) can red kidney beans, drained and rinsed
4 spring onions, trimmed and finely chopped
1 garlic clove, skinned and crushed
60 ml (4 tbsp) chopped fresh mint
30 ml (2 tbsp) chopped fresh parsley
60 ml (4 tbsp) olive oil
juice of 1 lemon
salt and pepper
175 g (6 oz) cooked chicken meat, skinned and chopped
lettuce leaves and mint and parsley sprigs, to serve

1 Soak the bulgar wheat in cold water for 35–40 minutes or until soft. Drain off the excess liquid, pressing the bulgar to squeeze out the moisture. This can be done by putting the drained bulgar into a clean tea towel and lightly squeezing the towel.
2 Mix together the prepared bulgar wheat, the kidney beans, spring onions, garlic, mint and parsley.
3 Mix the oil with the lemon juice and salt and pepper to taste, then stir into the bulgar wheat and beans. Mix in the cooked chicken and leave for at least 30 minutes to let the flavours develop. Serve the tabouleh on a bed of lettuce leaves garnished with herb sprigs.

FARMHOUSE CHICKEN BREASTS

SERVES 4
Portions per serving: **3p, 1f&o**

15 ml (1 tbsp) polyunsaturated margarine
½ small carrot, scrubbed and finely chopped
½ small onion, skinned and finely chopped
½ celery stick, trimmed and finely chopped
½ leek, finely chopped
1 garlic clove, skinned
4 boneless chicken breasts, each about 200 g (7 oz), skinned
200 ml (7 fl oz) chicken stock
50 ml (4 tbsp) low-fat natural yogurt
salt and pepper
cooked carrot slices and celery sticks, to garnish

1 Melt the margarine in a heavy-based casserole. Add the carrot, onion, celery, leek and whole garlic clove. Cook for 5 minutes or until softened but not browned.
2 Place the chicken breasts on top of the vegetables and add the stock. Cover and simmer for 15 minutes or until the breasts are cooked through. Transfer the chicken breasts to a warm plate with a slotted spoon and keep warm.
3 Discard the garlic clove, then pour the mixture into a blender or food processor and purée until smooth. Return to the pan and reheat. Just before serving, mix in the yogurt and salt and pepper to taste. Serve the chicken breasts with a little sauce spooned over them and garnished with cooked carrot slices and celery.

CHICKEN AND SPINACH LOAF WITH CARROT ORANGE SAUCE

Serve this colourful layered chicken loaf with the carrot sauce either hot or cold. Fresh tarragon lifts the flavour of the dish.

SERVES 4
Portions per serving: **2p**

350 g (12 oz) spinach, stalks removed and washed
2 boned chicken breasts, skinned
30 ml (2 tbsp) chopped fresh tarragon
black pepper
45 ml (3 tbsp) chicken stock

FOR THE CARROT SAUCE
5 ml (1 tsp) sunflower oil
1 small onion, skinned and chopped
225 (8 oz) carrots, peeled and roughly chopped
juice of 1 orange
pinch of freshly grated nutmeg
pepper

1 Blanch the spinach leaves in boiling water for 10 seconds. Drain thoroughly and dry. Slice the chicken breasts horizontally.
2 Grease a non-stick 450 g (1 lb) loaf tin with polyunsaturated margarine. Line the base and sides of the tin with spinach. Reserve four leaves and roughly chop the remaining spinach.
3 Layer the chicken breasts, tarragon, black pepper to taste and chopped spinach, ending with a layer of the reserved spinach leaves. Pour over the chicken stock and cover with damp greaseproof paper. Place the loaf tin in a roasting tin half-filled with hot water. Bake at 180°C (350°F) mark 4 for 1 hour.

4 Drain off any excess liquid into a measuring jug, put weights on top of the loaf and allow to cool.
5 Pour off any liquid into the jug before turning out. Invert a serving dish over the loaf tin and then turn both the dish and the tin over together. Give both a sharp shake and remove the tin.
6 Heat the oil in a non-stick pan. Add the onion and cook for 5 minutes or until soft. Meanwhile, make the liquid from the loaf up to 300 ml (½ pint) with the orange juice. Add the carrots, chicken juices, nutmeg and pepper to taste to the pan. Bring to the boil, cover and then simmer for 30 minutes or until tender.
7 Allow to cool slightly, then purée in a blender or food processor. If the sauce seems too thick add water. Sieve the sauce. The sauce can either be chilled and served cold or reheated and served hot.

CHICKEN WITH MUSTARD SAUCE

Whole grain mustard is a hot, pungent mustard made from whole mustard seeds, allspice, black pepper and white wine. The liquid, in this case the white wine, brings out the flavour of the mustard.

——————— SERVES 4 ———————
Portions per serving: **2p**

4 chicken portions, each weighing about 175 g (6 oz), skinned
20 ml (4 tsp) whole grain mustard
juice of 1 small lemon
150 ml (¼ pint) low-fat natural yogurt
fresh coriander leaves, to garnish

1 Put the chicken in a roasting tin and spread the mustard equally on each portion. Sprinkle over the lemon juice.
2 Roast at 200°C (400°F) mark 6 for about 40 minutes, turning once, until cooked through and tender.
3 Remove the chicken with a slotted spoon and arrange on warmed serving plates. Keep warm. Add the yogurt to the roasting tin and stir to mix with any juices and excess mustard from the base of the tin. Heat the sauce without boiling, stirring, then pour over the chicken. Garnish with fresh coriander.

TANDOORI CHICKEN

Skinning the chicken dramatically reduces the fat content of this popular Indian-style dish.

———————— SERVES 4 ————————
Portions per serving: **4p**

4 chicken quarters, skinned
30 ml (2 tbsp) lemon juice
1 garlic clove, skinned
2.5 cm (1 inch) piece of fresh root ginger, peeled and chopped
1 green chilli, seeded
60 ml (4 tbsp) low-fat natural yogurt
5 ml (1 tsp) ground cumin
5 ml (1 tsp) garam masala
15 ml (1 tbsp) paprika
5 ml (1 tsp) salt
lemon wedges and onion rings, to serve

1 Using a sharp knife or skewer, prick the flesh of the chicken pieces all over. Put in an ovenproof dish and rub the lemon juice into the chicken flesh. Cover and leave for 30 minutes.
2 Meanwhile, put the garlic, ginger, chilli and 15 ml (1 tbsp) water in a blender or food processor and blend to a smooth paste.
3 Add the yogurt, cumin, garam masala, paprika and salt and mix together. Pour over the chicken so that it is completely covered. Cover and leave to marinate at room temperature for 5 hours. Turn once or twice during this time.
4 Barbecue or grill the chicken for 20–25 minutes or until tender, basting with the marinade and turning occasionally. Serve with the lemon wedges and onion rings.

CHINESE CHICKEN WITH RICE

———————— SERVES 4 ————————
Portions per serving: **2p, 1c, 1½f&o**

75 g (3 oz) brown rice
30 ml (2 tbsp) corn or olive oil
1 garlic clove, skinned and crushed
1 onion, skinned and thinly sliced
1 large red or green pepper, cored, seeded and cut into thin strips
75 g (3 oz) button mushrooms, sliced
450 g (1 lb) cooked chicken meat, skinned and cut into strips
3–4 canned water chestnuts or bamboo shoots, sliced
225 g (8 oz) fresh beansprouts (optional)
10 ml (2 tsp) cornflour
15 ml (1 tbsp) soy sauce
150 ml (¼ pint) chicken stock
15 ml (1 tbsp) dry sherry
lime slices and fresh coriander, to garnish

1 Put the brown rice in 450 ml (¾ pint) boiling water. Cover and simmer for about 30 minutes, until tender and liquid has been absorbed.
2 Heat the oil in a large frying pan or wok. Add the garlic, onion, red or green pepper and mushrooms. Cook for 3 minutes, stirring.
3 Add the rice and cook for 2 minutes. Stir in the chicken, water chestnuts or bamboo shoots and beansprouts if using. Cook for 2–3 minutes stirring frequently.
4 Dissolve the cornflour in the soy sauce and mix with the chicken stock and sherry. Add to the pan and bring to the boil, stirring. Cook for 2–3 minutes, stirring, until the liquid has thickened. Garnish and serve.

MEAT DISHES

Many diets rely heavily on lean meat, which is tough on those who don't like to eat a great deal of it, or on those who don't always want to have to cook what they eat. A diet that consists of a little meat alongside plenty of other ingredients such as vegetables is becoming increasingly popular. All the recipes below are interesting combinations of meat together with complimentary foods. Meat is relatively high in calories, so combining it with less fattening foods can help make it more slimming.

Recipe	p	c	d	f&o	f
AT-A-GLANCE PORTION GUIDE (per serving)					
Stir-fried Liver	2			1	
Rabbit with Prunes	2	½		1½	1
Mustard Rabbit	2		½	1½	
Greek-style Kebabs	1½	1		1½	
Baked Beef and Vegetable Crumble	2	1½		1½	
Beef Olives with Mushroom Stuffing	6			1	
Savoy Pork Chops	3			1½	1½
Lamb Chops with Rosemary	2				1
Stuffed Vine Leaves	2	½		1	
Minted Lamb Meatballs	4				
Pork with Apricots	5			1	1

STIR-FRIED LIVER

This flavourful dish will not only appeal to people who enjoy eating liver, but may also tempt those who do not usually care for it.

─────── SERVES 4 ───────
Portions per serving: **2p, 1f&o**

15 ml (1 tbsp) corn oil
8 button onions, skinned
15 ml (1 tbsp) plain wholemeal flour
pepper
225 g (8 oz) lamb's liver, cut into thin strips
1 red pepper, cored, seeded and cut into thin strips
1 green pepper, cored, seeded and cut into thin strips
100 g (4 oz) button mushrooms
2 fresh rosemary sprigs
25 ml (1½ tbsp) soy sauce
150 ml (¼ pint) vegetable stock
100 g (4 oz) beansprouts

1 Heat the oil in a large frying pan or wok and cook the onions for 5–7 minutes or until browned. Remove from the pan and keep hot.
2 Season the flour with pepper and coat the liver strips. Quickly cook in the oil left in the pan for about 3 minutes, until browned. Return the onions to the pan with the red and green peppers and mushrooms. Add the rosemary sprigs, the soy sauce and the pepper to taste.
3 Pour the stock over and cook quickly for 5 minutes, stirring occasionally. Add the beansprouts and continue to cook for a further 2–3 minutes or until the beansprouts are heated through. Discard the rosemary and check the seasoning. Place on a warmed serving dish and serve hot.

RABBIT WITH PRUNES

A good source of fibre, prunes make an interesting addition to a casserole. The type of plum grown for drying is usually late-ripening and black skinned.

─────── SERVES 4 ───────
Portions per serving: **2p, ½c, 1½f&o, 1f**

6–8 back fillets of rabbit, about 450–550 g (1–1¼ lb)
10 ml (2 tsp) wholegrain mustard
30 ml (2 tbsp) plain wholemeal flour
15 ml (1 tbsp) chopped mixed fresh herbs, such as basil and parsley
pepper
15 ml (1 tbsp) sunflower oil
15 g (½ oz) polyunsaturated margarine
12 shallots or pickling onions, skinned
3 medium carrots, scrubbed and sliced
450 ml (¾ pint) chicken stock
5 ml (1 tsp) tomato purée
12 no-cook dried stoned prunes
fresh herb sprig, to garnish.

1 Brush the rabbit fillets lightly with mustard. Mix together the flour and herbs and add pepper to taste. Use to coat the rabbit fillets; reserving the excess flour mixture.
2 Heat the oil and margarine in a flameproof casserole and cook the shallots or pickling onions, carrots and rabbit fillets for about 5 minutes, turning frequently, until the rabbit is sealed. Remove the rabbit and set aside.
3 Stir the reserved flour mixture into the casserole and cook for 1 minute. Gradually add the stock and tomato purée and bring to the boil, stirring.

Remove from the heat. Return the rabbit to the casserole and cover.
4 Cook at 190°C (375°F) mark 5 for 50 minutes. Gently stir in the prunes. Cover again and cook for a further 30 minutes or until the rabbit is tender and cooked through. Garnish with a fresh herb sprig.

MUSTARD RABBIT

Rabbit is a tasty and very lean meat; its flavours are complemented well by the sharpness of the mustard.

SERVES 4
Portions per serving: **2p, ½d, 1½f&o**

15 g (½ oz) polyunsaturated margarine
15 ml (1 tbsp) corn oil
2 carrots, scrubbed and sliced
2 leeks, trimmed and sliced
1 large onion, skinned and chopped
900 g (2 lb) rabbit pieces, thawed if frozen
25 ml (1½ tbsp) plain wholemeal flour
600 ml (1 pint) chicken stock
30 ml (2 tbsp) Meaux mustard
150 ml (¼ pint) Greek strained yogurt

1 Melt the margarine and oil in a flameproof casserole. Add carrots, leeks and onion and cook for 5 minutes.
2 Toss the rabbit joints in the flour, shaking off the excess and reserving. Add rabbit to pan and cook for 5 minutes, turning, until sealed. Add reserved flour, stock and mustard to pan and stir well. Bring to the boil, lower the heat, cover and simmer for about 1 hour, stirring occasionally.
3 Using a slotted spoon, transfer rabbit and vegetables on to a plate. Simmer the liquid until reduced by half, stirring occasionally. Remove from heat, stir in the yogurt and return the rabbit and vegetables to the pan. Reheat gently and serve.

GREEK-STYLE KEBABS

SERVES 4
Portions per serving: **1½p, 1c, 1½f&o**

14 stoned black olives
175 g (6 oz) lean minced leg of lamb
1 garlic clove, skinned and crushed
1 onion, skinned and finely chopped
75 g (3 oz) fresh brown breadcrumbs
25 ml (1½ tbsp) tomato purée
15 ml (1 tbsp) sesame seeds
pepper
8 shallots or small onions, skinned
1 red pepper, cored, seeded and cubed
30 ml (2 tbsp) olive oil
45 ml (3 tbsp) lemon juice
10 ml (2 tsp) chopped fresh coriander

1 Finely chop 6 of the olives and put in a mixing bowl with the lamb, garlic, onion, breadcrumbs, tomato purée and sesame seeds. Add pepper to taste and mix together well. Form into 12 small sausage-shapes, cover and chill for 30 minutes.
2 Thread 4 kebab skewers with the lamb rolls, shallots or small onions, pepper and reserved olives. Blend the olive oil, lemon juice and coriander together and brush over the kebabs.
3 Cook under a moderately hot grill for 8–10 minutes or until cooked, turning and brushing occasionally with the oil mixture.

BAKED BEEF AND VEGETABLE CRUMBLE

Leaving the skins on the jacket baked potatoes increases the fibre content of this substantial dish.

―――― SERVES 4 ――――
Portions per serving: **2p, 1½c, 1½f&o**

225 g (8 oz) cold cooked lean beef or other meat, cut into strips
175 g (6 oz) cold baked or boiled potatoes, cut into 1 cm (½ inch) cubes
3 spring onions, trimmed and finely chopped
175 g (6 oz) cold cooked courgettes or other green vegetable, thinly sliced
10 ml (2 tsp) grated fresh or bottled horseradish
pepper
300 ml (½ pint) beef stock
25 g (1 oz) polyunsaturated margarine
40 g (1½ oz) fresh wholemeal breadcrumbs
40 g (1½ oz) rolled oats
5 ml (1 tsp) paprika
10 ml (2 tsp) chopped fresh parsley

1 Put the meat, potatoes, spring onions and courgettes into a bowl. Add the horseradish, pepper to taste and 150 ml (¼ pint) of the stock. Put the mixture into a 1.1 litre (2 pint) ovenproof serving dish.
2 Rub the margarine into the breadcrumbs in a bowl, then stir in the oats, paprika and parsley. Sprinkle over the meat mixture.
3 Bake at 190°C (375°F) mark 5 for 40–45 minutes or until the top is crisp. Warm the remaining stock and serve with the crumble.

BEEF OLIVES WITH MUSHROOM STUFFING

―――― SERVES 4 ――――
Portions per serving: **6p, 1f&o**

8 thin slices topside, 75 g (3 oz) each
15 g (½ oz) polyunsaturated margarine
150 ml (¼ pint) dry red wine
salt and pepper
15 ml (1 tbsp) tomato purée
finely chopped fresh parsley, to garnish

MUSHROOM STUFFING
75 g (3 oz) button mushrooms, finely chopped
5 ml (1 tsp) Dijon mustard
1 small carrot, scrubbed and grated
1 courgette, grated
15 ml (1 tbsp) bran
10 ml (2 tsp) tomato purée

1 Beat the beef slices between sheets of damp greaseproof paper until almost double in size.
2 To make the stuffing, mix together mushrooms, mustard, carrot, courgette, bran and tomato purée. Divide mixture between the beef slices and spread evenly over. Roll up and secure at both ends with fine string.
3 Melt the margarine in a flameproof casserole and brown the prepared beef olives over a medium heat. Pour over the red wine and salt and pepper to taste. Cover and cook for 45 minutes, until tender. Transfer beef olives to a serving dish, discard the string and keep hot.
4 Skim the fat from the cooking liquid, then add the remaining tomato purée and adjust seasoning. Heat through and pour over beef olives. Garnish and serve at once.

SAVOY PORK CHOPS

Apples complement pork and here they are cooked with the chops.

———————— SERVES 4 ————————
Portions per serving: **3p, 1½f&o, 1½f**

4 lean pork chops
30 ml (2 tbsp) oil
4 medium onions, skinned and sliced
4 medium to large cooking apples, peeled, cored and sliced
pinch of ground sage
pinch of dried tarragon
30 ml (2 tbsp) sultanas
300 ml (½ pint) chicken stock or dry cider
salt and freshly ground black pepper

1 Trim the pork chops of any fat or gristle. Heat 15 ml (1 tbsp) of the oil in a non-stick frying pan and quickly seal and brown the chops on both sides. Lift them out and keep hot. Add the remainder of the oil and gently soften the onions without browning. Remove.
2 Soften the apples in the same way, lift out and keep them hot with the onions. Raise the heat a little, put the chops back into the pan and continue frying until cooked well through.
3 Pour off any excess oil and return the onion and apple to the pan, together with the herbs and sultanas. Mix well, then add the stock and simmer until the sauce thickens slightly and all the ingredients are well cooked. Season to taste.

LAMB CHOPS WITH ROSEMARY

Redcurrants and apple complement the flavour of lamb.

———————— SERVES 4 ————————
Portions per serving: **2p, 1f**

4 lean lamb chops, well trimmed
150 ml (¼ pint) unsweetened apple juice
15 ml (1 tbsp) chopped fresh rosemary or 7.5 ml (½ tbsp) dried
salt and pepper
1 garlic clove, skinned and chopped
2 large eating apples
juice of 1 lemon
60 ml (4 tbsp) redcurrants, thawed if frozen
fresh rosemary sprigs, to garnish

1 Put the lamb chops into a shallow dish with the apple juice, rosemary, salt and pepper to taste and garlic. Cover and marinate in the refrigerator for 3–4 hours.
2 Halve the apples crossways, then core and brush with the lemon juice. Stand the apple halves in an ovenproof dish and cover with foil. Bake at 190°C (375°F) mark 5 for 12–15 minutes, until just tender.
3 Meanwhile, remove the lamb chops from the marinade and grill for 5–6 minutes. Turn the chops over, brush with a little marinade and grill for a further 5–6 minutes.
4 Fold back the foil from the apples, fill each half with redcurrants and return to the oven for 3 minutes.
5 Arrange the cooked chops on a serving dish, with the apple halves placed around them, and garnish with rosemary sprigs.

STUFFED VINE LEAVES

———— SERVES 4 ————
Portions per serving: **2p, ½c, 1f&o**

225 g (8 oz) packet vine leaves, drained and rinsed
15 ml (1 tbsp) corn or olive oil
1 onion, skinned and grated
225 g (8 oz) minced lean lamb
50 g (2 oz) fresh wholemeal breadcrumbs
50 g (2 oz) canned or bottled chestunuts, drained and finely chopped
grated rind and juice of 1 orange
10 ml (2 tsp) chopped fresh mint or 5 ml (1 tsp) dried
pepper
200 ml (7 fl oz) vegetable stock
orange slices, to garnish

1 Separate the vine leaves, put into a mixing bowl and pour boiling water over. Set aside until ready to use.
2 Heat the oil in a saucepan and cook the onion for 2 minutes or until transparent, then add the lamb and cook quickly, stirring, for a further 3 minutes or until browned. Remove from the heat, drain off any fat and mix in the breadcrumbs, chestnuts, orange rind and juice, mint and pepper to taste. Mix together.
3 Drain the vine leaves and remove the stems. Put each leaf, shiny side down, on a flat board and spoon about 1 dessertspoon of the lamb mixture into the centre. Fold the leaf over to encase the filling completely, forming a neat parcel. With the smaller leaves, overlap 2 or 3 of the leaves together before adding the stuffing and folding.
4 Put the stuffed leaves close together in a shallow 1.1 litre (2 pint) ovenproof dish, pour the stock over, cover and cook at 190°C (375°F) mark 5 for 35–40 minutes or until the filling is cooked through. Serve hot, garnished with orange slices.

MINTED LAMB MEATBALLS

———— SERVES 4 ————
Portions per serving: **4p**

225 g (8 oz) crisp cabbage, trimmed and finely chopped
450 g (1 lb) lean minced lamb
100 g (4 oz) onion, skinned and finely chopped
2.5 ml (½ tsp) ground allspice
salt and freshly ground pepper
397 g (14 oz) can tomato juice
1 bay leaf
10 ml (2 tsp) chopped fresh mint or 5 ml (1 tsp) dried
15 ml (1 tbsp) chopped fresh parsley

1 Steam the cabbage for 2–3 minutes or until softened.
2 Place the lamb and cabbage in a bowl with the onion, allspice and salt and pepper to taste. Beat well to combine all the ingredients.
3 With your hands, shape the mixture into 16–20 small balls. Place the meatballs in a shallow large ovenproof dish.
4 Mix the tomato juice with the bay leaf, mint and parsley. Pour over the meatballs. Cover the dish tightly and bake in the oven at 180°C (350°F) mark 4 for about 1 hour until the meatballs are cooked.
5 Skim any fat off the tomato sauce before serving, and taste and adjust seasoning. Serve hot.

PORK WITH APRICOTS

Dried apricots are used in this spicy pork dish.

─────── SERVES 8 ───────
Portions per serving: **5p, 1f&o, 1f**

30 ml (2 tbsp) oil
1.4 kg (3 lb) shoulder of pork, trimmed, boned and cubed
4 medium onions, skinned and sliced
2 garlic cloves, skinned and chopped
5 ml (1 tsp) ground ginger
5 ml (1 tsp) ground coriander
5 ml (1 tsp) ground cumin
150 ml (¼ pint) dry white wine or chicken stock
225 g (8 oz) dried apricots, soaked for 4 hours in water to cover
salt and freshly ground black pepper or crushed green pepper
50 g (2 oz) almonds, blanched and halved
chopped fresh parsley, to garnish

1 Heat the oil in a large frying pan and, when it is really hot, seal and brown the meat cubes, a few at a time. Remove the meat from the pan as it browns and keep hot. When all the meat cubes are browned, lower the heat and soften the onions and garlic, without letting them take colour.

2 Pour away any excess fat from the pan and add the spices and wine, stirring vigorously to mix. Return the meat cubes to the pan, add three-quarters of the soaked apricots together with all of the soaking water. Cover and simmer for 45–55 minutes until the pork is tender. Season to taste.

3 Lightly brown the blanched, halved almonds in a hot dry pan, shaking them continuously. Chop and add the remaining apricots to the browned almonds. Heat through and use to garnish the dish with the parsley. Serve with boiled brown rice cooked with a pinch of saffron, if available.

THE RECIPES

VEGETARIAN DISHES

The dishes below aren't what most people tend to think of as vegetarian food. To many of us the word 'vegetarian' still conjures up images of leaden cardboard pastry, and dreary, ill-assorted mixtures of stewed vegetables doused in miso. The current trend in vegetable cooking is much less heavy-handed, however, and truly delicious, as you'll discover when you try these recipes. Vegetables are the natural ally of the slimmer – so many are Free Foods.

AT-A-GLANCE PORTION GUIDE (per serving)					
Recipe	p	c	d	f&o	f
Herbed Twice-baked Potatoes	1	2			
Spinach and Cheese Quiche with Crisp Potato Crust	2	1½		2	
Scrambled Eggs with Tomato	1½	1		1	
Souffleed Rarebits	2	1		1	
Onion Quiche	½	2		4	
Basil and Tomato Tartlets	3	3		3	
Spiced Bean Sausages	1	½			
Summer Vegetable Flan	1	1½	½	2	
Goat's Cheese Tarts	1	2		3	
Slimming Fish Pie	2½	1½		1	
Vegetarian Pancakes	1½	1		1	
Curried Tofu and Vegetables	½	1		½	
Stuffed Mushrooms	1	1½			
Piperade	1			1	

134

VEGETARIAN DISHES

Vegetarian Tofu Kebabs	1½		2
Stuffed Cabbage Rolls	1		½
Peppery Cheese Souffles	2		
Carrot, Onion and Egg Loaf	1	½	
Spinach and Egg Crumble	2	2½	4
Hot Mushroom Mousse	1	1	3
Onion Tart	2	½	1½
Carrot Quiches	1	2	2
Pizza Chilli	1	4	

HERBED TWICE-BAKED POTATOES

These potatoes may be cooked and filled ahead, and reheated when required. The herbs may be varied according to taste.

——————— SERVES 4 ———————
Portions per serving: **1p, 2c**

four 150 g (6 oz) potatoes, scrubbed
30 ml (2 tbsp) chopped fresh mixed herbs, such as chives, parsley, marjoram and basil
3 spring onions, trimmed and chopped
100 g (4 oz) natural Quark
2 tomatoes, finely chopped
salt and pepper
50 g (2 oz) low-fat Cheddar cheese, grated
extra fresh herb sprigs and tomato slices, to garnish

1 Prick the potatoes all over with a fork. Bake at 200°C (400°F) mark 6 for 50–60 minutes, until tender.

2 Cut a thin slice horizontally from the top of each potato, then carefully scoop out most of the potato into a bowl, leaving shells about 0.5 cm (¼ inch) thick.

3 Mix the potato with the herbs, onions, Quark, chopped tomatoes and salt and pepper to taste. Spoon the mixture back into the potato shells and place in a shallow ovenproof dish.

4 Sprinkle the filling with the grated cheese and return to the oven to bake for 25 minutes, until lightly golden. Garnish each potato and serve at once.

SPINACH AND CHEESE QUICHE WITH CRISP POTATO CRUST

The potato crust can be prepared in advance and stored, covered, in the refrigerator.

———— MAKES 6 SLICES ————
Portions per slice: **2p, 1½c, 2f&o**

275 g (10 oz) trimmed spinach leaves, finely shredded
3 eggs
225 g (8 oz) ricotta cheese
100 g (4 oz) low-fat soft cheese
30 ml (2 tbsp) grated Parmesan cheese
5 ml (1 tsp) grated nutmeg
finely grated rind of 1 lemon
juice of ½ lemon
pepper
50 ml (2 fl oz) semi-skimmed milk
paprika, for sprinkling

CRISP POTATO CRUST
100 g (4 oz) plain wholemeal flour
50 g (2 oz) polyunsaturated margarine
100 g (4 oz) potatoes, scrubbed and finely grated
½ small onion, skinned and grated
salt and pepper
5 ml (1 tsp) corn oil

1 To make the crust, put the flour in a bowl and rub in the margarine until the mixture resembles fine breadcrumbs. Squeeze the grated potatoes well, to remove as much excess moisture as possible. Add to the flour mixture with the onion and salt and pepper to taste. Mix to a firm dough.
2 With lightly floured fingers, thinly press the dough over the base and sides of a 20 cm (8 inch) flan tin or dish. Bake at 200°C (400°F) mark 6 for 20 minutes. Brush with the corn oil and bake for a further 10 minutes, until the crust is crisp.
3 Meanwhile, place the spinach in a steamer over boiling water. Cover tightly and steam for 1 minute, until just tender. Set aside.
4 Beat together the eggs, ricotta cheese, low-fat soft cheese, half the Parmesan cheese, the nutmeg, lemon rind and juice, pepper to taste and milk until smooth. Add the spinach and gently mix.
5 Reduce the oven to 180°C (350°F) mark 4. Spoon the spinach and cheese mixture into the cooked crust and level the surface. Sprinkle over the remaining Parmesan cheese and paprika. Bake for 30–35 minutes, until lightly coloured and set. Serve warm or cold.

SCRAMBLED EGGS WITH TOMATO

———— SERVES 4 ————
Portions per serving: **1½p, 1c, 1f&o**

6 eggs
150 ml (¼ pint) semi-skimmed milk
15 g (½ oz) polyunsatured margarine
2 tomatoes, coarsely chopped
dash of Worcestershire sauce
four 25 g (1 oz) slices wholemeal toast, to serve

1 Beat together the eggs and milk. Melt the margarine in a non-stick saucepan over a low heat. Add the eggs and cook, stirring occasionally, until the eggs begin to scramble.
2 Add the tomatoes and Worcestershire sauce and continue cooking until set but still creamy. Serve at once with toast.

SOUFFLEED RAREBITS

Easy to make, these are a delicious variation of the traditional Welsh rarebit, with a piquant taste.

———— SERVES 4 ————
Portions per serving: **2p, 1c, 1f&o**

four 25 g (1 oz) slices wholemeal bread
15 g (½ oz) polyunsaturated margarine, plus a little extra for spreading
15 ml (1 tbsp) poppy seeds
15 ml (1 tbsp) plain flour
150 ml (¼ pint) semi-skimmed milk
5 ml (1 tsp) Dijon mustard
5 ml (1 tsp) Worcestershire sauce
100 g (4 oz) Edam or Gouda cheese, grated
2 eggs, separated
tomato wedges and watercress sprigs, to garnish

1 Spread the slices of bread lightly with margarine. Sprinkle each slice with poppy seeds and bake at 190°C (375°F) mark 5 for 5 minutes.
2 Melt 15 g (½ oz) margarine in a saucepan, stir in the flour and cook for 1 minute.
3 Gradually stir in the milk and bring to the boil. Stir over a low heat until the sauce has thickened. Remove from the heat.
4 Beat in the mustard, Worcestershire sauce, grated cheese and egg yolks.
5 Whisk the egg whites until stiff, then fold into the cheese mixture.
6 Spoon the mixture on top of each slice of bread and return to the oven for a further 15 minutes, until puffed and golden. Serve immediately, garnished with the tomato wedges and watercress sprigs.

ONION QUICHE

———— MAKES 6 SLICES ————
Portions per serving: **½p, 2c, 4f&o**

75 g (3 oz) plain wholemeal flour
75 g (3 oz) plain flour
75 g (3 oz) polyunsaturated margarine
30 ml (2 tbsp) corn oil
3 onions, skinned and thinly sliced
6 spring onions, trimmed and cut diagonally into 2.5 cm (1 inch) pieces
75 ml (5 tbsp) semi-skimmed milk
3 eggs
2.5 ml (½ tsp) cayenne

1 Put the flours into a mixing bowl and rub in the margarine until the mixture resembles fine breadcrumbs. Mix to a firm but pliable dough with about 30 ml (2 tbsp) cold water. Knead on a lightly floured surface.
2 Roll out the dough and use to line a 20 cm (8 inch), loose-based flan tin. Chill for 30 minutes.
3 Place a sheet of greaseproof paper in the base of the flan case, cover with baking beans and bake at 200°C (400°F) mark 6 for 15 minutes. Remove the beans and paper, then bake for 5 minutes more.
4 Meanwhile, heat the oil in a saucepan and cook the onions and spring onions for 6–8 minutes, until transparent. Drain off the oil, then place the onions in the partially baked flan case.
5 Beat the semi-skimmed milk with the eggs and add the cayenne. Pour into the partially baked flan case and bake for 25–30 minutes, until the filling is set and golden.

BASIL AND TOMATO TARTLETS

Make these tarts in the summer when fresh basil is available. Don't be tempted to use dried basil instead as the flavour is quite different. These tartlets are particularly high in calcium.

―――――― SERVES 4 ――――――
Portions per serving: **3p, 3c, 3f&o**

75 g (3 oz) plain wholemeal flour
75 g (3 oz) plain white flour
50 g (2 oz) polyunsaturated margarine
50 g (2 oz) Cheddar cheese, grated
1 egg yolk
6 tomatoes, roughly chopped
200 g (7 oz) medium fat Mozzarella cheese, cut into 1 cm (½ inch) cubes
45 ml (3 tbsp) chopped fresh basil
salt and pepper
basil leaves, to garnish

1 To make the pastry, put the flours in a bowl and rub in the margarine until the mixture resembles fine breadcrumbs.
2 Stir in the Cheddar cheese and the egg yolk mixed with 30 ml (2 tbsp) water. Knead on a lightly floured surface to form a smooth, firm dough.
3 Divide the dough into four equal pieces and roll out each piece on a lightly floured surface. Use to line four 10 cm (4 inch) flan tins or dishes.
4 Place a sheet of greaseproof paper in the base of the flan case, cover with baking beans and bake at 200°C (400°F) mark 6 for 10 minutes. Remove the beans and paper and bake for a further 10 minutes. Cool, then remove from the tins.
5 Mix together the tomatoes, Mozzarella and chopped basil and add salt and paper to taste. Divide the filling between the pastry cases, garnish with basil and serve at once.

SPICED BEAN SAUSAGES

Cumin and coriander give these unusual sausages made from haricot beans a delicious spicy flavour.

―――――― MAKES 12 ――――――
Portions per serving: **1p, ½c**

225 g (8 oz) dried haricot beans, soaked overnight
1 small onion, skinned and grated
15 ml (1 tbsp) lemon juice
5 ml (1 tsp) freshly ground cumin
5 ml (1 tsp) fresh ground coriander
15 ml (1 tbsp) chopped fresh coriander
pepper
1 egg, beaten
50 g (2 oz) fresh wholemeal breadcrumbs
15 ml (1 tbsp) sunflower oil

1 Drain the beans and rinse. Put in a saucepan with plenty of fresh water and cook for 1¼ hours or until tender. Drain well, then press the beans through a sieve or purée in a food processor.
2 Add the onion, lemon juice, spices and fresh coriander. Add pepper to taste and mix well. If the mixture is a little soft, chill for 15 minutes.
3 Divide the bean mixture into 12 and roll each piece into a sausage shape about 5 cm (2 inches) long, dusting your hands with a little flour if necessary. Coat the sausages in the egg and breadcrumbs.
4 Heat the oil in a non-stick frying

pan and cook the sausages on all sides for about 5–10 minutes until evenly browned and crisp. Drain on absorbent kitchen paper and serve hot.

SUMMER VEGETABLE FLAN

The usual quantity of fat used in pastry-making is halved in this crisp, light, yeasted pastry. The secret is to roll out the dough very thinly as the yeast will raise it.

———————— SERVES 6 ————————
Portions per serving: **1p, 1½c, 2f&o**

FOR THE PASTRY

50 g (2 oz) plain unbleached flour
50 g (2 oz) wholemeal flour
5 ml (1 tsp) easy mix dried yeast
pinch of salt
25 g (1 oz) polyunsaturated margarine
45–60 ml (3–4 tbsp) skimmed milk, warmed

FOR THE FILLING

15 g (½ oz) polyunsaturated margarine
25 g (1 oz) wholemeal flour
300 ml (½ pint) skimmed milk
pepper
10 ml (2 tsp) sunflower oil
1 large onion, skinned and thinly sliced
225 g (8 oz) courgettes, trimmed and thinly sliced
100 g (4 oz) button mushrooms
225 g (8 oz) runner beans, trimmed and thinly sliced
1.25 ml (¼ tsp) dried rosemary, oregano or mixed herbs
4 tomatoes, skinned and quartered
50 g (2 oz) walnuts, chopped

1 For the pastry, mix the flours, yeast and salt in a bowl. Rub in the margarine until the mixture resembles fine breadcrumbs. Gradually add enough milk to make a soft dry dough. Knead until smooth.

2 Grease a 25.5 cm (10 inch) flan ring. Roll out the dough on an unfloured work surface and use to line the flan ring. Cover with greased polythene and leave in a warm place while preparing the filling.

3 For the filling, put margarine, flour and milk into a saucepan. Heat, whisking continuously, until the sauce thickens, boils and is smooth. Simmer for 1–2 minutes. Add pepper to taste, leave to cool.

4 Heat the oil in a non-stick saucepan and cook the onion and courgettes for about 8 minutes or until just cooked. Remove with a slotted spoon. Leave to cool. Cook the mushrooms in the remaining liquid for 3–4 minutes. Put the beans in a pan containing the minimum of boiling water and cook for about 5 minutes, then drain.

5 Remove the polythene and cover the base of the flan with crumpled greaseproof paper, weighed down with dried beans. Bake blind at 200°C (400°F) mark 6 for 10 minutes. Remove the beans and paper and bake for a further 5 minutes.

6 Arrange the onion, beans and courgettes over the base of the flan, sprinkle with the herbs and spoon over the sauce. Arrange the tomatoes, cut side down, in a circle around the flan. Fill the centre with the whole mushrooms.

7 Bake for 20 minutes. Sprinkle with the chopped nuts and bake for a further 5 minutes. Serve hot.

GOAT'S CHEESE TARTS

Goat's cheese is available from delicatessens and large supermarkets.

———— SERVES 4 ————
Portions per tart: **1p, 2c, 3f&o**

50 g (2 oz) plain wholemeal flour
50 g (2 oz) plain flour
salt
50 g (2 oz) polyunsaturated margarine
fresh coriander sprigs, to garnish

CHEESE FILLING

50 g (2 oz) soft goat's cheese, any coarse rind removed
1 egg, separated
100 ml (4 fl oz) semi-skimmed milk
salt and pepper
one of the following flavourings:
1 small red pepper, cored, seeded and finely chopped;
30 ml (2 tbsp) snipped fresh chives;
8 green and 8 black olives, stoned and chopped with 15 ml (1 tbsp) drained capers

1 Put flours and salt into a bowl. Rub in margarine until mixture resembles fine breadcrumbs. Add water to form a dough. Chill for 30 minutes.
2 Divide the dough into 4. Roll out each piece to a round and use to line individual Yorkshire pudding tins. Prick with a fork, bake blind at 200°C (400°F) mark 6 for 5 minutes. Lower oven temperature to 190°C (375°F) mark 5.
3 Meanwhile, cream the cheese with a fork. Beat in the egg yolk and gradually add milk. Add salt and pepper to taste and add one of the flavourings. Whisk egg white until stiff. Fold into mixture.
4 Divide filling between pastry cases and bake for a further 25 minutes. Garnish and serve warm.

SLIMMING FISH PIE

This versatile dish may be served with piped potatoes in individual gratin dishes or as a starter in ramekins.

———— SERVES 4 ————
Portions per serving: **2½p, 1½c, 1f&o**

450 g (1 lb) potatoes, peeled
45 ml (3 tbsp) skimmed milk
300 ml (½ pint) skimmed milk
1 slice onion
1 slice carrot
6 peppercorns
1.25 ml (¼ tsp) ground mace
15 g (½ oz) polyunsaturated margarine
35 g (1¼ oz) plain flour
salt and pepper
225 g (8 oz) firm-fleshed white fish, skinned
juice of ½ lemon
75 g (3 oz) peeled prawns
50 g (2 oz) button mushrooms, finely sliced
30 ml (2 tbsp) freshly grated Parmesan cheese

1 For the gratin, put the potatoes in a saucepan of water and cook for about 20 minutes. Drain and mash them very thoroughly with the 45 ml (3 tbsp) milk. Lightly grease 4 individual gratin dishes and pipe or spoon the potato around the edge. Set aside.
2 For the ramekins, lightly grease six 100 ml (4 fl oz) ramekins.
3 Put the 300 ml (½ pint) milk, the

onion, carrot, peppercorns and mace in a saucepan and heat through until almost boiling. Allow the milk to cool, then strain into a pan. Add the margarine and flour. Heat, whisking continuously, until the sauce thickens, boils and is smooth. Simmer for 1–2 minutes. Season liberally with pepper and add a little salt if required.

4 Cut the fish into thin strips, divide between the dishes and pour over the lemon juice. Arrange the prawns and mushrooms over the fish. Pour over the sauce and sprinkle with Parmesan cheese.

5 Bake at 180°C (350°F) mark 4 for 20–25 minutes or until golden.

VEGETARIAN PANCAKES

The nuts, wholemeal flour and vegetables make these pancakes relatively high in fibre.

———————— SERVES 8 ————————
Portions per serving: **1½p, 1c, 1f&o**

50 g (2 oz) wholemeal flour
50 g (2 oz) plain flour
1 egg, beaten
300 ml (½ pint) skimmed milk
15–30 ml (1–2 tbsp) sunflower oil
snipped fresh chives, to garnish

FOR THE NUT FILLING
100 g (4 oz) low-fat cottage cheese
50 g (2 oz) unsalted cashew nuts, chopped
50 g (2 oz) unsalted Brazil nuts, chopped
1 small red pepper, cored, seeded and finely chopped
1 bunch spring onions, cut into 2.5 cm (1 inch) pieces
15 ml (1 tbsp) snipped fresh chives
30 ml (2 tbsp) low-fat natural yogurt

1 Put the flours into a bowl and make a well in the centre. Add the egg and 150 ml (¼ pint) of the milk and gradually mix in the flour from the sides of the bowl, whisking until smooth. Slowly whisk in the remaining milk.

2 Heat 5 ml (1 tsp) of the oil in a 20 cm (8 inch) non-stick frying pan and pour in 45 ml (3 tbsp) of the batter. Tilt the pan so that the batter flows evenly over the base. Cook over a medium heat for 2 minutes or until golden brown. Toss or turn the pancake and cook for a further 2 minutes. Place on a plate, cover with foil and put in the oven at 170°C (325°F) mark 3 to keep hot while cooking the remaining pancakes.

3 For the filling, put all the ingredients into a small saucepan and heat through gently, stirring occasionally, until piping hot.

4 To serve, place 15–30 ml (1–2 tbsp) of the filling on each pancake, roll up and serve at once, garnished with chives.

CURRIED TOFU AND VEGETABLES

Tofu is an excellent source of low-fat protein. In a dish, it provides an interesting texture, but as it has a slightly bland taste it has to be prepared with a tasty sauce.

─────── SERVES 4 ───────
Portions per serving: ½p, 1c, ½f&o

15 ml (1 tbsp) sunflower oil
1 large onion, skinned and chopped
2 garlic cloves, skinned and crushed
10 ml (2 tsp) freshly ground coriander
10 ml (2 tsp) freshly ground cumin
5 ml (1 tsp) ground turmeric
5 ml (1 tsp) ground ginger
5–10 ml (1–2 tsp) chilli powder
5 ml (1 tsp) freshly ground fenugreek
300 ml (½ pint) vegetable stock
juice of 1 lemon
2 carrots, scrubbed and diced
100 g (4 oz) cauliflower, divided into florets
2 courgettes, trimmed and diced
4 tomatoes, chopped
100 g (4 oz) French beans, trimmed and cut into 2.5 cm (1 inch) pieces
175 g (6 oz) firm tofu, cut into 1 cm (½ inch) cubes
30 ml (2 tbsp) low-fat natural yogurt
chopped fresh coriander, to garnish

1 Heat the oil in a large non-stick saucepan and cook the onion and garlic for 3 minutes until soft. Add the spices and keep cooking for a further 5 minutes, stirring occasionally.
2 Stir in the stock and lemon juice with the carrots, cauliflower and courgettes. Bring to the boil, cover and simmer for 10 minutes. Add the tomatoes and beans and cook for a further 5 minutes.
3 Add the tofu and continue cooking for 5 minutes. Stir in the yogurt and heat through, without boiling. Garnish with coriander and serve hot.

STUFFED MUSHROOMS

This recipe may be prepared up to the grilling stage several hours ahead, then left covered with plastic wrap and refrigerated. The mushrooms may then be grilled immediately prior to serving.

─────── SERVES 4 ───────
Portions per serving: 1p, 1½c

four 25 g (1 oz) slices wholemeal bread
4 large, open brown-gilled mushrooms, stalks removed and finely chopped
50 g (2 oz) low-fat Cheddar cheese, grated
2.5 ml (½ tsp) Dijon mustard
2.5 ml (½ tsp) curry powder
5 ml (1 tsp) minced onion
30 ml (2 tbsp) low-fat natural yogurt
30 ml (2 tbsp) chopped fresh parsley, to garnish

1 Using a round pasdtry cutter the same size as the mushrooms, cut 4 rounds from the bread.
2 Mix together the mushroom stalks, cheese, mustard, curry powder, onion and yogurt in a bowl. Spoon the mixture into the mushroom cups.
3 Cook the mushrooms under a hot grill until the cheese bubbles and browns. Just before they are cooked, grill the bread rounds on both sides.
4 Place the toast on 4 small warmed

plates and top each with a mushroom. Garnish with chopped parsley and serve immediately.

PIPERADE

Besides being a nutritious, egg-based snack, this traditional Basque dish is colourful and easy to prepare. The basil provides a warm, pungent fragrance.

———————— SERVES 4 ————————
Portions per serving: **1p, 1f&o**

15 ml (1 tbsp) sunflower oil
1 medium onion, skinned and finely chopped
1 garlic clove, skinned and crushed
1 small green pepper, cored, seeded and cut into thin strips
1 small red pepper, cored, seeded and cut into thin strips
pepper
5 ml (1 tsp) chopped fresh basil or 2.5 ml (½ tsp) dried
4 eggs, beaten
175 g (6 oz) tomatoes, cut into wedges
basil leaves, to garnish

1 Heat the oil in a non-stick frying pan and cook the onion, garlic and green and red peppers for 5 minutes.
2 Add pepper to taste, basil and 15 ml (1 tbsp) water to the eggs and pour into the pan. Stir lightly, then leave to cook for 3 minutes.
3 Add the tomatoes, stir again and gently shake the pan from side to side, allowing the uncooked mixture to flow underneath the cooked egg mixture. Cook for 3–5 minutes or until the eggs are set. Cut into quarters, garnish with basil leaves and serve immediately.

VEGETARIAN TOFU KEBABS

———————— SERVES 4 ————————
Portions per serving: **1½p, 2f&o**

450 g (1 lb) tofu, cut into 2.5 cm (1 inch) cubes
1 large red pepper, cored, seeded and cubed
1 large green pepper, cored, seeded and cubed
grated rind and juice of 2 limes or 1 lemon
45 ml (3 tbsp) olive oil
salt and pepper
30 ml (2 tbsp) low-fat natural yogurt
30 ml (2 tbsp) soy sauce, preferably naturally fermented shoyu
1 garlic clove, skinned and finely chopped
1.25 ml (¼ tsp) ground cumin
1.25 ml (¼ tsp) curry powder
8 cherry tomatoes or 4 tomatoes, cut into wedges
shredded lettuce, to serve

1 Put the tofu and pepper cubes into a shallow dish. Mix together the lime or lemon rind and juice, olive oil, salt and pepper to taste, yogurt, soy sauce, garlic and spices. Spoon evenly over the tofu and peppers. Cover and chill for 3–4 hours, turning the tofu and peppers occasionally.
2 Remove the tofu and pepper cubes from the marinade and thread on to skewers, alternating with the tomatoes. Grill for 3–4 minutes, turn, brush with the marinade and cook for a further 3–4 minutes. Serve on a bed of shredded lettuce.

STUFFED CABBAGE ROLLS

Lentils are a good source of protein; unlike many other pulses, they do not have to be soaked before cooking.

--- MAKES 8 ---
Portions per roll: **1p, ½f&o**

175 g (6 oz) green lentils
8 large green cabbage leaves
1 large onion, skinned and finely chopped
15 ml (1 tbsp) sunflower oil
30 ml (2 tbsp) tomato purée
1 red pepper, cored, seeded and finely chopped
5 ml (1 tsp) ground mixed spice
400 g (14 oz) can chopped tomatoes
150 ml (¼ pint) vegetable stock
few drops of Tabasco sauce or to taste

1 Place the lentils in a small saucepan, add cold water to cover and bring to the boil. Lower the heat and simmer for about 20 minutes, until tender, then drain.
2 Meanwhile, in another saucepan, blanch the cabbage. Place in boiling water and cook for 4–5 minutes. Drain and set aside to cool.
3 In a clean saucepan cook the onion in the oil for about 3 minutes until soft. Add the tomato purée, red pepper and mixed spice and cook for 2–3 minutes, stirring occasionally. Add the lentils and remove from the heat.
4 Place a little of the mixture into the centre of each cabbage leaf and fold to form a parcel. Place in a shallow ovenproof dish in a single layer.
5 Mix the tomatoes and their juice with the vegetable stock, season with a little Tabasco and pour over the parcels.
6 Cover with a piece of aluminium foil and bake at 180°C (350°F) mark 4 for 40 minutes, until tender. Serve immediately.

PEPPERY CHEESE SOUFFLES

These light soufflés are quick to prepare and are perfect before a simple beef or poultry meal, or on their own as a simple late-night supper.

--- SERVES 4 ---
Portions per serving: **2p**

100 g (4 oz) low-fat soft cheese
50 g (2 oz) mature Cheddar cheese, finely grated
15 ml (1 tbsp) grated Parmesan cheese
1.25 ml (¼ tsp) mustard powder
5 ml (1 tsp) green peppercorns in brine, drained and roughly chopped
50 ml (2 fl oz) dry sherry or white wine
2 eggs, separated

1 Lightly grease 4 ramekins and set aside. Mix the cheeses with the mustard and peppercorns. Mix in the sherry or wine and the egg yolks.
2 Whisk the egg whites until stiff, then carefully fold 15 ml (1 tbsp) into the cheese mixture, to soften. Fold in the remainder.
3 Spoon into the ramekins and bake at 200°C (400°F) mark 6 for about 15 minutes, until puffed and golden brown on top. Serve immediately.

VEGETARIAN DISHES

CARROT, ONION AND EGG LOAF

──────── MAKES 12 SLICES ────────
Portions per slice: **1p, ½c**

1 parsnip, peeled and halved
2 carrots, scrubbed and grated
2 courgettes, trimmed and grated
2 onions, skinned and chopped
100 g (4 oz) fresh wholemeal breadcrumbs
salt and pepper
1 egg, beaten
100 g (4 oz) Double Gloucester or mature Cheddar cheese, grated
3 eggs, hard-boiled and shelled

1 Lightly grease a 900 g (2 lb) loaf tin and line with lightly greased greaseproof paper. Cook the parsnip in boiling water for 5 minutes. Drain and leave to cool slightly, then grate.
2 Put the parsnip, carrots and courgettes into a bowl. Mix in the onions, breadcrumbs and seasoning. Add the beaten egg and 50 g (2 oz) of the grated cheese. Combine the ingredients throughly.
3 Place one-third of the vegetable mixture in the tin and spread out evenly. Arrange the hard-boiled eggs down the centre.
4 Cover with the remaining vegetable mixture and press firmly to level the surface. Sprinkle over the remaining cheese and press lightly.
5 Bake, on a baking sheet, at 180°C (350°F) mark 4 for 1 hour. If necessary, cover loaf with foil during cooking to prevent overbrowning.
6 Leave the loaf to cool in the tin for 1 hour. To serve, turn out on to a serving plate and remove lining paper, then slice.

SPINACH AND EGG CRUMBLE

──────── SERVES 4 ────────
Portions per serving: **2p, 2½c, 4f&o**

1 onion, skinned and chopped
15 g (½ oz) margarine
2 garlic cloves, skinned and crushed
450 g (1 lb) chopped frozen spinach, thawed
5 ml (1 tsp) grated nutmeg
4 eggs

CRUMBLE
100 g (4 oz) plain wholemeal flour
50 g (2 oz) plain flour
5 ml (1 tsp) mustard powder
pinch of cayenne
50 g (2 oz) polyunsaturated margarine
50 g (2 oz) mature Cheddar cheese, grated

1 Put the onion and margarine in a saucepan over a gentle heat. Cover and cook until the onion is translucent, shaking the pan occasionally to prevent sticking.
2 Add the garlic, spinach, nutmeg and pepper to taste and cook gently for 2–3 minutes, stirring occasionally.
3 To prepare the crumble, mix the flours with mustard powder and cayenne rubbing in margarine and cheese.
4 Divide the spinach mixture between 4 small heatproof dishes, making a well in the centre of each. Break an egg into each and cover with the crumble mixture.
5 Bake at 200°C (400°F) mark 6 for 15–20 minutes, until the crumble begins to brown and the eggs are set but not too hard.

HOT MUSHROOM MOUSSE

---SERVES 4---
Portions per serving: **1p, 1c, 3f&o**

20 g (¾ oz) polyunsaturated margarine
20 g (¾ oz) plain wholemeal flour
300 ml (½ pint) semi-skimmed milk
salt and pepper
75 g (3 oz) button mushrooms, finely chopped
75 g (3 oz) fresh wholemeal breadcrumbs
2 eggs, separated
30 ml (2 tbsp) chopped fresh parsley
30 ml (2 tbsp) grated Parmesan cheese
12 small button mushrooms

CHIVE SAUCE
45 ml (3 tbsp) low-fat natural yogurt
45 ml (3 tbsp) mayonnaise
1.25 ml (¼ tsp) lemon juice
15 ml (1 tbsp) snipped fresh chives

1 Lightly grease and line a 450 g (1 lb) loaf tin or 15 cm (6 inch) soufflé dish with greaseproof paper.
2 Melt the margarine in a saucepan. Stir in the flour and cook for 1 minute. Stir in the milk and bring to the boil. Add salt and pepper to taste and the chopped mushrooms. Simmer for 5 minutes.
3 Beat the breadcrumbs, egg yolks, parsley and cheese into the sauce. Whisk the egg whites until stiff, then fold into the mixture.
4 Spoon the mixture into the prepared loaf tin, adding the whole mushrooms at random. Level the surface and cover with a piece of lightly greased aluminium foil.
5 Stand in a roasting pan and add hot water to come halfway up the sides of the loaf tin. Bake at 170°C (325°F) mark 3 for 45 minutes, until the mousse is set.
6 Meanwhile, make the sauce. Mix together the yogurt, mayonnaise, lemon juice and chives. Cover and chill until ready to serve.
7 Turn the loaf out on to a warm serving dish. Serve, cut into slices, accompanied by the sauce.

ONION TART

This low-fat, yeasted pastry can be made with all wholemeal flour, white flour or, as below, a mixture of the two.

---SERVES 4---
Portions per serving: **2c, ½d, 1½f&o**

FOR THE PASTRY
50 g (2 oz) plain unbleached flour
50 g (2 oz) wholemeal flour
5 ml (1 tsp) easy mix dried yeast
pinch of salt
25 g (1 oz) polyunsaturated margarine
50 ml (3–4 tbsp) skimmed milk, warmed

FOR THE FILLING
700 g (1½ lb) onions, skinned and finely sliced
60 ml (4 tbsp) skimmed milk
large pinch of dried thyme
pepper
25 g (1 oz) very strong Cheddar cheese, grated

1 For the pastry, mix the flours, yeast and salt in a bowl. Rub in the margarine until the mixture resembles fine breadcrumbs. Gradually add enough milk to make a soft dry dough. Knead until smooth.

2 Grease a 25.5 cm (10 inch) flan tin. Roll out the dough on an unfloured work surface and use to line the flan tin. Cover with greased polythene and leave in a warm place while preparing the filling.

3 For the filling, put the onions into a saucepan and add 150 ml (¼ pint) water. Bring to the boil, cover and simmer gently for 25–35 minutes or until the onions are soft. Drain. Mix in the milk and thyme. Add pepper to taste.

4 Remove the polythene and cover the base of the flan with crumpled greaseproof paper, weighed down with dried beans. Bake at 200°C (400°F) mark 6 for 10 minutes. Remove the paper and beans and bake for a further 5 minutes.

5 Fill the flan with the onion mixture and sprinkle over the cheese. Bake for 15–20 minutes or until browned. Serve hot or warm.

CARROT QUICHES

Low-fat Quark is used here to add a creamy cheese taste to these quiches.

SERVES 4
Portions per serving: **1p, 2c, 2f&o**

100 g (4 oz) carrots, scrubbed and finely diced, with a few thin slices reserved
200 g (7 oz) low-fat Quark
1 egg, beaten
5 ml (1 tsp) ground mace
15 ml (1 tbsp) dried oregano
pepper

FOR THE WHOLEMEAL PASTRY
100 g (4 oz) wholemeal flour
pinch of salt
40 g (1½ oz) polyunsaturated margarine

1 For the pastry, put the flour and salt into a bowl. Rub in the margarine until the mixture resembles the fine breadcrumbs. Gradually add 25 ml (1½ tbsp) cold water and mix to form a smooth dough.

2 Divided the dough into 4 equal pieces. Roll out each on a lightly floured work surface and use to line 4 individual quiche moulds or Yorkshire pudding tins. Cover and chill for 25 minutes.

3 Cook the carrots in a saucepan of boiling water for 5 minutes or until just tender. Drain well. Reserve the carrot slices for garnish.

4 Put the diced carrots, Quark, egg, mace, 10 ml (2 tsp) of the oregano in a bowl and mix well. Add pepper to taste. Divide the mixture between the pastry-lined tins and lightly sprinkle with the remaining dried oregano.

5 Bake at 200°C (400°F) mark 6 for 10–15 minutes or until risen and set. Serve hot, garnished with the reserved carrot slices.

PIZZA CHILLI

Italian pizzas are traditionally made with white flour but are equally delicious and more nutritious made with wholemeal flour.

SERVES 4
Portions per serving: **1p, 4c**

FOR THE BASE
225 g (8 oz) wholemeal or plain flour
pinch of salt
5 ml (1 tsp) easy mix dried yeast
50 ml (2 fl oz) boiling water
150 ml (¼ pint) cold water

FOR THE TOPPING
5 ml (1 tsp) sunflower oil
1 small onion, skinned and finely chopped
1 garlic clove, skinned hand very finely chopped (optional)
200 g (7 oz) can tomatoes with their juice, chopped
15 ml (1 tbsp) dried or fresh basil
pepper
chilliflakes
3 black olives, stoned and chopped
100 g (4 oz medium fat Mozzarella cheese, very thinly sliced

1 For the base, combine the flour, salt and yeast in a bowl. Mix the hot and cold water together and stir sufficient into the flour mixture to make a soft dry dough.
2 Turn the dough on to a lightly floured work surface and knead for 5 minutes. Place in a lightly oiled bowl, cover with polythene and leave to rise in a warm place until dubbed in size.
3 Meanwhile, for the filling, heat the oil in a non-stick saucepan and gently cook the onion for about 5 minutes until soft. Add the garlic, if using, tomatoes and tomato purée and simmer gently for about 10 minutes or until thick. Cool.
4 When the dough has risen, lightly grease 2 baking sheets. Knead the dough until smooth and divide in half. Roll out each piece into a 23 cm (9 inch) round and transfer to a baking sheet. Cover again with polythene and leave in a warm place to prove for 20–30 minutes until the bases are well risen and puffy.
5 Spread the tomato sauce over the pizza bases, leaving a 1 cm (½ inch) border around the edges. Sprinkle with basil, pepper and chilli flakes to taste, the black olives and Mozzarella.
6 Bake at 230°C (450°F) mark 8 for 10–15 minutes or until the top is bubbling and the base looks cooked. Serve piping hot.

PUDDINGS

Sometimes we might not actually be hungry, but we still crave something sweet. The recipes below are nearly all based on fruit which means they're healthier alternatives to conventional puddings and lower in calories.

AT-A-GLANCE PORTION GUIDE (per serving)

Recipe	p	c	d	f&o	f
Barbecued Bananas			½	2	1½
Raspberry Tofu Ice Cream	½			1	
Golden Peach Soufflé	½				1
Plum Clafoutis	2			3	1
Almond and Mango Ice Cream	1				½
Apricot and Kiwi Fruit Cups	½	½	½	2	1
Orange Mousses			½	½	1
Apricot and Orange Coupe			½		2
Strawberry Cream	½				1
(with honey)	½			½	1
Ginger Fruit Salad			½		1½
Fruit Kebabs with Yogurt and Honey Dip				1½	3½
Dried Fruit Compote					1½
Spiced Dried Fruit Compote				1½	3

BARBECUED BANANAS

———— SERVES 4 ————
Portions per serving: ½d, 2f&o, 1½f

4 large bananas
25 g (1 oz) demerara sugar
grated rind and juice of 1 large orange
granted rind and juice of 1 lime
2.5 ml (½ tsp) ground cinnamon
25 g (1 oz) polyunsaturated margarine
orange and lime slices, to decorate
300 ml (½ pint) thick natural yogurt, to serve

1 Cut four large rectangles of kitchen foil. Peel the bananas, then place one on each piece of foil. Prick them in several places with a fine skewer.
2 Mix together the sugar, orange rind and juice, lime rind and juice and cinnamon. Pour slowly over the bananas, dividing it equally between them. Dot with the margarine.
3 Bring the two long sides of the foil up over one banana, then fold the join over several times to seal thoroughly.
4 Fold up the ends of the foil so that the banana is enclosed completely and the juice cannot run out during cooking. Repeat with the remaining three bananas.
5 Place the parcels on the barbecue or grill and cook for 15 minutes, turning them once during cooking.
6 To serve, open the parcels carefully and transfer the bananas to individual serving dishes. Pour over the juices which have collected in the foil and decorate with the orange and lime slices. Serve with thick natural yogurt.

RASPBERRY TOFU ICE CREAM

Tofu is made from ground soya beans and water and is extremely rich in protein. Buy it at Chinese grocers' or health food shops.

———— MAKES 12 SLICES ————
Portions per slice: ½p, 1f&o

625 g (1 lb 6 oz) tofu
1 egg, separated
100 g (4 oz) golden granulated sugar
90 ml (6 tbsp) Greek strained yogurt
few drops of vanilla essence
100 g (4 oz) raspberries
a few raspberries, to decorate

1 Drain excess liquid from the tofu. Place in a blender or food processor with the egg yolk and 75 g (3 oz) of the sugar and blend until smooth. Add the yogurt and vanilla essence and blend again briefly.
2 Pour the mixture into a freezer container and freeze for about 1 hour until beginning to set. Meanwhile, press the raspberries through a nylon sieve to make a purée.
3 Whisk the egg white until stiff and gradually whisk in the remaining sugar. Carefully fold in the purée.
4 Remove the tofu mixture from the freezer. Gently swirl in the raspberry mixture to create a marbled effect. Pour the mixture into a 900 g (2 lb) loaf tin and freeze until firm. To serve, dip the tin in hot water, then invert on to a serving plate. Slice and decorate with raspberries.

GOLDEN PEACH SOUFFLE

This fruit soufflé is perfect after a large meal because it is made without a flour base. Serve it as soon as it is cooked, as it will collapse quickly.

———— SERVES 4 ————
Portions per serving: **½p, 1f**

425 g (15 oz) can unsweetened peaches, drained
15 ml (1 tbsp) clear honey
2 egg yolks, beaten
3 egg whites

1 Lightly grease a 1.1 litre (2 pint) soufflé dish. Place the peaches and honey in a blender or food processor and purée until smooth.
2 Mix into the egg yolks. Whisk the egg whites until stiff, then carefully fold them into the peach mixture until well incorporated.
3 Pour into the prepared dish and bake at 190°C (375°F) mark 5 for 40–50 minutes, until golden and well risen.

PLUM CLAFOUTIS

Serve the clafoutis hot, straight from the oven, or chilled.

———— MAKES 6 SLICES ————
Portions per slice: **2p, 3f&o, 1f**

450 g (1 lb) plums, halved and stoned

BATTER
50 g (2 oz) low-fat cheese
50 g (2 oz) ground almonds
25 g (1 oz) light muscovado sugar
2 eggs, lightly beaten
60 ml (4 tbsp) semi-skimmed milk
50 g (2 oz) polyunsaturated margarine, melted

1 Lightly grease a 20.5 cm (8 inch) round flan dish and arrange the plums in it in a circular pattern.
2 To make the batter, beat the cheese, ground almonds and sugar together, then gradually whisk in the eggs and milk. Fold in the margarine and pour the batter over the plums.
3 Bake at 200°C (400°F) mark 6 for 25–30 minutes, until set.

ALMOND AND MANGO ICE CREAM

———— SERVES 8 ————
Portions per serving: **1p, ½f**

2 medium ripe mangoes, peeled, stoned and coarsely chopped
297 g (10 oz) silken tofu
300 ml (½ pint) semi-skimmed milk
finely grated rind and juice of 1½ limes
50 g (2 oz) blanched almonds, toasted and chopped
lime slices and toasted flaked almonds, to decorate

1 Put half the mango in a blender or food processor with the tofu, milk and lime rind and juice. Blend well until smooth.
2 Pour the mixture into a shallow freezer container and freeze for about 2 hours or until ice crystals form around the edges.
3 Turn into a large, chilled bowl and mash the ice crystals with a fork. Fold in the remaining mango and the chopped almonds. Return to the freezer and freeze for 3–4 hours or until firm.
4 About 30 minutes before serving, remove from the freezer and leave the ice cream to soften at room temperature. Serve decorated with lime slices and toasted flaked almonds.

APRICOT AND KIWI FRUIT CUPS

Non-stick silicone paper is useful when baking biscuits that are fragile. The fine film of oil on the paper makes it easy to lift off the cooked biscuits. Greased greaseproof paper is a good alternative.

———————— SERVES 4 ————————
Portions per serving: ½p, ½c, ½d, 2f&o, 1f

1 egg white
25 g (1 oz) light muscovado sugar
25 g (1 oz) plain wholemeal flour
25 g (1 oz) flaked almonds, chopped
25 g (1 oz) polyunsaturated margarine, melted
60 ml (4 tbsp) whipping cream
60 ml (4 tbsp) Greek strained yogurt
1 kiwi fruit, peeled and finely chopped
2 kiwi fruit, sliced, to decorate
3 apricots, stoned and finely chopped

1 Line 2 baking sheets with non-stick silicone paper. Whisk the egg white until stiff, then lightly fold in the sugar, flour and almonds with a metal spoon. Fold in the margarine.
2 Place 8 spoonfuls of the mixture, spaced well apart, on the baking sheets. With the back of the spoon smooth out each spoonful thinly to a 7.5 cm (3 inch) round. Bake at 190°C (375°F) mark 5 for 8–10 minutes, until golden.
3 Using a palette knife, quickly lift the biscuits, one at a time, from the baking sheets and place over a small orange or the base of a small glass so that they will set in a cup shape. Allow a moment or two for each biscuit to harden, then remove to a wire rack to cool. If the remaining biscuits begin to harden before being shaped, return them to the oven for a few minutes.
4 Whip the cream until quite thick, then lightly whisk in the yogurt. Fold in the chopped kiwi fruit and apricots.
5 Fill each biscuit cup with the fruit cream and serve decorated with kiwi fruit slices.

ORANGE MOUSSES

———————— MAKES 4 ————————
Portions per serving: ½d, ½f&o, 1f

4 sweet oranges
15 ml (1 tbsp) gelatine
15 ml (1 tbsp) light muscovado sugar
75 ml (3 fl oz) Greek strained yogurt
50 ml (2 fl oz) whipping cream
a few orange segments and mint sprigs, to decorate

1 Over a large bowl, cut the top third off the oranges to make a zigzag edge. Remove all the flesh from the oranges and press through a sieve, then make the juice up to 300 ml (½ pint) with a little water if necessary. Reserve the orange shells.
2 Put half the juice into a saucepan, add the gelatine and leave for 5 minutes. Over a low heat, dissolve the gelatine by stirring, then add the sugar, stirring until dissolved. Pour into a bowl. Stir in the remaining juice and leave until the mixture sets around the edges of the bowl.
3 Fold the yogurt into the orange mixture. Whip the cream until it forms soft peaks and fold in to the mixture. Leave for 10–15 minutes, until it holds its shape. Pile into the

reserved orange shells. Chill for 2–3 hours or until set. Serve chilled, decorated with orange segments and mint sprigs.

APRICOT AND ORANGE COUPE

Dried, canned or fresh apricots can be used to make this dessert.

───────── SERVES 4 ─────────
Portions per serving: ½d, 2f

225 g (8 oz) dried apricots, soaked overnight, or 400 g (14 oz) canned, stoned and drained, or fresh apricots, cooked and stoned
grated rind of 1 orange
100 ml (6½ tbsp) freshly squeezed orange juice
50 g (2 oz) low-fat curd cheese or Quark
30 ml (2 tbsp) low-fat natural yogurt
15 g (½ oz) flaked almonds

1 Cook the apricots in the water in which they were soaked, making it up to 300 ml (½ pint) with water if needed, for about 20 minutes or until soft. Add the grated orange rind and three-quarters of the orange juice to the cooked or canned apricots. Cool a little, then purée in a liquidiser. Divide this between 4 or 6 stemmed, wide glasses (or coupes).
2 For the topping, purée the cheese with the remaining orange juice and the yogurt. Spoon over the apricot purée and scatter with the almonds. Chill before serving.

VARIATION

This recipe works very well with many fresh stoned fruits, such as peaches or plums as well as with soft fruits like strawberries, raspberries, loganberries or mulberries. Of course, fresh fruit will not need soaking but, if using the soft fruits, it is advisable to sieve them after cooking (they need only 5 minutes simmering) to remove the small pips.

STRAWBERRY CREAM

───────── SERVES 6 ─────────
Portions per serving: ½p, 1f, (with honey, ½f&o)

100 g (4 oz) cottage cheese
150 ml (¼ pint) low-fat natural yogurt
5 ml (1 tsp) clear honey, to taste (optional)
700 g (1½ lb) fresh strawberries

1 Purée the cottage cheese in a blender or food processor until smooth. Alternatively, work it through a fine wire sieve by pushing with the back of a metal spoon.
2 In a bowl, beat the cheese and yogurt together with honey to taste (optional). Set aside.
3 Hull the strawberries and slice thinly, reserving 6 whole ones to decorate.
4 Divide the sliced strawberries equally between 6 individual glasses or glass serving dishes.
5 Pour the cheese mixture over the strawberries and chill in the refrigerator for about 1 hour. Serve chilled, decorated with the reserved whole strawberries. Accompany with wholemeal shortbread biscuits, if liked.

GINGER FRUIT SALAD

———— SERVES 4 ————
Portions per serving: ½d (optional), 1½f

2 apricots
2 eating apples
1 orange
241 ml (8½ fl oz) bottle low-calorie ginger ale
50 g (2 oz) white grapes
2 bananas
30 ml (2 tbsp) lemon juice
300 ml (½ pint) low-fat natural yogurt, to serve (optional)

1 Plunge the apricots into a bowl of boiling water for 30 seconds. Drain and peel off the skin with your fingers.
2 Halve the apricots, remove the stones and dice the flesh. Core and dice the apples, but do not peel them. Peel the orange and divide into segments, discarding all white pith.
3 Put the prepared fruits in a serving bowl with the ginger ale. Stir lightly, then cover and leave to macerate for 1 hour.
4 Cut the grapes in half, then remove the seeds by flicking them out with the point of a knife.
5 Peel and slice the bananas and mix them with the lemon juice to prevent discoloration.
6 Add the grapes and bananas to the macerated fruits. Serve in individual glasses topped with yogurt, if liked.

FRUIT KEBABS WITH YOGURT AND HONEY DIP

———— SERVES 4 ————
Portions per serving: 1½f&o, 3½f

1 small pineapple
3 large firm peaches
2 large firm bananas
3 crisp eating apples
1 small bunch large black grapes, seeded
finely grated rind and juice of 1 large orange
60 ml (4 tbsp) brandy or orange-flavoured liqueur
200 ml (7 fl oz) low-fat natural yogurt
45 ml (3 tbsp) clear honey
few fresh mint sprigs, to decorate

1 Prepare the fruit. Cut the top and bottom off the pineapple. Stand the fruit upright on a board. Using a large, sharp knife, slice downwards in sections to remove the skin and 'eyes'. Slice off the flesh, leaving the core. Then cut the flesh into small cubes.
2 Skin and halve the peaches and remove the stones. Cut the flesh into chunks.
3 Peel the bananas and then slice them into thick chunks. Quarter and core the apples, but do not peel them. Cut each quarter in half crossways.
4 Put all the fruit in a bowl. Mix together the orange rind and juice and the brandy or liqueur. Pour over the fruit, cover and leave for at least 30 minutes.
5 Thread the fruit on to kebab skewers. Place under the grill or on a barbecue and cook for 10–15 minutes, turning and basting frequently.
6 Meanwhile make the dip. Whisk together the yogurt and 30 ml (2 tbsp)

PUDDINGS

of the honey. Pour into a serving bowl and drizzle over the remaining 15 ml (1 tbsp) of honey. Decorate with fresh mint sprigs.
7 Serve the fruit kebabs immediately with the yogurt dip handed separately in a small bowl.

DRIED FRUIT COMPOTE

SERVES 6
Portions per serving: **1½f**

50 g (2 oz) dried apple rings
50 g (2 oz) dried apricots
50 g (2 oz) dried figs
300 ml (½ pint) unsweetened orange juice
300 ml (½ pint) water
25 g (1 oz) hazelnuts

1 Cut the dried apples, apricots and figs into chunky pieces and place in a bowl.
2 Mix together the unsweetened orange juice and water and pour over the fruit in the bowl. Cover and leave to macerate in the refrigerator overnight.
3 The next day, spread the hazelnuts out in a grill pan and toast under a low to moderate heat, shaking the pan frequently until the hazelnuts are browned evenly on all sides.
4 Tip the hazelnuts into a clean tea-towel and rub them while they are still hot to remove the skins.
5 Chop the hazelnuts roughly using an automatic chopper or large cook's knife. Sprinkle over the compote just before serving.

SPICED DRIED FRUIT COMPOTE

Although more portions per serving are used up with this recipe than the previous one, there is a greater quantity of fruit per serving here.

SERVES 4
Portions per serving: **1½f&o, 3f**

15 ml (1 tbsp) jasmine tea
2.5 ml (½ tsp) ground cinnamon
1.25 ml (¼ tsp) ground cloves
300 ml (½ pint) boiling water
100 g (4 oz) dried apricots, soaked overnight, drained
100 g (4 oz) dried prunes, soaked overnight, drained and stoned
100 g (4 oz) dried apple rings
150 ml (¼ pint) dry white wine
toasted flaked almonds, to decorate

1 Put the tea, cinnamon and cloves in a bowl and pour in the boiling water. Leave for 20 minutes.
2 Put the dried fruit in a saucepan, then strain in the tea and spice liquid. Add the wine and sugar and heat gently until the sugar has dissolved.
3 Simmer for 20 minutes until tender, then cover and leave for 1–2 hours until cold.
4 Turn the compote into a serving bowl and chill for at least 2 hours. Sprinkle with almonds just before serving.

CHAPTER 7

A REGULAR EXERCISE PLAN

TAKING REGULAR EXERCISE CAN reduce your weight without ever having to cut back on food. The slow but steady rise in our weight over the last 50 years isn't just due to dietary changes, but also to the decreasing amounts of exercise we take. For those who haven't a lot of weight to lose, exercise alone could solve a weight problem. Our attitude to exercise has begun to change, however, as we realise how much it can contribute to both health and appearance. Increasing numbers of people regularly visit a gym, exercise class or dance studio. Combining diet with exercise is now recognised as being the only really effective way to lose weight – or fat – and keep it off. Exercise guards against the inevitable drop in metabolism that dieting causes, and while helping to burn up fat it also helps to tone up lean muscle tissue which uses up calories faster.

The effects of exercise on our health and well-being are well known. Regular aerobic exercise done at least three times a week for 20–30 minutes can significantly reduce risks of heart disease. Our bodies respond to exercise by increasing in strength, stamina and suppleness. Bones, joints and their supporting ligaments are strengthened, helping to keep the whole body strong and supple until late into life. Exercise is also an excellent way to relieve stress and tension. Indeed, some psychiatrists even use the 'high' experienced after 15 or 20 minutes of vigorous exercise, when endorphins, the body's 'pleasure hormones', are released, as a kind of natural remedy for depression. Exercise can help you feel more alert and able to concentrate better, gives you more energy and helps you to sleep at night (providing it isn't done too close to bedtime).

A recent discovery is that exercise also helps long term weight loss, by helping to keep it off once you have lost it – maybe because it makes you more aware of your body and its changing shape.

It is easy to make good resolutions about exercise – much harder to stick to them. Because of this, it is vital to find an activity that you really enjoy, that fits easily into your life. It's pointless signing up for an aerobics class, if you don't really like aerobics and haven't much free time on your hands.

This chapter, then, is all about finding out how fit and active you are, and finding out how much exercise you need to do and from there, building an exercise routine to suit you. In Chapter 3, on page 23, we asked you to keep an activity log at the same time as you kept your diet diary. If you didn't do so then, do so now.

HOW FIT ARE YOU?

If you are fit you should be able to:
1 Walk briskly up and down a flight of about 15 steps three times and still hold an ordinary conversation without being out of breath.
2 Run on the spot lifting feet at least six inches from the ground for three minutes with ease.
3 Do step-ups for three minutes and hold a conversation afterwards.
4 Jog gently and easily for one mile in 10 minutes (if under 45 years), in 12 minutes (if under 55 years), and be able to hold a conversation without being too out of breath.
5 After 2 or 3 deep breaths hold your breath for over 50 seconds with ease (it's not necessary to hold longer than one minute)
6 Have a resting pulse rate that is right for your age group (see box below).

ASSESS YOUR FITNESS LEVEL

Check your pulse rate after exercise: it should not go above the beats per minute range outlined below. Those who are less fit should aim for the lower end of the range after exercise and move to the higher by about five beats a week, slowly building up.

Take your pulse by placing the first two fingers of your other hand on the thumb side of your inside wrist. Count the beats for 10 seconds then multiply by six.

AGE	BEATS/MINUTE
20–29	120–180
30–39	114–171
40–49	108–162
50–59	102–153
60–69	96–144
70 and over	90–135

Record every single activity you do in your normal daily routine for a whole week, including cleaning and stair climbing as well as any exercise classes you've been to or sports you've played. Write down details of your daily activities in the chart below.

	YOUR ACTIVITY LOG		
	Exercise/activity	Time taken	Distance covered (if relevant)
Mon			
Tues			
Wed			
Thurs			
Fri			
Sat			
Sun			

Now, with your log in front of you, answer the following questions, ticking the most appropriate response.

1 During your day's work do you spend time:
sitting 0
sitting/standing 1
standing 2
moving 3
heavy manual 4

2 Do you take a brisk walk lasting about 20 minutes?
every day 3
3–4 times a week 2
1–2 times a week 1
never 0

3 Do you take regular aerobic exercise for 20 minutes (e.g. swimming, cycling, running or an exercise class)?
every day 3
3–4 times a week 2
1–2 times a week 1
never 0

4 Is your resting pulse rate less than:
60 beats a minute 2
60–80 a minute 1
more than 80 0
*see pulse test box below

5 Do you spend 20 minutes gardening or grass cutting?
twice a week or more 2
once a week 1
never 0

6 Do you do housework e.g. making beds, dusting hoovering?
every day 1
not every day 0

7 Do you have stairs at home?
yes 1
no 0

8 When at work or out shopping do you:
climb stairs 1
take the lift or escalator 0

9 Do you walk on the escalator even though it is moving?
yes 1
no 0

10 If you have children do you play actively with them?
every day 2
1–2 times a week 1

Now add up your scores

0–3 Subtract 15 per cent from your daily calorie requirements you calculated on page 32 (working out your metabolic rate). You lead a very inactive life. Your job is probably totally sedentary and you take no exercise outside your working day.

You need to totally re-evaluate your attitude to exercise. You must realise how important it is to your health and how it can increase your energy and feelings of well being. It can also influence your rate of weight loss.

To build more activity into your daily routine, start taking stairs instead of lifts or escalators, swapping a bus journey (or 1 or 2 stops) for a brisk walk. On top of this try to take on one of the activities outlined below, whichever one you feel suits you, on a regular basis.

4–7 Subtract 10 per cent from your metabolic rate calculation. You are still too inactive and need to increase your score to reach the next category. You also need to introduce more activity into your daily routine, do more gardening, work about the house, climb stairs rather than taking the lift, walk or cycle to work. On top of this, take up a regular activity, two to three times a week. Choose from those outlined below.

8–12 Don't adjust the chart reading of your normal daily calorie requirements. You live an active life. Your work probably involves some physical movement and you are probably already health/exercise aware and consciously incorporate some activity into your life. You could possibly add one regular activity a week, such as a swim if the other exercise you take isn't particularly good for suppleness, or Yoga if you feel in need of a relaxing form of exercise.

13–16 Add 10 per cent to your reading on the chart on page 33. You lead an active life. You probably have a lot of natural energy and are already well aware of the benefits of exercise on your health and well being. Keep it up. You may also benefit from a relaxing form of exercise that aids suppleness (depending on your current activities) such as a once weekly swim or Yoga class.

17–20 Add 15 per cent to your daily calorie requirements. You are extremely active. Your work almost certainly involves a lot of physical exercise and you take a lot out of work as well. You might even be slightly addicted to exercise and may benefit from a relaxing Yoga class.

You should now know how fit you are, whether you need to take more exercise, and how much. Regular periods of activity can make a big difference to your total energy expenditure. Using up as little as an extra 500–1000 calories over the week can add up to the equivalent of 2–9 kg (4–20 lb) of fat over a year. Taking on more exercise has a snowball effect, it gradually makes you a more lively, energetic person – more likely to take the stairs than the lift – which means you naturally expend an increasing amount of energy in your daily life. Muscle will use energy in order to perform exercise and in doing so will be less likely to be used as a source of energy by the dieting body – and you'll lose more fat than you would by dieting alone. And after each bout of activity, your metabolic rate may remain raised for between 2 and 4 hours afterwards. People don't realise how exercise can improve their mood and feelings of energy, enthusiasm and well-being. It is one of its great unsung benefits and it has to be tried to be believed. You'll find, too, that you can cope more easily with the challenges of everyday life, and your sense of satisfaction with your lot will improve, and you will have more energy and optimism to change the parts of your life that should be changed.

CHOOSING YOUR EXERCISE

Money, class, sex and culture all influence what sort of exercise we take up. British schoolgirls don't play rugby, and working class men don't play squash. To enable you to stick at the exercise you choose, you must like it, it must fit in well with your life and preferably be close to either home or work.

The best type of exercise to help weight control isn't the most strenuous. People tend to think extremely vigorous forms of exercise burn up calories the fastest, when, in fact, low to moderate intensity exercise is best of all (gentle jogging or fast walking for instance), with the emphasis on duration rather than intensity. Any form of activity that you can maintain comfortably for 20–30 minutes at a time is ideal, and it should be done at least three times a week – five times a week is even better. This level of exercise, done little and often is the most effective in helping you lose weight, as well as improving cardiovascular fitness. Thus, taking more exercise doesn't necessarily mean taking up a sport or joining a class. Walking or cycling can be just as effective. Below is a description of the benefits of some of the most accessible forms of exercise and sport, as well as many others, plus our ratings as to their fat burning potential.

Fat burning potential
☆☆☆☆☆ Excellent
☆☆☆☆ Good
☆☆☆ Fairly Good
☆☆ Not enough to make significant difference
☆ Poor

WALKING ☆☆☆☆☆

For all-round fitness, walking is second only to a daily swim. It's safe for all ages and exercises almost every muscle in the body – heart included. It's particularly good for women, because calcium builds up around the bones at the point where tendons pull on them, helping prevent hip fractures in later life. (A cause of more deaths per year than breast and uterine cancer put together).

Walking is safer than most forms of exercise because the impact of each foot striking the ground is only one-and-a-half times the body weight, compared to three times or more for any running step. This means far less strain on joints, muscles and ligaments. Yet at around 5mph (a brisk walk), it burns up more calories than running. The advantage of walking is that it slots easily into daily routine. If you're city based, walk to work. It's a quick and less harassing way to get around, and you arrive fresh and alert. If you live in suburbs or countryside, possibilities are even better. It's also a great way to spend extra time with the children and encourage them to exercise. If possible, walk them to school, then walk back

AGE	AIM FOR	SPEED	FREQUENCY
25–35	30 min	4mph	4–7 times weekly
35–50	30 min	4mph	2–5 times weekly
50–65	20 min	3mph	2–4 times weekly
65–80	20 min	3mph	2–4 times weekly

These guidelines are approximate. The right amount of exercise should increase breathing without making you feel breathless.

quickly. Walk the dog, or walk to the shops, then bus back to avoid carrying heavy shopping. To find out your ideal pace in order to derive maximum benefit and push your heart rate into aerobic-training range, examine the chart above.

An added health bonus is that new findings reveal that in women walking an average of 2 miles in 30 minutes every day for a year, heart rates dropped, oxygen intake increased by 6 per cent, cholesterol levels dropped by 6 per cent and energy expenditure went up by 200 calories a day without an increased desire for food.

SWIMMING *****

Swimming can give your body a more thorough work out than any sport and is excellent for all ages as the water helps support your weight so little strain is placed on the joints. For this reason it is especially good for those with back problems, rheumatism and arthritis.

As you propel yourself through the water, you stretch and contract the muscles of arms, shoulders, trunk and, to a lesser extent, legs, all of which forces you to breathe deeply and regularly, good exercise in itself. This, combined with all the stretching involved, makes swimming deeply relaxing.

To improve strength, stamina and suppleness, you should aim to swim steadily without stopping for 20–30 minutes three times a week, starting with ten minute sessions if you aren't fit and gradually building up. Try to do a mixture of strokes so that you are exercising as many different muscles as possible. Backstroke and breaststroke expend more energy than crawl, but your legs get a better workout with breaststroke. However, the frog-like flicks can be uncomfortable if you have weak knees. If you can't swim it's never too late to learn. Ask about lessons at your local pool.

CYCLING ☆☆☆☆/☆

If you use a bicycle as transport, cycling can actually save you time rather than you having to make time for it. Also a particularly good form of exercise for the overweight, it places little strain on joints, unlike jogging which jars all the weight-bearing joints each time the feet touch the ground. Cycling works all the extensor muscles – those of the calves, thighs and buttocks – as well as the hips, back, shoulders and arms. By altering the gears on your bike you can vary the type of exercise you get: cycling in a low gear will be more of an aerobic exercise, good for weight loss and improving stamina. Cycling in a high gear will make it more of a resistance exercise which will firm up and strengthen muscles.

STATIONARY CYCLING ☆☆☆☆☆

This is ideal for people at all levels of fitness. It builds up your stamina, helping you to burn off calories and build up your muscles but it doesn't overwork you. It also means you can cycle in all weathers.

TENNIS OR BADMINTON ☆☆☆/☆

The benefits of tennis or badminton vary according to the level and speed at which you play. Movements tend to be short and explosive with moments of idling in between, so it's important to keep your legs moving all the time in order to make it a more aerobic exercise and improve stamina and the amounts of calories it uses up. Tennis helps to improve hand/eye co-ordination and tones up the muscles of calves, thighs and buttocks. It also improves the flexibility of the upper body and strengthens the arm muscles (particularly the racquet arm), shoulders, chest, waist and back. It is important to warm-up shoulder muscles gently in preparation for serving as a sudden wrench to cold muscles can cause injuries. Apart from tennis elbow, players are prone to hurt their knees from sudden twisting movements. This happens when non-slip tennis shoes grip tightly to a non-slip court. The slightly slippery surfaces of grass, or tarmac coated with grit courts enable the foot to slide and prevent the knee from having to bear the brunt of the twisting movement.

TEAM SPORTS ****
Most team games such as football, hockey and cricket are very good for stamina and strength and many are good for suppleness too. As many involve twisting and turning and sudden movements, it's as well to be fit before you start to play, the exercises below or a keep fit class will help to reduce risks or damaging muscles or joints.

DANCING *****
Dancing is a creative and satisfying way to exercise. It is excellent for strength, especially for the legs and is good for stamina and burning up calories. It is also excellent for helping to keep you supple. It also helps improve balance.

JOGGING *****
Jogging or running is fun, free and a quick way to get fit. It is excellent for stamina, improving the function of heart and lungs, and for building up strength in the leg muscles, but less good for all over suppleness and strength in the upper body. Run on soft surfaces if you can to help prevent the risk of injury to feet, knees, ankles and hips. Jog at a gentle pace for short periods at first and slowly build up. You should never be out of breath, however. Breathing should be increased but you should still be able to carry on a conversation. If you have arthritis or are very overweight, try cycling, swimming or walking instead.

WEIGHT TRAINING ★★★★

Weight training can build up strength, stamina and suppleness. You should always join a class or be taught how to use the weights safely and correctly before you start. Then you can specify what you want out of your workout. Slow movements with heavy weights help strengthen and tone muscles, repeated lifts with light weights help build up stamina.

GOLF ★★★

Combining all the benefits of walking with movements that build up strength in arms, back and shoulders, golf keeps the whole upper body mobile and supple. In fact, in an 18 hole game you may walk up to five miles and have delivered between 40–50 shots. The best thing about golf is that you can adapt the game to suit your skill or your energy.

EXERCISING AT HOME

You may find it easiest of all to do an exercise routine at home, in your own time. Overleaf is a safe, simple workout. It is the one used by some of our eight dieters featured earlier in the book. To give yourself a rhythm to work to, put on some music.

PRECAUTIONS

Most people, even the elderly, do not need a medical check-up before starting regular exercise. There are no risks in regular rhythmic exercise as long as the programme begins gently and increases gradually in vigour. Begin very gently and gradually work up the amount of exercise you take, day by day, week by week, and you will gain all the benefits without straining yourself. It is wise to consult your doctor if:
- You have ever had high blood pressure or heart disease.
- You have chest trouble, like asthma or bronchitis.
- You are troubled with joint pains, severe back pain or arthritis.
- You are recovering from an illness or operation.
- You are worried whether exercise may affect any other aspect of your health.

> ## KNOW YOUR EXERCISE PERSONALITY
> Are you a sprinter, a trotter, a hurdler or a stroller? Identifying which type you are may help point you towards the right form of exercise for you.
>
> The sprinter is the person who is enthusiastic to experience life, who has short sharp bursts of energy, who sleeps little and is perhaps in nervous overdrive. Competitive sports where short, sharp bursts of energy are involved should appeal, *e.g.* squash, tennis, windsurfing, sand yachting, skiing, sprinting.
>
> A trotter is more realistic, knows their highs and lows and is more able to sense their body signs and symptoms to maximise their efforts. A trotter should enjoy gentle jogging, tennis and badminton, swimming, dancing, cycling, aerobics, callanetics and even golf.
>
> Hurdlers are governed more by emotions like anger, and shuttle between extremes. They should choose a good blend of indoor and outdoor activities and will probably enjoy gardening, tennis, golf, running, walking (in particular hill walking), and some forms of dancing.
>
> The low energy which characterises a stroller may be an asset since high energy does not guarantee success. Leisurely or repetitive activities suit them best such as walking, cycling, bowls, swimming or jogging.

It is essential not to allow your heart rate to increase too quickly, to ensure that your heart is not over-exerted.

If you are starting on a fitness programme in your later years, it is important to proceed very slowly. The same principles apply in this age-group as they do earlier on – the way to avoid injury is to build up slowly. Few people in their seventies will want to take up running, although there is no particular reason why they should not, but walking, cycling, and especially swimming, are as effective in the later years as they are earlier in life.

As you get older, sports carry greater risk of injury. However, a group of 200 runners over the age of 70 years were able to avoid almost all trouble by sticking to a programme of gently performed stretching exercises. It is not necessary to push yourself hard physically all the time. The idea is to keep your body moving, and to keep the heart and lungs working a little harder than they do at rest. Activities such as gardening, ballroom dancing and bowls are more than sufficient. They are enough to keep the aerobic system working well and they certainly help to keep you supple.

THE 30-DAY DIET EXERCISE ROUTINE

The following exercises are divided into three groups – warming up, the exercise programme, and cooling down. All those exercises in the first and last group should be done every time you follow this routine, but choose between six and ten of the main programme – try them all out the first time and decide which ones are the most suitable for you.

WARMING UP

SWEEP

1 Stand with your feet wide apart, bend your knees slightly, and curve your arms with your left arm up and right arm down.
2 Bend to the right, pressing your left arm to the right. Change arm positions and, with the right arm up and left arm down, lean to the left. Continue in a swinging, flowing movement alternating to the right and left. Repeat 25 times.

FLOW THROUGH

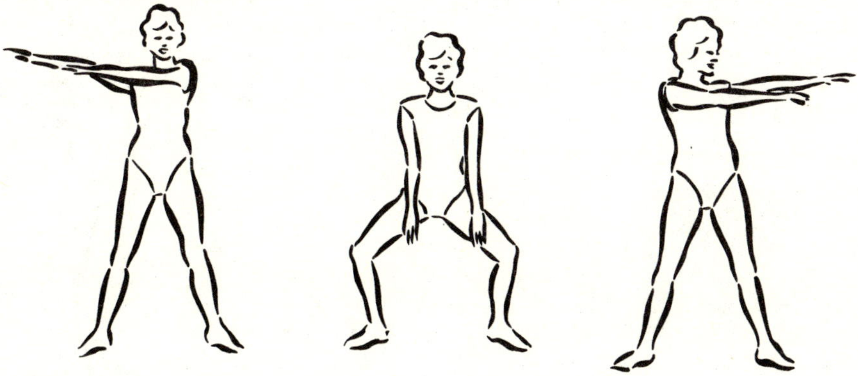

1 Stand with your feet wide apart, with your knees slightly bent and both arms to the right.

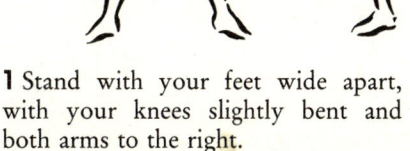

2 Bend your knees a little more and swing both arms down in front.

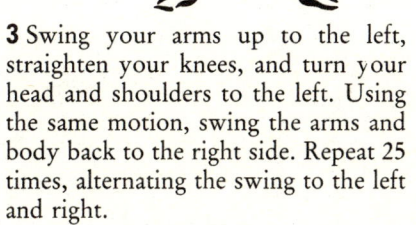

3 Swing your arms up to the left, straighten your knees, and turn your head and shoulders to the left. Using the same motion, swing the arms and body back to the right side. Repeat 25 times, alternating the swing to the left and right.

BACK STRETCH

1 Stand with your feet crossed, toes turned in and your hands at the side.

2 Slowly bend from the waist. Place your hands on your knees, flatten your back and lift your head. Hold this position for between 5 and 10 counts.

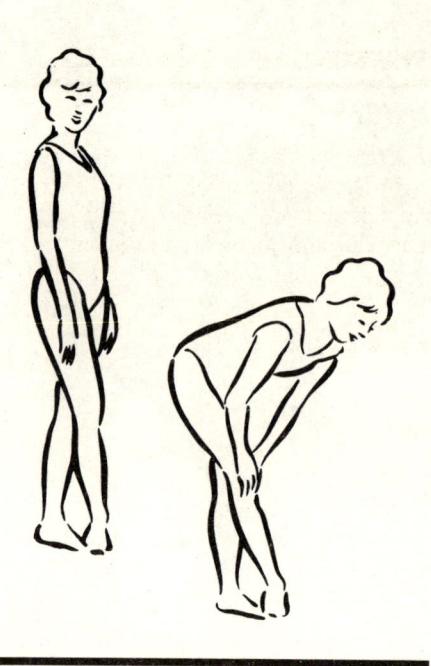

AEROBIC RUN

1 Stand with your feet slightly apart. Bend your knees slightly and bend your arms at waist height.
2 Run in place, kicking the legs up high to the back. At the same time, clap your hands in time to the movement. Run for 1 minute. Gradually work up to 6 minutes.

Check your pulse immediately after this exercise and refer to the chart on page 157 to see if you are within your correct heart rate range.

THE EXERCISE PROGRAMME

KICK UP

1 Stand with your weight on your right leg, with your left leg slightly to the side and your weight on your toes. Let your arms hang at your sides.

2 Raise your left leg forward and up as high as possible. At the same time, swing both hands forward and try to touch your left ankle. Return to the starting position. Repeat 8 times with each leg.

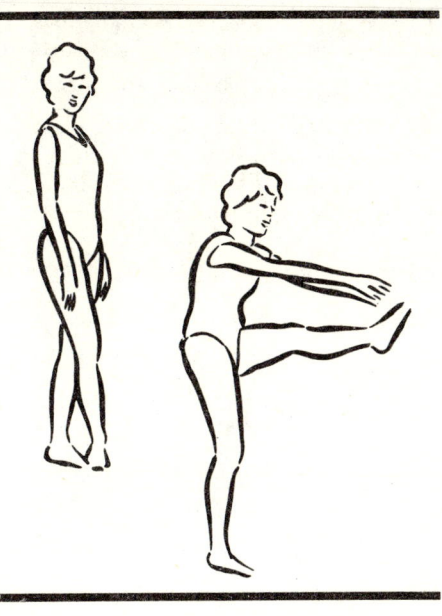

WAISTLINE WHITTLER

1 Stand with your weight on your right leg, bend your left knee and turn to the side with your weight on your toes. Your left hand is on your hip and your right arm at the side.

2 Keeping your knee turned out, raise your left leg as high as possible. At the same time, extend your right arm and lean toward the right. Return to the starting position. Repeat 8 times with each leg.

LEAN

1 Stand with your feet wide apart, and your knees slightly bent and with your hands clasped behind your head.

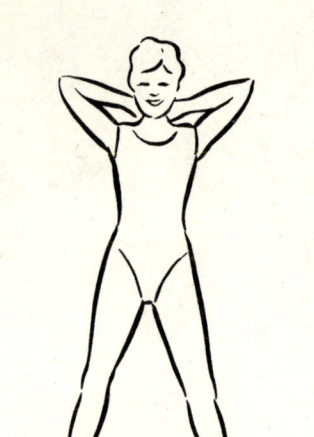

2 Bend your left knee to the side and lean to the left. Return to the starting position and repeat to the right. Repeat the whole movement 10 times, alternating left and right.

THE BOXER

1 Stand with your feet wide apart and with your right hand on your hip. Bend your left arm up with your fist clenched.

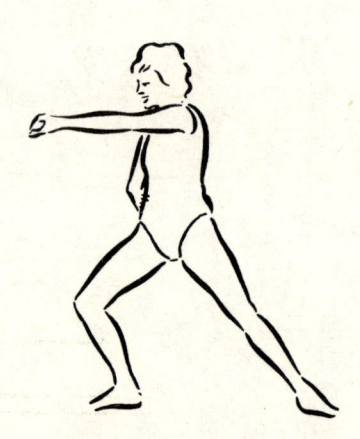

2 Bend your right knee, and extend your left arm across your body to the right. Return to the starting position. Repeat 10 times with each arm.

TOUCH UP

1 Stand with your weight on the right leg with your left leg to the side. Ensure your weight is on your toes. Place your right hand behind your head and your left hand on your hip.

2 Bend your left knee up towards your chest and touch your right elbow to the knee. Return to the starting position. Repeat 10 times with each leg.

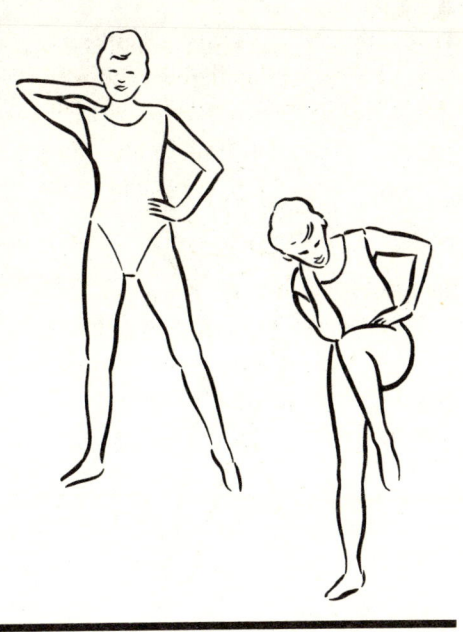

HURDLER'S CIRCLE

1 Sit in a hurdler's position with your left leg bent back and your right leg extended to the side. Place your hands on the floor at the sides.

2 Raise your right leg and circle it 10 times. Reverse the leg positions and circle your left leg 10 times.

A TOUGH ACT

1 Sit with your legs apart, knees bent, feet flat on the floor and arms folded across your chest.

2 Slowly lower your back to the floor keeping your shoulders and head up off the floor.

3 Sit up and swing your left leg out to the side. Return to the starting position. Repeat 8 times with each leg.

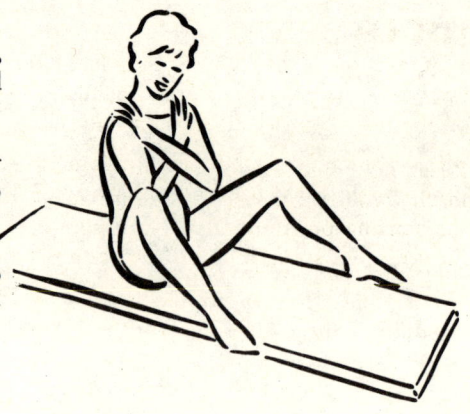

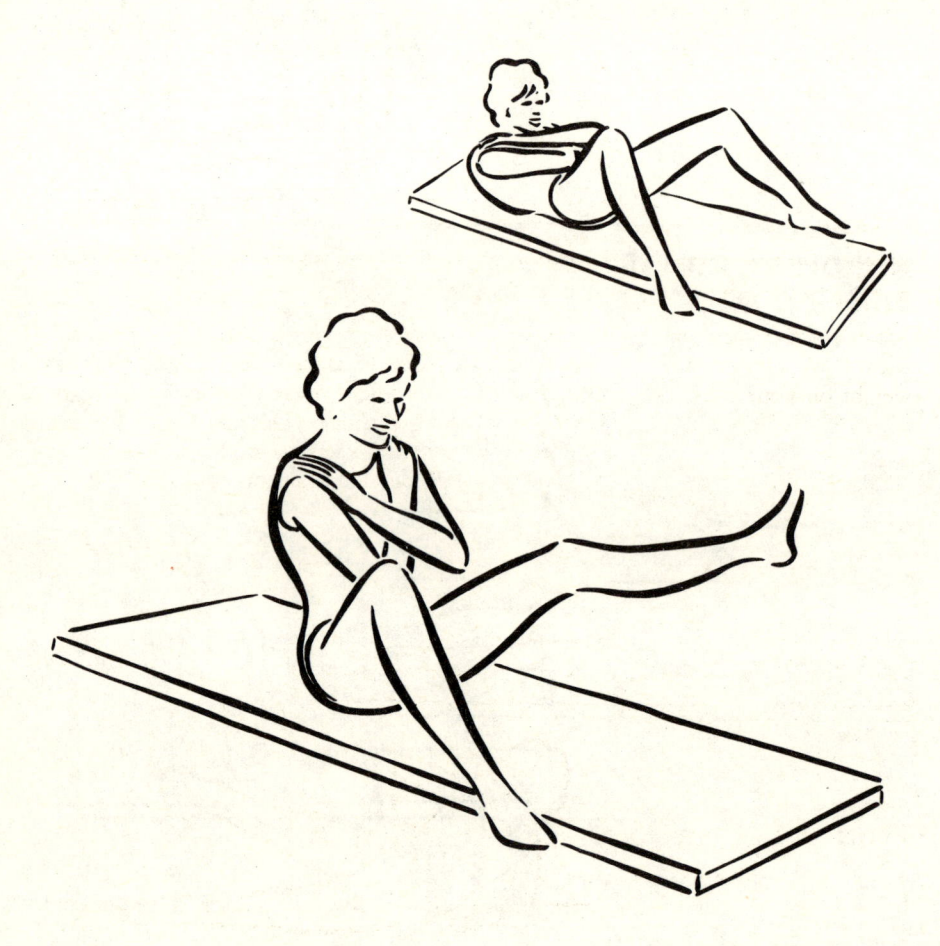

LIFT UP

1 Sit on the floor with your legs extended forward, toes up and hands on the floor parallel to the hips.

2 Lift your hips and pull in the stomach. Hold for 5 counts. Return to the starting position. Make sure you lift your hips straight up off the floor. Repeat 5 times.

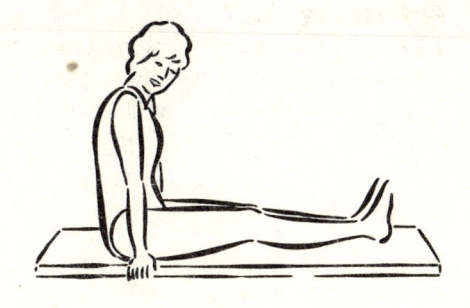

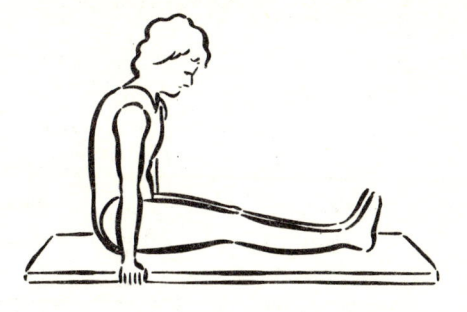

SIDELINE SQUEEZE

1 Lie on your right side on the floor with your legs extended. Place your weight on your right elbow and with your left hand on your hip.

2 Keeping the foot flat (not pointed), raise your left leg up as high as possible. Lower your leg to the starting position. Do not turn your leg, always keep it in the side position. Repeat 10 times on each side.

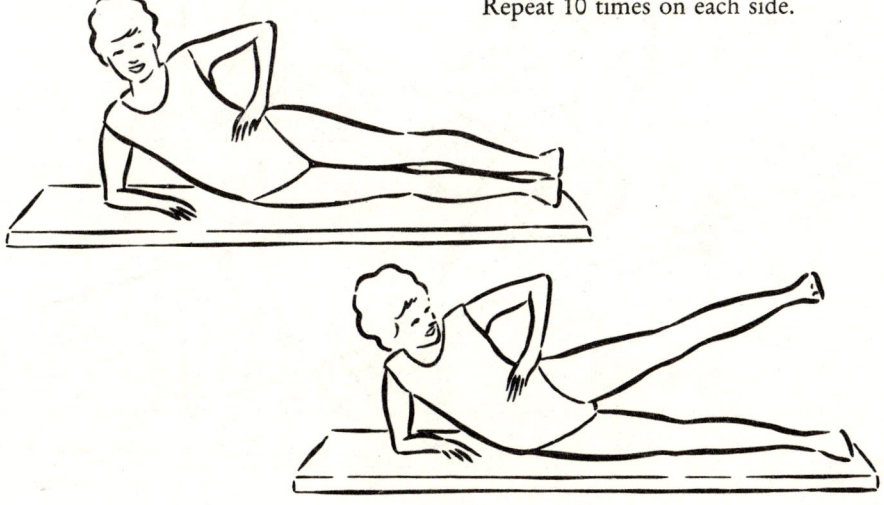

SWING IT

1 Lie on your left side with your weight on the left elbow and right hand. Keep both feet off the floor and bend your right knee in toward your chest.

2 Extend your right leg forward.

3 Then swing your leg back. Bend your knees in again to return to the starting position. Repeat 10 times on each side.

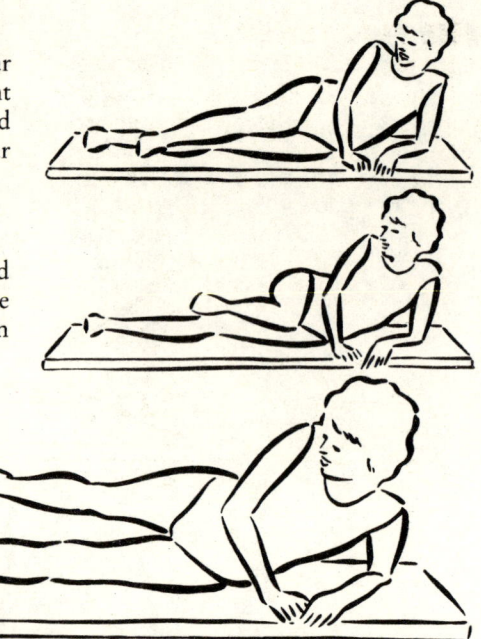

TWIST AND TOUCH

1 Sit with your feet wide apart, knees bent and feet flat on the floor. Clasp your hands behind your head.

2 Twist and touch your right elbow to the outside of your left knee. Return to the starting position and repeat to the right side. Repeat 10 times in all, alternating left and right.

THE FLATTENER

1 Lie on your back with your left leg off the floor and extended straight out. Place your right foot on your left knee, hands holding the right knee, and keep your head up off the floor.

2 Gripping your knee, sit up. Return to the starting position. Repeat 8 times with each leg.

TONE UP

1 Lie on your back with your hands clasped behind your head. With your head off the floor, bend your knees so that your feet are off the floor, too.

2 Pull your right knee in towards your chest and touch your left elbow to your right knee. At the same time, extend your left leg straight out. Then touch your right elbow to your left knee and extend your right leg. Do 10 to 15 times, alternating right and left.

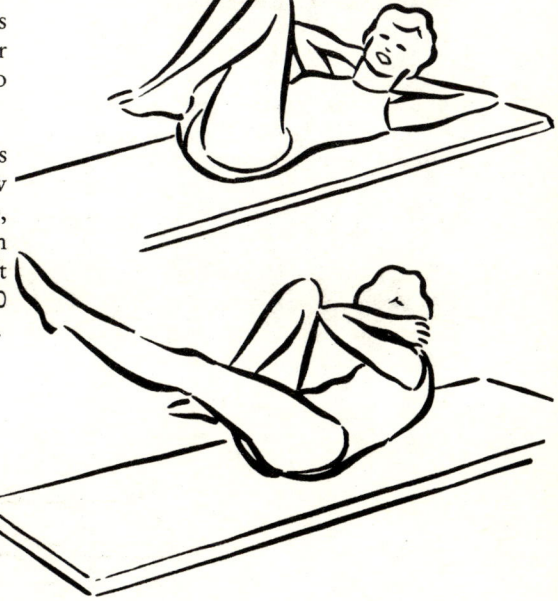

TRY HARDER

1 Sit with your weight on your hands, or the elbows, legs extended up, toes turned out to the sides.

2 Slowly lower your legs to the floor.

3 Bend your knees in towards your chest. Then extend your legs up to return to the starting position. Repeat 8 times.

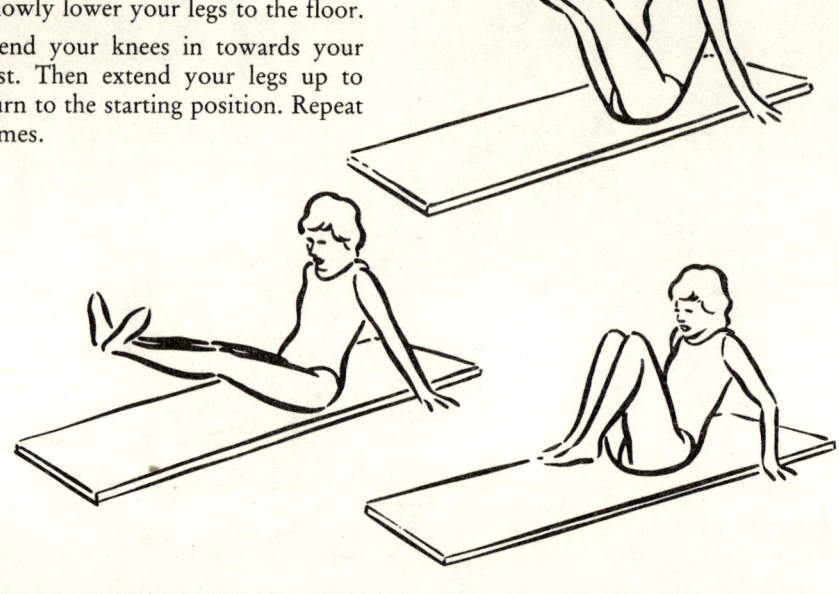

OVERHEAD SWINGS

1 Lie on your back with your knees bent, feet flat on the floor and arms at your sides.

2 Lift your hips as high as possible. Then lift your left leg straight up. Hold for 5 counts and then return to the starting position. Repeat 3 times with each leg.

Do not lift your leg so high that you are placing pressure on the back of your neck. If you feel pain in your neck, stop doing this exercise.

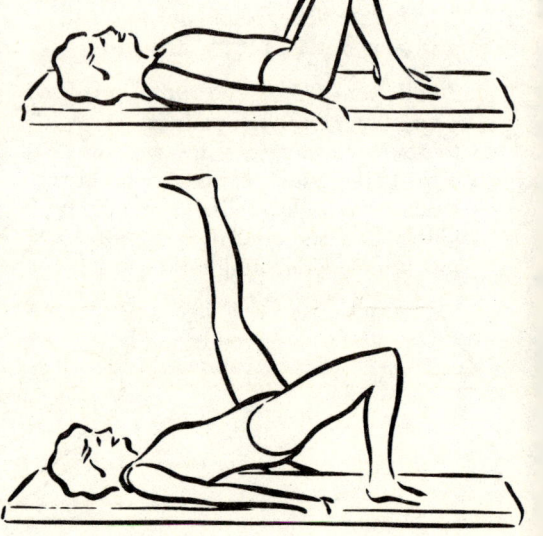

COOLING DOWN

THE TILT

1 Lie on your back with your knees bent and feet flat on the floor and wide apart. Rest your head on the floor and clasp your hands behind your head.

2 Pressing your back into the floor, lift your hips slightly off the floor. Do not lift your hips too high as this could place too much pressure on the back of your neck.

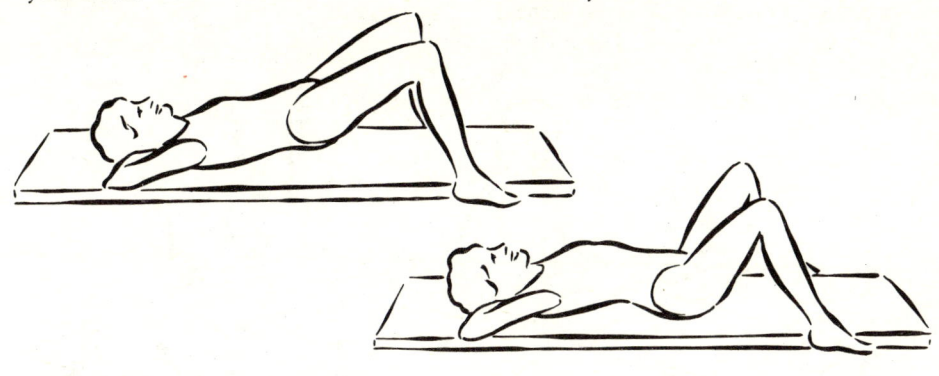

DROP-OFF

1 Lie on your back with your legs up, feet flat and hands clasped behind your head. Your head may be up off the floor or resting on the floor – whichever feels more comfortable for your back.

2 Slowly lower your left leg to within a few inches of the floor. Hold for 5 counts. Bend your knee in toward your chest and return your leg up to the starting position. Do 10 times with each leg.

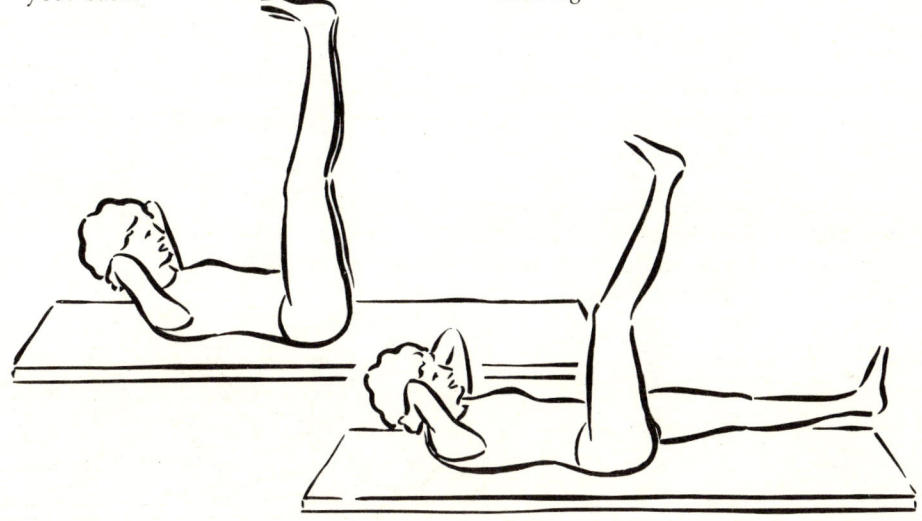

KNEE SWINGS

1 Stand facing the back of a sturdy chair, holding to the back of it. Place your weight on your right left and bend your left knee so that your weight is on your toes.

2 Lift your left knee up to the side.

3 Then rotate your hips and turn your knee in front of your body towards the right side. Return your knee to the starting position. Repeat 10 times with each leg.

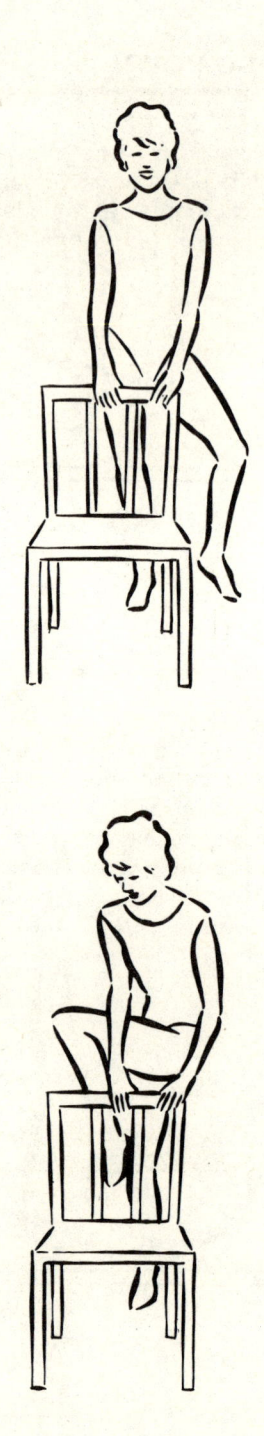

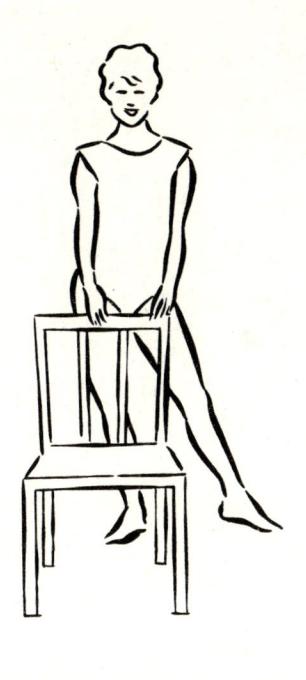

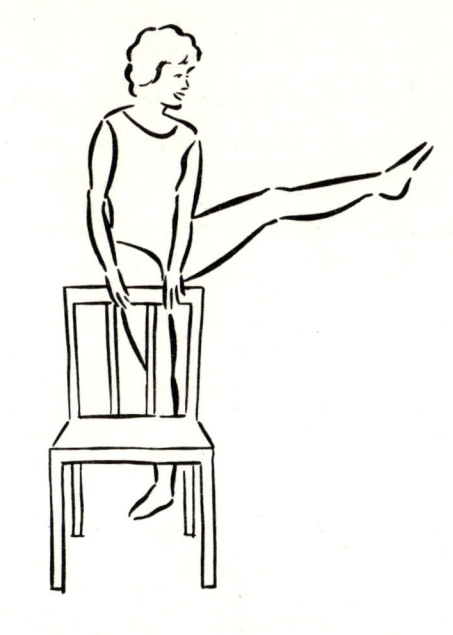

LEG SWINGS

1 Stand facing the back of a sturdy chair, hands holding the back of the chair and weight on the right left. Move your left leg to the side with your weight on the toes.

2 Keeping your left leg straight, lift it up as high as possible to the left side.

3 Then lower your leg and cross it in front of your body to the right side. Be careful not to hit your toes on the chair as your leg crosses! Swing each leg to the left and to the right 10 times.

CRISSCROSS

1 Lie on your back with your legs up and wide apart, hands clasped behind your head. Your head may be up off the floor or resting on the floor – whichever feels more comfortable for your back.

2 Alternately cross your legs and then open them 10 times while gradually lowering your legs towards the floor. Then raise them again to the starting position. For this exercise, point your toes.

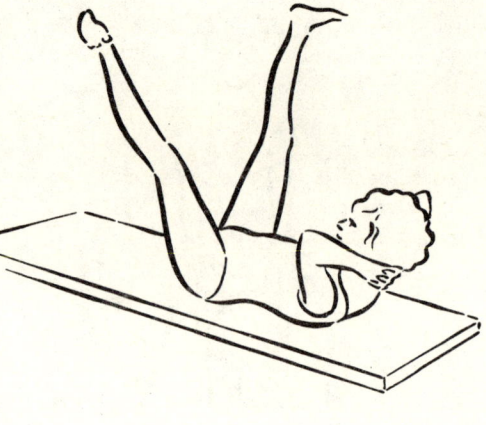

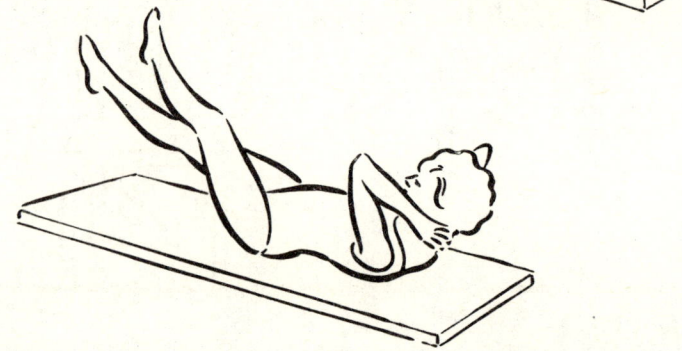

STRESS RELIEF

1 Kneel on your hands and knees with your head up.

2 Pull your right knee in towards your chest, clasp it with your right hand and press your head down towards your knee. Hold for 5 counts. Repeat 3 times, alternating right and left.

KICK OUT

1 Stand with your hands on the seat of a sturdy chair, gripping the side of the chair and with your right knee bent up towards your chest.

2 Extend your right leg out to the back, bending your leg up. Return to the starting position. Repeat 10 times for each leg.

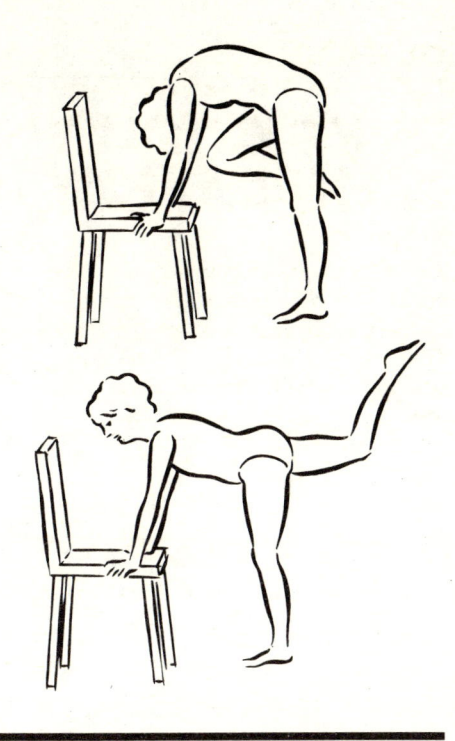

THE ARCH

1 Stand with your hands on the seat of a sturdy chair, gripping the sides of the chair and make sure your back is flat.

2 Push your hips forward, and round your back as high as possible. Hold for 5 counts. Return to a flat back. Repeat 3 times.

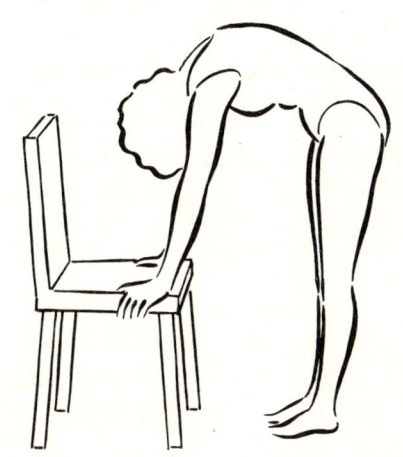

CHAPTER 8

NOW YOU'VE LOST WEIGHT HERE'S HOW TO KEEP IT OFF

SOMETHING HAPPENS WHEN you've lost weight, you feel quite differently about yourself. You feel more attractive, you want to buy new clothes that show off your figure instead of hunting down those that hide it or create the illusion of slimness. You take an interest in your appearance and feel pleased with it. Compare this new feeling with how you felt before you lost weight. You may have ceaselessly craved new clothes because you wanted something to make your body look better, fast. You probably ate foods such as sweets or biscuits out of boredom – the questionnaires in Chapter 3 will have made you realise this.

If you think about it, some of that boredom can be attributed to boredom with yourself and the way you looked. When you've lost weight, though, these feelings vanish. Suddenly you are interested in yourself again, want to dress yourself attractively, and realise that lots of clothes you already have are actually perfectly okay. You see them as such because you look so much better in them.

Because you have dieted at a sensible rate, cutting your calories enough to lose you no more than 1 kg (2 lb) a week (though you may have lost more, depending on your own individual rate of weight loss, and on the amount of exercise you pursued), you'll find that you won't have to struggle to keep your weight down once you've finished. You'll find it much easier to maintain your weight than ever before.

> **TIPS TO HELP YOU KEEP WEIGHT OFF**
> - Most people have good and bad spells in their eating habits, the bad often triggered by times of worry, depression or boredom – with life or with yourself, sometimes both. Answering the questionnaires in Chapter 3 should have helped you realise when your bad times were and why they occurred and to cater for them either by giving yourself a treat food, or supplying slimming alternatives such as dried fruit.
> - Most of our eight dieters found that having been on the 30-Day Diet made them much more aware of changes in their body shape and size. The moment they felt fatter they would take action, and as eating by portion was so simple, they found it very easy to slip back into the way they ate while on the weight loss programme. Don't ignore slight increases in your size, remember it's easy to lose a pound or two.
> - Keeping up the exercise also played a major part in preventing the dieters' weight regain. Those who let it slip, and who then got out of the exercise habit, were the ones that regained some weight. This tended to happen to those who had hectic lives who couldn't map out a clear routine into which they could fit the exercise. When your routine changes it is best to rethink what exercise you can cope with and adapt accordingly, taking up a new activity that you can fit in better.
> - Make exercise a social activity, too. Enlist the support of a friend, not only will it be more fun, but you will feel bad about letting her or him down if you failed to go, and there's always someone else to encourage you.

REASSESSING YOUR DAILY REQUIREMENTS

The most common cause of weight regain is that most dieters revert to the amount they were eating before they lost weight. There are two things wrong with this. First, it was these eating habits that made you gain weight in the first place, and they are guaranteed to do it again. Secondly, if you assess your calorie requirements again, you will see that they are less than when you first started dieting. This is because there is now less of you to fuel, as you are carrying less metabolically active tissue. Exercise can help here, by increasing your energy requirements which will enable you to eat more without gaining weight. The point of the Good Housekeeping 30-Day Diet, is that it is a way of eating that has been designed to suit you so well that you can stick to its basic principles once you have finished losing weight. You should have learnt new eating habits, let them guide you from now on.

Find out how much food you now need to eat to maintain your new weight by using the chart on page 32. Perform the original calculation, using your new weight instead of your starting weight. Make sure you include your new activity level in your calculations too – do the activity questionnaire on page 159 again if necessary.

This time, don't subtract any calories, because you don't want to lose weight any more. Exchange your new daily calorie requirements for the portion selection you like most (see pages 35–6), and eat this way for a few weeks until it becomes second nature. If you find you begin to gain weight, switch to a lower portion amount until you find your weight has leveled off and you are maintaining it with ease.

HOW EXERCISE CAN MAINTAIN WEIGHT

Just keeping up with your exercise will help you ward off weight regain. New research shows that exercise is a major factor in helping dieters keep weight off once they've lost it. Researchers studied the weight of two groups of dieters, one of which had combined exercise with their diet, the other which had dieted alone. One year later, the dieters who had also exercised had kept their weight off, those who hadn't had regained all or most of it. By improving your figure, making it firmer and more supple, exercise may help make us more aware of and interested in our bodies, preventing the boredom and loss of interest that makes us feel we just can't be bothered to watch our weight and might as well eat another tube of Smarties. It may also be that taking an active step towards keeping fit and healthy helps us to feel in control of our lives, which in turn helps us to control other aspects of our life, such as diet.

TEN GOOD REASONS TO KEEP THE WEIGHT OFF

- You look better
- Your face looks ten years younger
- You are less limited in your choice of clothes – all clothes look better on you.
- You will be healthier and run less risk of being ill, now or in later life
- You will feel happier with yourself
- You will have more confidence
- You will probably live longer
- Succeeding and being positive in this area of your life will help you to achieve more in others
- All this will increase your self esteem yet further!
- You will never have to diet again!

CONTINUING DIETING AFTER THE 30 DAYS

If you still have weight to lose after 30 days (and you are fit and healthy and have consulted your doctor before starting if you are under 18 or over 60) there is no reason why you shouldn't continue to diet until you reach the size you want to be. You may find you want to give yourself a rest, stop dieting, and maintain your weight for a few weeks and then begin again. This can also help counteract the drop in metabolism caused by the body thinking it's being starved. A period of normal eating appropriate to your new size should maintain you at your new level, then you can begin to diet again at a later stage. Remember that dieting can get slower once you have lost some weight as the difference between what you need and the amount of calories in the diet is not so big any more. However, increasing the amount of exercise you do will increase the amount of food that you need and so continue to maintain the difference between the calories you need and the calories in the diet you have developed.

Stopping dieting and maintaining your weight by eating healthily, before continuing to diet will also help you establish better long-term eating habits, helping you to maintain your weight in the future.

THE EIGHT DIETERS – HOW WELL THEY MAINTAINED THEIR WEIGHT

Rowena Wilson: The Good Life

'I've carried on dieting because I had more to lose and I've since lost another 19 kg (3 st) – making 25 kg (4 st) lost altogether! I've tried lots of diets before, but I've always regained the weight, and often put on more than I'd lost. This is the first diet that's really worked for me, I think because it fits in with my lifestyle so well. I know I can be naughty at weekends, that it doesn't matter because I can cut back on weekdays when it is easier for me. I've kept off alcohol and puddings, helped by following tips for making one's drink stretch – mixing wine with soda or fruit juice. The diet is part of my life now. It is the individual approach that has made it so successful.'

Mary Cadogan: Working Mother

'My weight stayed off successfully for a few months until my working life became so hectic that I gave up the exercise. Then my weight began to creep up. However, I immediately slipped back into my portion eating routine just over a week ago and I've already lost 1 kg (2 lb). The swimming is hard for me to do at the moment so I'm taking up badminton with another mother. We're going to play every morning after dropping the children off at school. I really enjoyed the exercise. It made me feel so much better, I don't want to let it drop again, I felt so much healthier while I was doing it.'

Daniela Brandler: Young Mother at Home

'Once my life got back on an even keel I was able to diet again and I've since lost another 1.5 kg (3 lb). I've found it very easy to keep the lost weight off. I realise why I want to eat lots of sweet things at some times and not at others. So now I let myself. I don't feel guilty about it, and just cut back later when it's easier. I've kept up with the exercise too, I go for more walks and do an exercise routine while watching breakfast television each day.'

Sue Webster: Foodie

It was the portions that made the diet so easy to handle, there's no weighing food and counting endless calories – you know a sausage is 2p – it's simple! I was surprised at what I was able to eat, it was very flexible and enjoyable, and I really became aware of just what I was putting into my mouth in a way that I wasn't before. I've since lost more weight. I'm now below 63 kg (10 st) and I still go running. I've found my weight loss easy to maintain – it will soon be a year. Knowing you can be bad at the weekend if you are good all week helps.'

Penny Nathan: Vegetarian Working Mother
'I've found it easy to keep my weight off since the diet. Because the diet allowed one to eat a reasonable amount, and because I was allowed treats such as baby Mars Bars, I didn't have the urge to rush out and pig myself silly when I finished the diet.'

Alice Lane: Teenage Junk Foodie
'I found the diet good because it made me eat healthily. I'd always assumed eating healthily meant eating nastily and it wasn't the case at all. The food I was able to eat and the recipes I tried were really tasty. Because of this I'm finding it easier to live on more slimming healthy foods than before. I'm still tempted to pig on sweets, but I'm more aware of what foods are fattening and what aren't.'

Liz Warner: Busy Journalist
'I've managed to maintain my weight (give or take a pound or two) because I've become aware of the dreadful things I was eating and drinking on a regular basis – particularly alcohol. My diet was terribly high in fat which I hadn't realised was so fattening, now I'm really conscious of butter, milk and cheese and have really cut down the amounts I eat and have traded high-fat foods for low-fat versions. I felt so much better for doing the exercise, and it makes me more conscious of my shape and what I'm doing to it when I over eat. I still snack a lot, but on satsumas or something better for me than croissants or chocolate.'

Carl Caddick: Designer with Own Business
'I found it easy to maintain my weight at first and enjoyed keeping up the exercise. But then I injured my knee which has meant I haven't been able to exercise for several weeks and I've gained weight again. Once I'm better though I'll get fit again and shed the weight now I know how easy it is.'

USEFUL ADDRESSES

British Cycling Federation,
36 Rockingham Road,
Kettering,
Northampton NN16 8HG
Telephone: 0536 412211

British Sports Association for the Disabled,
The Mary Glen Haig Suite,
34 Osnaburgh Street,
London NW1 3ND
Telephone: 01 383 7277

Keep Fit Association,
16 Upper Woburn Place,
London WC1H 0QG
Telephone: 01 387 4349

British Wheel of Yoga,
1 Hamilton Place,
Boston Road,
Sleaford,
Lincolnshire NG34 7ES
Telephone: 0529 306851

British Amateur Weight Lifters Association,
3 Iffley Turn,
Oxford OX4 4DU
Telephone: 0865 778319

Rambling Association,
1–5 Wandsworth Road,
London SW8 2LJ
Telephone: 01 582 6878

The Long Distance Walkers Association,
Alan Castle,
Wayfarers,
Moorings Close,
Parkgate,
South Wirral L64 6TL
Telephone: 058 087 341

The Sports Council,
16 Upper Woburn Place,
London WC1H 0QP
Telephone: 01 388 1277
(Always enclose an sae when writing)

INDEX

activity log, 158
alcohol allowance, 34, 82
Almond and Mango Ice Cream, 149, 151
Apricot
    and Kiwi Fruit Cups, 149, 152
    and Orange Coupe, 149, 153
Asparagus with Orange Sauce, 90, 97
Avocado and Chick-pea Salad, 98, 102

Badminton, 164–5
Baked Beef and Vegetable Crumble, 127, 130
Baked Gingered Chicken, 119, 121
Baked Smoked Salmon Mousses, 112, 114
Barbecued Bananas, 149, 150
Basil and Tomato Tartlets, 134, 137
Bean and Chicken Tabouleh, 119, 123
Beef Olives with Mushroom Stuffing, 127, 130
Brandler, Daniela, 47–52, 188
Breakfast Ideas, 84–5
Broad Noodles with Smoked Salmon, 105, 109
Burghul Wheat Salad, 98, 103

Caddick, Carl, 70–4, 188
Cadogan, Mary, 42–7, 188
calories
    calculating daily requirements, 32–4
    reassessing daily requirements, 185–6
    your personal requirement, 34
calorie savers, 31
Carrot
    and Orange Soup, 90, 96
    Onion and Egg Loaf, 135, 145
    Quiches, 135, 147
Cereal Portion Counter, 77–8
Chicken
    and Chicory Sandwiches, 119, 122
    and Spinach Loaf with Carrot Orange Sauce, 119, 124
    Dishes, 119–26
    in Yogurt, 119, 120
    Kebabs, 119, 123
    Stir-fry Salad, 98, 101
    with Mustard Sauce, 119, 125
Chinese Chicken with Rice, 119, 126
Chunky Vegetable Soup, 90, 91
continuing dieting after the 30 days, 187
Crispy Baked Mushrooms with Garlic Dip, 90, 91
Curried Chicken Toasts, 119, 122
Curried Tofu and Vegetables, 134, 142
Cycling, 164
    stationary, 164

Dairy Portion Counter, 78–9
Dancing, 165
Diet Notes, 82
dietary assessment
    making changes, 30
    questionnaire, 28–9
Dieting Vegetarian, 60
Dried Fruit Compote, 149, 155

Eating Out, 83
exercise
    choosing, 161–66
    importance of, 17–18
    maintaining weight, 186
    precautions, 166–8
    routine, 169–83
Extras, 80

Farmhouse Chicken Breasts, 119, 124
Fats & Oils Portion Counter, 79
Fettuccini with Clam Sauce, 105, 109
Fish Dishes, 112–18
fitness
    assessing your level, 157
    questionnaire, 159–61
food diary, 24–5
    assessing it, 27
    how to make it, 23
food preferences chart, 26
Foods to Avoid, 82
Free Foods, 81
Fresh Pea Soup, 90, 92
Fresh Tomato Sauce, 105, 111
Fruit Kebabs with Yogurt and Honey Dip, 149, 154
Fruit Portion Counter, 80
Fruited Cheese Salad, 98, 102

Gazpacho, 90, 95
Ginger Fruit Salad, 149, 154
Goat's Cheese Tarts, 134, 140
Golden Peach Souffle, 149, 151
Golf, 166
Greek-style Kebabs, 127, 129

Haddock-stuffed Courgettes, 112, 114
Hedgerow Salad, 98, 100
Herbed Twice-Baked Potatoes, 134, 135
Hot Chicken Liver Salad, 98, 99
Hot Mushroom Mousse, 135, 146

Jogging, 165–6

Kedgeree, 112, 117
keeping weight off
    tips to help, 185

Lamb Chops with Rosemary, 127, 131
Lane, Alice, 61–6, 188
Lemon Sole in Lettuce, 112, 115
Lettuce and Mange-tout soup, 90, 97

INDEX

Lunch Ideas, 85–6
Luncheon Salad, 98, 103

Mango Chicken Parcels, 119, 121
Marinated Steak Salad, 98, 100
Meat Dishes, 127–33
Mediterranean Fish Stew, 112, 116
Menu Suggestions, 88–9
Minted Lamb Meatballs, 127, 132
Monkfish and Mussel Brochettes, 112, 113
Mustard Rabbit, 127, 129

Nathan, Penny, 56–61, 188
Neapolitan Tortelloni, 105, 106

Onion Quiche, 134, 137
Onion Tart, 135, 146
Orange Mousses, 149, 152

Pasta
    con le Zucchine, 105, 110
    Dishes, 105–111
    Giorgio, 105, 110
    with Pesto, 105, 107
    with Tomato Sauce, 105, 107
Peppery Cheese Souffles, 135, 144
Piperade, 134, 143
Pizza Chilli, 135, 148
Plum Clafoutis, 149, 151
Pork with Apricots, 127, 133
portion combinations
    choosing your own, 35–6
Protein Portion Counter, 76–7
psychology of eating, 14–15
Puddings, 149–55

Questionnaire 1, 28–9
Questionnaire 2, 30
Quick Chicken Liver Pate, 90, 93

Rabbit with Prunes, 127, 128
Raspberry Tofu Ice Cream, 149, 150

Salads, 98–104
Sauces, 111
Savoy Pork Chops, 127, 131
Scrambled Eggs with Tomato, 134, 136
Seafood Spaghetti, 105, 108, 112, 116
Simple Tomato Sauce, 105, 111
Singapore Noodles, 105, 108
Slimming Fish Pie, 134, 140
Smoked Chicken and Mint Salad, 98, 104
Smoked Trout Mousse in Lemon Shells, 112, 113
smoking and fat, 11

Souffleed Rarebits, 134, 137
Soups, 90–97
Spiced Bean Sausages, 134, 138
Spiced Chicken, 119, 120
Spiced Dried Fruit Compote, 149, 155
Spicy Bean Pate, 90, 93
Spicy Scallops, 112, 115
Spinach
    and Cheese Quiche with Crisp Potato Crust, 134, 136
    and Yogurt Soup, 90, 92
    and Egg Crumble, 135, 145
    Salad, 98, 104
    Soup, 90, 96
Starters, 90–7
Stir-fried Liver, 127, 128
Strawberry Cream, 149, 153
Stripy Avocado and Cheese Mousses, 90, 94
Stuffed Cabbage Rolls, 135, 144
Stuffed Mushrooms, 134, 142
Stuffed Vine Leaves, 127, 132
Summer Vegetable Flan, 134, 139
Supper Ideas, 86–7
Swimming, 163–4

Tandoori Chicken, 119, 126
Taramasalata, 90, 94
Team sports, 165
Tennis, 164–5
Tuna
    and Bean Salad with Orange Dressing, 98, 101
    and Haricot Bake, 112, 117

Uncooked Tomato Sauce, 105, 111

Vegetable Lasagne, 105, 106
Vegetarian
    diets, 60
    Dishes, 134–48
    Pancakes, 134, 141
    Tofu Kebabs, 135, 143

Walking, 162
Warm Vegetable Salad, 98, 99
Warner, Liz, 66–70, 188
water retention, 19–20
Watercress Soup, 90, 95
Webster, Sue, 52–5, 188
weight/height chart, 20
Weight training, 166
West Country Cod, 112, 118
What constitutes a healthy diet?, 13
Wilson, Rowena, 38–42, 188